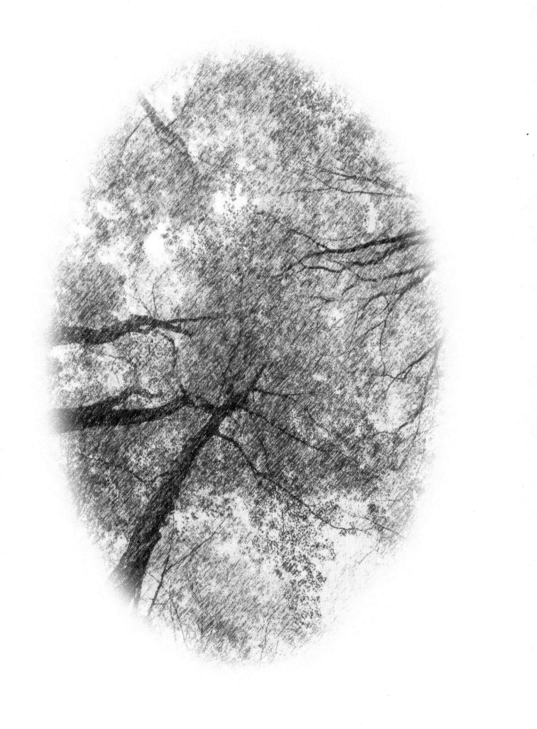

By Our Design:

A Human Manual to the Evolutionary Process of Fifth Dimension Ascension.

By James Anthony Curtis

DEDICATION

To Michael,

and all the beauty in each of us that desires only to shine.

INTRODUCTION

Almost nightly for the last ten years or so of my mother's life, I would receive a phone call and upon answering would hear, "It's me!" Mom had a wonderful light she lived by, and just listening to her voice invoked a smile in the soul; my reply was always, "Hello, Me!" Her spirit always brightened the room, and as she aged, her humor, self-confidence, and good nature became a staple of love that I looked forward to being with. Mother's unique way of living life, her background growing up, and her love of family gave me a deeply rooted sense of self from an early age, where I experienced the nurturing necessary to explore my own life path with vulnerability. She had come from a home of five children (four sisters and one brother), my grandmother raising them as a single mom, and was no stranger to hardship. During World War II, Mom insisted on working before it was coming-of-age to do so and changed the date on her birth certificate to receive early employment (although mistakenly did so in the opposite direction making herself a year younger, which we joked about). She had a strong will, a huge heart, and when my two older sisters and I arrived, much of life became dedicated to caring for us, especially after a divorce when she found herself a single mother raising children.

It really wasn't until later in life after Frank (her third husband) had passed and all of us had grown up that she really came into her own. My stepfather Frank had left her a nice inheritance upon passing, and she really began to explore simple pleasures that were difficult early in life to pursue. Several of her favorites included bingo at a nearby fire hall, going to a local weekly auction, and sharing bus trips with seniors on mini adventures up to the casino to eat at the buffet. Frequently she would arrive back to her house late at night, and I would receive a phone call letting 'me' know she was safely home. When I had to get up early for work in the morning, that phone call would trigger some minor irritation, but the feeling quickly subsided upon hearing the warmth in her cheerful voice of, "it's me!!"

A mother's love transmitted the simplicity of divine mystery for many years in those two simple words, "it's me." They described every longing we will ever have or find fulfilled in some degree of reflection: to be acknowledged, feel safe, feel content, and know the connection of who we are in a profound certainty of love.

When my mom passed in January of 2015, it was a part of a culmination of events that were so precise in reflection, that there was no room left for doubt in understanding that greater forces were at work behind the scenes. The loneliness that came into my life was far beyond anything ever experienced before; not only was there the loss of my mother after she went into the hospital on Christmas Eve, but a divorce pending, the painful passing of a dear friend by cancer, death of my dog, and a myriad of deprivations which provoked feelings of utter abandonment. The devastation to my reality was so complete, it was unlike anything ever felt before, and so excruciatingly painful the heart was unable to be restored to its former state. Even long-term relationships of support seemed distant and foreign in form, as if they had been a wisp of illusion the entire time. And as the intensity of circumstances increased, deeper issues of betrayal, rejection, and unworthiness began to surface in the loneliness which was felt. All of this transpired for someone who had a firm foundation of faith, family, and several spiritual practices, who worked consistently in a community fellowship for well over 20 years, who only a year prior had stable, sound, relationships with everyone he knew.

When we are overwhelmed in suffering, it is common to grasp for relief in any form, where we may find ourselves incessantly repeating behaviors, the mind wrestling to find a solution to the pieces our awareness is missing. Egoic constructs will intensify in these repetitious energies, both to protect the nervous system from the emotional turbulence we feel, and to ensure if and when we are ready to move into resolve. Often what we perceive as pain, suffering, or loss in human terms is only addressed in relation to outer circumstances, but, whether we realize it or not, we are energetic beings on a much larger journey of integration, where what we experience three-dimensionally is working in coordination with our soul multi-dimensionally. This doesn't mean we will not grieve, or form meaningful personal relationships which we miss, but that we will have the freedom to do so in the expression of resolve, rather than feeling like a victim of circumstances held behind the walls of egoic entrapments created for stability.

In each life path, there will be numerous relationships which effect every one of us deeply, where synchronicities, resonation, and alignment are no strangers in connection with what we feel, but at some point, as part of the human evolutionary process, we will realize something at work within the layers. In my personal experience, this 'something' had become more orchestrated, focused, and intensified synchronistically. In the years leading up to and through my mother's death, circumstances had become so perfect in coordination that the devastation was not random, nor was it something to move through solely by grieving. As humans, when we face overwhelming loss on this scale, where reality as we know it collapses and the pain of living becomes so unbearable that existence serves only as a state of deep bewilderment, we will question everything: our faith, if we want to go on living, if things can get any worse, what reality is, who we are, and if there is a purpose in our life. Although this place may be filled with depression, loneliness, and despair, these are only indications that we are ripe for something remarkable. Where one leaps to their end, another takes flight inward in transformation.

The most common misconception we have as humans is to the 'why' of suffering, and the most prevalent practice currently is the endeavor to eradicate pain altogether, but therein burns the fire of transformative nature, and the humility of divine power: even though all of the uncomfortable, afflictive, chaotic energies we feel as human beings may seem to be adversarial, hidden within the layers of them are their purpose; one which, as we are ready, is revealed by the advocation of the soul. The reasoning mind, based in egoic logic, will want to separate the energies of suffering categorically for some sense of stability to reality, but the energy of suffering is simply the energy of suffering, regardless of how it has arisen. And in an inclusive universe, no amount of suffering is ever in vain, wasted, or without greater purpose, even though we may question the method in which it unfolds.

As evolving beings, we are living lives far beyond what we often view as circumstances in relation to our incarnation, which are intertwined deeper energetically in the vibrational fabric of a much vaster existence. But because we live in the third dimension many of us will continually attempt to shift our circumstances through various tactics of negotiation, self-effort, and reasoning. Since these solely focus on the outer, we inadvertently neglect the potentials that are within our field as beings of multi-dimensional capability. This one incessant loop purposefully repeats in each life path until energies are aligned for awakening; it's only when our shadows overtake us that what we suspect lingers beneath the surface comes to fruition and we are offered the potential shift vibrationally which previously eluded us. As we are ready, we discover a different purpose in outer circumstances, one in which 'something' is working alongside them. And instead of a singular focus directed at changing outcomes linearly, we start to listen reflectively to what they are provoking within us, both for resolve and as a part of our empowerment as beings of manifestational potential.

When devastation entered my life path in orchestrated terms, it did so with such perfection that it revealed two lives: one that had formed beautiful relationships on spiritual principles and meaningful interactions with the world around me, and another that existed beneath the surface, waiting to be fulfilled, awakened, and empowered by a universal love which was always suspected to exist. But in order for the second life to be fulfilled, this type of shift in consciousness will destroy or see the death of the former reality, although only to the point it must as a part of a 'birthing' process— not necessarily in three-dimensional fleshy matter, but rather as a vibrational transformation in perception. This might sound simple, like just looking in a different direction, or from an alternate point of view, and it is, but confusing 'simple' with 'easy' is an incredible underestimation of the human evolution that is taking place in this process. So if you can imagine our perception based on a vibrational frequency, then in order to see a different reality, that frequency must shift.

This can be a precarious time, because consciousness exists between worlds and, from a perspective of three-dimensional solutions, appears insane by logical reasoning. Society has done its best to cope with this as it perceives it as a malady, whether in physical, mental, or emotional form, introducing everything from antidepressants to mood stabilizers with treatments varying from counseling to institutionalization in extreme cases, each of which have stopped short of resolve for what ails the one in the experience of affliction. Although sometimes it's imperative to be medicated, institutionalized, or in treatment, it's not necessarily for the reasons we believe, but rather as a component to what is in an adjustment process vibrationally. What groans as instability in the flesh frequently is rooted in deeper issues asking for our attention, and if we sleep spiritually, the pain we feel is recognized only as adversarial in nature. But even when only the symptoms are treated, from an inclusive point of view we are becoming primed to receive what we have been asking for in resolve and will undoubtedly manifest as each one of us is ready.

In the near future, there will be some changes each of us will notice, where we may or may not find ourselves experiencing a certain amount of trepidation and even feelings of great sadness, which we may view as apocalyptic in divination. At first we may find great difficulty, particularly when questions arise concerning the unknown, but we will also discover in this place that we are open to expansion, which may feel uncomfortable, and even painful if in resolve of deep wounds. And while we may not recognize pain as a bearer of healing balm, in spiritual terms it is an indication we are ready to receive transformation. The articulate nature of pain is such that not only does it call or redirect our attention to what is in need, but it also carries the necessary energies for transformation in its 'askings', even fulfilling requests we may or may not be aware of. Whether what we feel afflictively is in the physical, mental, or emotional realm of experience, these energies only manifest on our behalf.

One of the purposes of this book is to address the struggle in ideology we have come to know through a paradigm based in third- and even some fourth-dimensional living, and although that 'struggle' is a part of our evolutionary process, as any shift is experienced, we will inherently draw to us perceptions no longer solely based in 'finite' description. When in the dark night the saving grace revealed is not in terms of a former faith, but rather an integration of the doubts that present themselves to us in the terror of 'wanting'. Although we are never forced to ascend until we are ready, if we are experiencing great pain, trauma, or affliction in our life, there will come a point when we simply cannot deny the truth of universal arrangement and what we are in relation to it. This is not unlike the caterpillar, cocoon, and butterfly in journey, and although our initial reaction may be to flinch, escape, or overcome various stages, as we develop a relationship with the soul, we will notice a face-to-face metamorphosis with these energies— not in any sense of defeating or controlling them, but a willingness to abide with them as part of the evolutionary process we must undergo in emergence. This process is not limited in temporal resolve or healing, but literally is our vibrational field shifting through our physical being on the temporal plane and offers resolution completely, which is exactly why it can be so difficult or painful— because we are changing the very structure of our vibrational threads in resolution.

Bliss is also a part of our evolutionary process, and will be discussed further, but the reason it tends to fall from the conversation early on is due to its quality of vibrational signature and intensity. When early on in awakening or evolutionary unfolding, bliss carries an energy signature that tends to pull us in the direction of awakening or alignment, but it doesn't have the pushing energies required for revealing or birthing, which are in pain. For the vibrational field to shift, often we require the intensity of emotional debris that arise to not only clear, but while doing so, they carry with them the transformative power for adjustment. The same bliss that I felt in the recognition of my mother's voice of, "It's Me!!" was unrecognizable in suffering, and indeed felt absent in presence. But in the creation of loss or death as a conduit for awakening, this process allowed me to move deeper into the relationship potential with her (and me) beyond three-dimensional constraints.

The process discussed here is not to minimize what we feel or move quickly through it, but to abide with what we feel in loving compassion by granting space for what flows, which honors all circumstances as purposeful in energy (shifting our belief system or vibration from one of doubt to faith) and provides relief as emotional debris are cleared by the integration of what desires acknowledgement in our field. Societally, the belief lingers that if we do this practice of embracing, we are somehow condoning the hurt that was caused in deep trauma, suffering, or loss, and are honoring the action rather than the energy of what was felt in reaction. As humankind evolves, though, it will continue to search for meaning, because meaning or purpose is built into us by our very nature. And because we live in an inclusive universe, we can never eradicate anything— it can only be integrated, transformed, and repurposed in process as the pure source material from which it came. We may witness this somewhat in nature through the circle of life on a base level three-dimensionally, but as we expand or ascend dimensionally, so will our narrative of what we are aware of in energy, time, and space. Even though this may sound incredibly far-reaching or complex at times, the most important thing to remember is that this is all proceeding with love: the love we offer, our soul working in conjunction with the universe, and greater self always moving on our behalf in benefit.

At some point in our life path, as we are ready, the universe will orchestrate an 'upgrade' for us, which entails the reconfiguring of the nervous system, allowing us to receive the energies necessary for transformation in consciousness. This upgrade may feel or have an appearance of insanity, as not only is our nervous system being upgraded, but the way we think and vibrate is completely rewired through this process. Imagine the old switchboard operators of the early telephone, which had to manually plug in cords to connect calls, and rather abruptly all the connections on the board are pulled out… this sudden shift in reception to our reality can feel deeply traumatic, full of loss and devastation. But slowly the upgraded version of our switchboard begins to be reconnected as the wiring is strengthened by cables more resilient to the downloads we are receiving. Although this is completely natural as part of the evolutionary process, what we feel may arguably be anything but pleasant. Being that we have incarnated into an experience of energetic sensations continuously pulsing in the body, it is not uncommon for the nervous system to become overwhelmed as it attempts to process waves of kinetic information on a three-dimensional level. And as we develop in our early years of life here, the innocence that we are in essence will present itself in an air of naivety, completely trusting the world until our view of reality is skewed to the finite for functioning in a somewhat closed system with 'others'. This is a necessary step in our evolutionary path which promotes the development of the ego in order to protect us from what is deemed as 'separation' in existence. Although feelings of inadequacy, worthlessness, and rejection are a part of this perception, the energy in these emotions are indications of the pending upgrade when we are ready for a spiritual (r)evolution of restoration. Although the time between our initial incarnation and when this takes place may seem somewhat arbitrary, every experience we will ever have whether fully present or not is part of a gestation period necessary for transformation to come to fruition. The soul will lead us into these energies at an appropriate time to abide, but as humans we can often focus so intensely on our emotions, many times we will miss the bigger picture of what is provided. This frequently leaves us feeling alone, without support, and isolated in a cycle of circumstances, which, although very far from the truth, can make it seem like we are spinning our wheels with little or no growth in our life path.

But if this is the case, there is always a benefit to being in this place where until we abide with what arises in loving compassion our perception will not shift in resolve. We will know this shift is occurring when we come to realize the nature of certain people, circumstances, and events in our life as universal benefactors, contracted to reveal our shadow side which has been asking for love.

Even though we may resist because of the uncomfortable and sometimes painful sensations that arise, as we learn to trust in universal arrangement, relief pours through the cracks of egoic construction, unraveling vibrational threads which have attached to emotional debris in our cellular memory. By learning our needs, feelings, and desires, we can provide the attention necessary for 'flow' to be restored in our experience. This clearing process is serving a dual purpose in resolve, both in this timeline as well as dimensionally, eternally providing empowerment to express who we are without hindrance or restraint. As one who has experienced resolve and healing as a byproduct of it, the one thing I can promise you without hesitation is that depression is not a sickness, pain is not purposeless, and the shadows work for our benefit. These are among some of the many indications that we are in deep transformation, evolving in the spiritual nature or the very fabric of any reality we are currently experiencing.

Although many of us may feel uneasy as we embrace the energy of 'uneasy' in loving compassion, integration, and as a revealer of divinity, the nature of our relationship with the universe becomes more and more apparent as the partnership we have long desired. By accepting personal responsibility in self-love, we come to know ourselves on a more intimate basis and realize that the energies we experience are all a part of evolvement. And when the protector ego is no longer necessary, although we will feel the pains of egoic death in the body of our incarnation, we will also come to know the bliss or freedom of its integration. We are passionate builders of the universe, both learning how it works in the utilization of its tools and in the pure expressing of that which we have come forth to be in creation. When transformative power appears in our life, it only does so upon our request in order that we may draw on the deep reserves we may have been sidestepping for fear of instability— those places of perpetual discomfort that will resurface in life until we are capable of embracing them, and will often be perceived as 'burdensome, troubling', or 'oppressive' in nature.

Early in awakening, a space of investigation or recognition may seem to yield little in results, but only because we are coming to know ourselves and those parts that may have been hidden or unknown before. We may even feel "this isn't working," or "maybe I'll look somewhere else," never realizing that was the feeling, the observation to be with— that aspect of the self that desired to be heard. What we may feel we are missing in a daily practice are those feelings themselves, which become our journey, until being with 'what we feel is missing' becomes our practice. Although this book may seem complex at certain times, really what it often alludes to is 'that one' in journey, and the simplistic nature of uncertainty in the process.

When we face uncertainty, it may not seem conducive to our spiritual wellbeing or process, but this space is universally created specifically for the expansion of faith, our ability to love, and grounding in relationship to the soul as we resolve doubt. Even though appearances in our circumstances may contradict what we are being offered, they are only manifested in direct proportion to what we desire on a deeper level in the soul. Whether we realize it or not, we have given the universe permission to do this on our behalf, even though what materializes may feel uncomfortable, unwanted, and out of our control. The purpose of this book is to move into this journey with the soul as 'pilgrims' coming to know ourselves, which we do not necessarily have to understand in order to reap the benefits. In fact, many times we can be so blinded by our own vision that we may be unable to see what we truly desire in our passions. The importance of uncertainty is exactly that— to trust, connect, and expand beyond three-dimensional outcomes, seeing situational relationships as opportunities to the infinite we have come to fulfill in larger perspective.

Being with 'me' (my mother and many other impactful relationships) was an integral part of rebirth in shifting vibrational threads of suffering that had been asking for resolve throughout my life path, possibly many lifetimes. And the simple nature of that one statement from mother, "it's me!!", energetically set the tone for a much deeper relationship universally that was coming; everything leading up to any loss experienced is always purposeful, and the inter-connections or relationships that precede in cellular memories are the transformative power coming forth in each of us. What had eluded me twenty years prior was really 'me', the one who needed the necessary time for evolution to move along life paths, forming connections, and enjoying the companionship of others while allowing the ego to build a reality only to be shattered as a part of the ascension process. Although in 3-D this sounds incredibly destructive (as we tend to view loss or death in human terms), the universe or divine nature of who we are feels the intimate evolvement of our relationships, and fulfillment of them on a higher dimensional plane of living. It's difficult to articulate the relationship I have today with my mother, because it spans across time dimensionally, where 'me' meets 'me' on a different plane of existence, one which extends beyond the finite of linear thinking in terms of energy. This isn't to say I don't miss her in physical form, but rather her physical form fulfilled a purpose multi-dimensionally, without which, as events unfolded in her death, neither of us would have evolved. A friend once shared with me his experience of this: "it's sort of like being on the phone with someone, and you get disconnected. It doesn't mean they are gone, only the form in which they were communicating no longer exists."

Currently humanity is undergoing an unmistakable transformation in reality, shifting in potential as we walk through the circumstances of our pain. And although much of our species resides in darkness, if we are experiencing deep suffering, we are not only awakening to our innermost selves, but are among those leading the front wave in human evolution. Now more than ever is a need for listening to the soul and a time of abiding with all that we feel, holding fast to the love our heart has desired to feel safe in for expansion. As we do so our body, mind, and energy will quicken, vibrationally shifting awareness through all that we feel as part of the transformational process of ascension. Old paradigms will no longer serve this new creation, and the physical sickness we may experience, along with depression, anxiety, and insanity, will be evidence of an egoic death taking place as we evolve dimensionally; awakening may look ugly in the healing aspect of our soul, but so does a butterfly emerging from its cocoon.

The proposals set forth in this book are garnered not only from personal experience, but from those among us who have awakened in self-realization as multi-dimensional beings. Originally this book was designed as daily readings of support for the one in the ascension process, but it quickly became apparent in working with others, workshops, and online meetings that a foundational manual was needed for terms like "egoic construction, shadow work, integration," and "multi-dimensional beings", just to name a few. I've attempted to articulate the downloads from not only my experiences while in process (much of which were written years later as awareness caught up with the energies), but also from what I call "future self." Although the concept of a relationship with our 'self' from the future may seem a little far-fetched (no pun intended), frequently I witness people having conversations with God, ascended masters, angels, themselves, and animal friends receiving similar results. The difference is in believability, and a willingness to follow that direction, guidance, or insight, which many of us do not trust— instead relying on egoic construction for stability. We all receive daily reflections of the soul where desires, expressions, and explorations come forth as emanations imparting wisdom or that which has been made manifest, but frequently the uninitiated may view them as separate and 'other' only in connection with outer circumstances. But when the process of ascension begins to unfold, this manual may help as a support to these communications that are accessible to us.

In a three-dimensional paradigm of egoic construction it will seem absurd to consider the perfection of our awakening under such circumstances, especially when we may experience intense suffering. And in our 'seeming' failure to comprehend how the current world crumbling beneath the weight of a former one in our belief system serves us, a new creation is literally forming within and around us as we ascend. It is perhaps one of the simplest, most beautiful, and most painful experiences in the universe, yet so complex in reflection that it can only be witnessed with childlike eyes.

Recently a friend had asked me about the dragonfly as his spirit guide and wondered what the spiritual significance or symbolism might be in his current circumstances. Many times, because the patterns of our relationships have been so rooted in ego, we view our messengers as 'other' rather than what we feel working in coordination with the soul. But as our ears, hearts, and eyes are opened, we expand in what we are able to receive in our awareness. As William shared his interaction with the dragonfly that day, and how it had been trapped inside the store where he worked, the tones in his voice carried an ache, and as his voice cracked as he became choked up saying, "he just kept flying into the window but couldn't get out, and it felt like I was the dragonfly, trapped, and wishing someone would come along and help."

Sometimes when we are shifting it is sort of like we "can't see the forest for the trees," because often we have a difficult time comprehending the simplicity of what we are experiencing.

When asking my friend, "who let the dragon fly out?" his response was, "I did."

It's all here to help, all of it. As human beings we have the capacity for greatness and awe in our movements, but only as we learn to endure our most afflictive of energies with loving embrace— those parts that come forth which are frequently perceived as 'unwanted', aching, and in pain, which will undoubtedly never go away until they are loved. Through the evolutionary process there will ultimately be a tipping point, and no matter what the ego presents, the desires within us will burst beyond the walls of egoic construction, presenting what we feel. And often the more traumatic the energies are, the bigger the resolve, and as a species we will move us beyond the dualism of 'right' and 'wrong', or 'good' and 'bad'. In other words, the outcomes, or circumstances related to them, are not the goal, but getting to know ourselves is. This doesn't mean we must stay where we are at, in the same relationship or career, but that the work we are doing shifts our perception from an outer focus to the inner, naturally creating a connection dimensionally with manifestational opportunities to reality.

While the law of attraction is indeed at work in our vibration, many of the current teachings of the day tend to lean towards 'feeling good' in order to shift outer circumstances. Although this has merit in the sense of what we vibrate the external will mirror, the 'greater self', which is us, works tirelessly to provide what we need in coordination with our vibrational field, often on a much deeper level than we are unaware of— where many times the actual request of what we are sending to the universe is misunderstood by us. The universe is a mirror teacher, and playground abundantly full of playmates for the soul, and it arises upon request, ultimately by our design. There is a wealth of life to be lived, and as we learn the language of compassion in viewing each reflection, we become open to what we feel; the fabric of reality shifts to meet each of us as 'me', and as we learn to hold the heart one "I love you" at a time, our messengers, friends, lovers, and family appear eternally in our embrace as *the one we already are.*

xxi

Table of Contents

Chapter 1

The Web of Life

There will be days when we may struggle with the simplest of tasks, like getting out of bed, showering, eating, and even waking. We may want to hide from the world, pulling the covers tight to us as we search for some sense of warmth and security. At times we will question life, observing it from a strange place of surreal perception, wondering how we came to be here, and what meaning there is in it all. Physically, mentally, and emotionally, our best efforts may be slowed to an arduous crawl, and we may feel as though we have blinders on to the world around us. We may even believe we have done something 'wrong' to feel this way or that we are unaware of any transformational value in what we discern, but this space is only one in a series of stages necessary for evolvement. And we may think we are alone, that no one knows the ache we endure, but there are forces in and around us that are consistently aware of our plight; when one thread is broken or disturbed, the entire web is affected by it.

Life can feel overwhelming at various times, but there are connections that exist beyond our present circumstances, even though we may be unaware of them. The sacred web of energy permeates every aspect of our existence. How we feel physically, mentally, and emotionally is bound to this web of life as it is to us, and no need goes unnoticed or unacknowledged energetically. Just as the earth senses magnetic fields, conditions, and variances that emerge in the system of the planet, universal forces also have an acute pulse throughout all of creation on a quantum scale that three-dimensionally is incomprehensible— which is why part of the darkness we experience often may be dismissed as weakness, laziness, inferiority, or some other negative characteristic applied by

1

egoic constructs in an attempt to protect our identity or known reality, especially as we start to experience activated energies from multiple points of view.

But by developing practices of love, the heart experiences relief and feels the safety necessary for our energy field to shift in transformation. Awareness also expands in self-realization of greater consciousness, which grows in connection over time by the love provided. When we are awakened, though, some energies will naturally have the appearance of conflict through the filter of the ego, and this view will only shift as we are ready to receive higher-vibrational data in our stream. This happens inadvertently in practices of self-love as we acknowledge energies in how we feel physically, mentally, and emotionally in our experience. In other words, as we allow the necessary space for "not feeling like getting out of bed, showering, eating, or even waking," paradoxically we acknowledge we are not abandoned, that all things are working together for wellness, and the love offered to the energies that have been asking for attention is maturing, all of which the universe responds to vibrationally. This doesn't necessarily mean we turn away from life responsibilities, but rather we allow ourselves to feel what is asking for support in us.

For many of us, this process might start as a small ache in the body, possibly feeling drained, or the need for space, but it will appear however is necessary to gain our attention. We receive guidance throughout our day, some subtle and some not-so-subtle, as to what we need when parts come forward in communication with us. The body works for us in coordination with the soul and universal forces, but because this may cause instability in our life, disrupting our daily routine of affairs, the ego will begin a regiment of thinking to reel us back from any notions of uncertainty, impressing upon us through its filter words like 'productivity' and 'responsibility'. Although personal responsibility is considered a part of any practice in self-love, as we go deeper into the web of life and how the universe manifests for wellbeing, *personal responsibility* shifts in applied meaning. Until it does, though, the ego will challenge any new belief system that feels unstable to egoic constructs or our current known reality, which depends on our focus of responsibility and productivity to remain intact as it is three-dimensionally. But as we will see throughout this book in the following chapters that this doesn't mean we are powerless with no ability to respond or be productive within the ascension process or our life path, but rather we allow ourselves to shift our attention to the energy of where we are being called to respond.

Although this may seem like a struggle between the needs within us and the ego, the evolutionary process allows the mind to race in apparent self-defeat for what arises on a deeper level in feelings to be resolved or expressed as desired. So, as we move deeper into what may feel or have an appearance of conflict when issues such as sickness, distress, or strong grasping arise, as we mature spiritually, we will become aware that the body is working cohesively with our environment to produce what is necessary for the transformational process of ascension. 'Set-backs' or afflictive circumstances in the third dimension are the paradoxical energies that the soul and universal forces have already worked out on multiple timelines and dimensions for wellbeing. Often, we are just in a state of waiting for our awareness to catch up to what has already happened for a shift in our vibration. Life may *seem* to work against us at times, especially when our shadows or fears expose themselves, but this is only a proving ground for our process. Once we are ready, we do not run, nor do we fight, we simply surrender trusting inherently in the nature of our creation.

Even when we are devastated, we are continuously made deeper in self, and we come to realize that what was suffered in the depths only did so that we might reclaim vibrationally what has asked for fulfillment. The healing many of us seek is in the acknowledgement of our own truth, in each of the feelings that come daily, whose whispers we hear in our own time. Society, friendships, children, lovers, work, and the body are the very fabric of reality, all of which are a part of the web of life, participating as necessary requirements for transformation. Incarnation is a wonderful system designed specifically for this that we may embrace vibrational issues which may not be so transparent otherwise. As we continue to interact with

3

the world, we begin to realize the contrast within us: the things that we do like, and the things that we don't like. And in coming to know the preferences within us, whether they be physical, ideal, or spiritually inspired, we start to see that our preferences are lined with emotional debris. These debris can be from a trauma we have experienced, the environment we were raised in, social conditioning, or even genetics passed down from our ancestors, but when they reach out for resolution, the natural process of these energies moves us further inward where we will begin to ask, "what is it that I truly desire through the emotional vortex arising in me?"

When we come to this place, we are nearing readiness for expansion. Old ideas of what we once thought of as a desired reality may begin to crumble, and belief systems of how things work begin to blur. The very nature of existence will come into question, along with what it means for us to be here on this journey, as well as the love we have for others in relation to our self. This is wonderful! We are opening access to a point of view where we are allowing truths to be challenged, one in which we can explore the deeper nature of energies in what we feel rather than mere surface reactions.

As we allow more and more space to abide with our feelings, giving attentive love for what arises, we begin to see the habitual patterns, and the egotistical structures in the subconscious thread of our vibration. The nature of our experiences of the world shift to become a school of reflection, teaching us about ourselves in the faces of others: those places within asking for nurturing, the love that we have been desirous of, and the aches deep in the heart which are triggered by our relationships. When we feel abandoned, rejected, or treated painfully, within the pain is a layer of our soul that is revealing a previously unacknowledged truth in the depth of the heart. This may feel like a great play at times as we experience universal reflection, where in one moment we are the actor, in another the director, or writer, possibly each in tandem or all at the same time. But as we learn how the universe works, with each scene and character fulfilling their lines, the more we explore, we discover the play has been carefully scripted as needed to evoke those places within us and others as needed. Even so, upon each stage is the temptation of comfort where egoic props become familiar, we review our performance, and there is a sense of feeling drawn into the illusion of permanence rather than what we know to be eternal. Whether we witness this in ourselves or others, the force of love is always active, and the world is not a dominating entity of oppression, but truly a living organism of love, scripting our most powerful passions in the reflections of the scenes we witness, consistently moving us towards higher destiny as it calls.

The approach we are looking at here might seem unorthodox in learning how the universe works, but when things don't line up the way we expect, and we or people in our lives act out, behaving in a manner that surprises us where we may feel hurt, disappointed, and alone, it's common to view life as an attack, like things are happening to us rather than for us. This one perception speaks volumes to the nature of what we believe in that, either the universe and creation has made our life a cosmic joke upon which we are the prey, or there is another possibility attempting to reveal itself in the paradoxical, energetic nature of what we feel.

As we abide with these energies, relief will slowly appear in unexplored avenues of intimacy we are developing with the soul. And often an awareness arises that our most difficult experiences have been filled with emotionally charged energies, each of which serves a purpose beyond what we have previously seen, where vibrational strands have been attempting to be heard, seen, and held by us in a way that no one else can. Although in an un-awakened state these energies or emotions may appear afflictive, to universal consciousness they are an invitation to intimacy.

Humanity has a deep need to share from the heart, exploring with other souls and the creation on an intimate level. Yet somehow, many of us are held prisoner by the corners of the mind, darkened emotional debris, captured in remarks of, "what if?" What if we share where we're at? What if we speak our truth? What if we follow our bliss? What if we surrender to what we have been resisting? What if we are more than our work, family, and friendships? These questions or vibrations and many more will more than likely

5

manifest energetically as anxiety, depression, obsession, and compulsory behaviors until acknowledged. They will frequently disguise themselves in the familiar faces of 'wall builders', or protectors of our reality, whose egoic constructs are a formidable castle commissioned for the stabilization of the one who needs love. We may wonder how intimacy with ourselves, others, and the creation is to be achieved when we view the defenses that have been built and the armies of each keep. But however unlikely it may seem, this is exactly how the universe works on manifestational terms to draw us further inward in relationship to love; in any attempt to escape desolation, we are only served with a deepening sense of 'soul famine' or despair. This despair leads to a vulnerability where being naked or transparent before the universe outweighs the need for protection and reveals those parts of the soul that have been desirous of attention, which vibrationally we have incarnated to resolve, express, and explore. The natural cycles in creation will support this by sending quakes to tumble high walls to ruin, floods to destroy dams, and fires for purging undergrowth. What we may view in three-dimensional terms as 'devastation' the universe sees as part of the evolutionary process, and at some point we are introduced to the uneasiness we feel as a form of deepening.

This may not be apparent at first in reaction with outer circumstances, but as vibrational strands resound throughout the sacred web, old friends, current employers, family and environment will begin to shift in recognition of any change in frequency. But any intimacy must start with our own inner path (the things we like or dislike), each truth being the great liberator of any perceived bondage, and the divine worker presiding over resolve. The energies within us already 'know' what we often seek to unravel or solve in the mind, and they are a direct communication of the soul, but they can only be approached with childlike humility as the ego faces certain death upon entering what it perceives as 'dark places'. Ironically, faith is only built upon uncertainty, and when reality becomes unstable the ego will do its best to create an environment where shadows do not exist, where we feel familiarity, and it is unchallenged by other worlds (this is thoroughly addressed in the next chapter).

Although abiding with strong energies is a simple direction, it is no easy task for the uninitiated. The importance of developing 'love practices' as we learn how to abide with these energies and how the universe works is paramount in providing relief to the nervous system, or to the overwhelming nature of the evolutionary process we are experiencing through our incarnation. One of these love practices we will refer to time and time again throughout this exploration is the importance of developing a relationship of compassion with the heart.

The heart generates the body's most powerful electromagnetic field, rippling out upon the earth's vibrational sphere: what we think, how we feel, all of our most intimate sharing vibrates magnetically even though we may not be aware of what is being transmitted. We are subject to the issues of our heart, and as our heart transmits, we communicate with the greater body of our self. Through our heart field we draw to us experiences that we need for wellbeing to occur. The earth, its people, and all things of the universe sense our needs in greater consciousness being a part of us, consistently listening, and feeling into our deepest vibrational desires to manifest on our behalf. As we learn to communicate with ourselves on this level, sharing experiences both of pleasure and pain, we begin to realize that throughout all that we feel, the heart is not only our companion, but a center, source, and comfort to us as we develop a nurturing relationship with it. It is a gateway to manifestational power, providing both insight and stability in a universe where uncertainty is the law to any emerging faith.

In shamanic practices, developing this relationship is key to awareness or self-realization in relation to the earth and the celestial body if we are to receive a fulfillment of existence. As we come to know and love the heart, we awaken to our humanity, which is a journey of birthing divine expression and a *coming forth* as what we already are. Through the tender nurturing of the heart, we begin to realize the deep nature of resolve manifesting in affliction, and how the universe is working in coordination with us for the liberation of what we desire.

Through our continued support and investment of love in holding the heart through all that is felt, we gradually shift the vibrational fields of imbalance which have been asking to be seen, heard, and held in compassion. Not only for our benefit, but for all beings as our heart field transmits this shift multi-dimensionally. Though we may doubt this in the beginning, as we see the effects of self-love reflected through manifestation, we will come to acknowledge the potential for resolve in the world universally. One of the supportive aspects to this evolutionary process in our incarnation is the experience of time, whereby we receive a reference point that we may view manifestation in our life path. This reference point gives us insight into our relationship with the universe as we come to know those parts on a more intimate basis that we have perceived either physically or spiritually as asking for attention in our circumstances.

As we proceed in time, we will receive glimpses of the one we are coming to know on a more personal basis. Each truth that is emerging gains ground as we practice holding the heart through all that we feel and observing what has manifested, or what we would like to manifest in the cycles of our vibrational field. We may be tempted to 'keep score', viewing our life path with a perception of progress, but if this happens, we remind ourselves that this particular part of the journey is about self-realization, and any emotions we may perceive as afflictive are a part of learning who we are. But if we go into judgment with strong emotion, rather than attempting to resist or stay the mind, we abide with the feeling of judgement, telling our heart, "even though I am feeling this judgement, I will not abandon you, or reject you, but part of my healing, exploration, and expression is to feel into this, and be with what judgement feels like."

As we sit with the feelings, we grow closer to ourselves in love, because as we allow space for what comes to the surface, we also grant the heart room to be with our soul, actively demonstrating that we will not abandon ourselves.

Even though we may not be aware of it at first, we may find differences or subtle shifts which have occurred in our vibration. The body will reveal these in our tone, the way we walk, and our overall sense of being over time. And if some of these seem to challenge our comfortability, we allow ourselves to observe the parts arising in what we feel, the likes and dislikes, noticing shifts that reveal more and more of who we are in any form of energy that surfaces. Self-expression will naturally come forth as we allow ourselves to move beyond habitual patterns into the energy itself. By granting ourselves permission to go here, we bring relief to a process of transformation that may have formerly been seen by us as afflictive in resistance. And although we may experience pain, as we begin to see joy or pain as energy in process, whether for resolve, exploration, or expression, we gradually come to know ourselves as in a partnership with universal manifestation, rather than as the victim of it.

While this partnership is indeed inherent in us, until we are awakened in awareness as to how the universe works, we may find ourselves in situations which feel or are unsafe, even violent, depending on our current state. Growing up, many of us learned that trust was an outward agreement, but inwardly, many of us were riddled with doubt, born into environments we couldn't comprehend, or circumstances we felt were beyond our control. This range of experiences from person to person is in the subtlest of energies where we feel insecure, unworthy, and abandoned to the most intensive in feeling abused physically, mentally, and emotionally.

Eventually these energies become powerful revealers of their reflections that, when explored, can provide vibrational shifts in all outer circumstances. But as we learn to embrace this awareness, we come to know the darker aspects of self: the fears, betrayal, and pain that arise in the mirrors of the world. This can be an onerous teaching in that it places full responsibility for each environment we experience squarely on our shoulders (meaning there are no monsters but the ones we conjure as a part of resolve), which works in coordination with the soul to reveal those places in us that cry out only to be heard, seen, and held in the arms of love. This may often feel like we are diminishing our demons, or making light of very real abuse issues that plague our world because these energies are so difficult to process. So, let me be as clear as I can on this specific teaching: *__if you are being abused, or if you are in danger, seek help immediately__* –this particular process can always be revisited when you are safe. And if you desire to go into it further, feel free to contact me or another who is experienced with this depth of resolve. There is relief, trust, and love to be revealed, but it can always wait until we are safe enough to begin.

As we are triggered, this teaching grants us the most powerful path, in that we are both greeted by our demons and given the opportunity to explore healing through them. 'Trust' becomes a watchword, not outwardly, but inwardly with the holding of the heart as we continue feeling what arises, addressing one by one those we see as enemies, and greeting them as long-lost aspects of the self that have come to seek out a peace with us in their afflictive energies. Where once we saw fiends, we attempt embracing friends, and in doing so we offer love to the heart as well as those that were once foes. Relief comes, but not as a destination or goal, but as a byproduct of the love we offer through the breathing in of our afflictions and easing of our mind as we surrender to 'greater self' developing trust with the divine which exists in all things. This bond that we form with creation is not one outwardly in trust, but by the trust we offer inwardly in coming to know the reflections that are given to us for our benefit. This same trust or agreement is what the creation operates on when we view the laws of the universe. Everything has a frequency, and when touched, plucked, dropped, or otherwise, will vibrate. Whether we realize it or not, we are frequently sending out a vibration to the universe full of requests, expressions, and gratitude for wellbeing— not only for ourselves, but by the same love that binds all things together cohesively in the web of life. Even in our darkest hours, when we might feel deeply depressed, or anxiously on edge, not only are these emotions indications of our most holy prayers, but they are continued aspects of healing sent forth to the universe as manifestational forces in request.

How then do we know our truths, what we are asking for, and what we are viewing in the web of life or our reflections?

If outer circumstances are a reflection of our inner chambers of the soul attempting to bring us into the reality we have desired, as we sit with our feelings and learn to abide in a space of offering through loving compassion, within the layers of emotional energy that surface are the deeper requests of the soul. These requests are in direct correlation with our desires, even though they may manifest in seeming opposition at times and appear afflictive in nature. They only do so to draw attention or reveal a part of ourselves, which, as we are energy beings, may be the most effective form of communication. This process of communication in energy is unique in that there is no 'right' or 'wrong', but simply how we feel in any situation. So as a practice, when we may meet any situation with love, observing and acknowledging what we feel, we naturally ground in our prayers or desires and inadvertently develop a greater awareness of the movements in the universe. This is a powerful realization in that as we engage our life path, allowing ourselves personal responsibility for what we feel, we not only see a fluidity with the web of life, but forces at work are revealed in our consciousness. No longer are we mere "victims of circumstance," but rather we are empowered by what we become aware of moving beneath the surface and by our role that incarnation has provided in coming to fulfill our destiny. The whole of our life path becomes a vibrating prayer of requests, and as we hone our senses to the reflections we experience, not only do we become aware of our requests on a deeper, subtler level, but we see the potential of what we have come to resolve, explore, and express in a much more intimate relationship with the universe.

But the process of enlightenment is not necessarily a peaceful experience. Prior to some of the most beautiful awakenings, it may have felt like someone hit us with a 2 X 4, turning the world completely upside down. One of my favorite spiritual mentors used to tell me, "Some people have ponies in their barn, others mules, and some pretty good riding horses. YOU have Clydesdales." I believe he was referring to my willful spirit at the time. These are those parts that, by nature, when they come forth often do so in a playful manner, but with a terrible amount of destructive force in an unruly state, all of which are characteristics that surface in need of expression.

In our current societal paradigm, these characteristics are often viewed with a form of distaste, frequently harmful (to our self and others), and might be categorized as either mentally or emotionally unstable, even criminal. And although we or others might be tempted to 'tame' these parts rather than befriend them, when we resist or work against these energies, we only increase their tenacity where they will push back in forceful retaliation. Why not instead develop a flow or partnership in working with them— the difference being an unruly, resentful 2,000-pound horse of self-will, or one that works for us, pulling great weight willingly with heart in desired measure.

It's not an easy thing, no matter what you have in the barn, to build a relationship with something that may have been ridiculed, ignored, and despised for years. But if we befriend our patterns, opening a path of love in offering, doors immediately start to appear in this acknowledgment. And the pain experienced in the 'breaking' process that may emerge are only those aspects of will that are subject to mending in our perceptions, which no longer serve the relationship of only the self or 'other', but rather the larger picture of the whole. In essence, the rider and the one being ridden see the benefit of a joint relationship or one energy in purpose, and the potential for great exploration, fellowship, expression, and healing resolution occurs.

All of creation hears us and responds in kind to what we are transmitting from our vibrational threads. Things may not appear as we would like, or as we think they should, but contained within these thoughts and feelings are our highest needs, desires, and expressions to the universe. The contrast we experience here on Earth in the body, mind, and emotions is how we come to both know our innermost life path and transmit it universally. So even though we may not feel as if we are making progress in what we desire, *that feeling is communicating to the universe what we desire.*

As we begin to look at life in terms of our reflections and move under the surface of circumstances into the matrix of energies that are presented, encoded in these vibrational fields of mirroring are the habitual patterns interwoven in our cellular memory for observing. These may include but are not limited to previous generational debris, past lives, current life traumas, or defense mechanisms developed by egoic cocooning prior to or in preparation of transformation. So, if we act out, rebel, or flee from what we feel, although it may seem as if egoic patterns are holding us captive, they are merely replaying the traumas in our cellular memory which have been encoded with the vibrational threads that desire attention, love, and healing.

Whether from past or present life circumstances, as events trigger these energies, they are necessary for furthering the evolutionary process or revealing those patterns resurfacing at our vibrational request when we are ready to address them. This readiness becomes apparent when we are willing to abide with the emotional debris arising in a space of holding the heart in loving compassion and feeling into the reflections that trigger us. As a practice, one of the most powerful offerings we can give to ourselves or others when experiencing strong energies is an affirmation of love. We may give this silently or out loud, but we speak directly to the heart saying, "I love you, and will not abandon or reject you; even though I am allowing myself to feel all that I feel, I am here for you, as one who loves you."

By developing a practice of love in whatever we may feel, be it strong emotions or otherwise, we allow an expansion of consciousness to occur, and we begin to see the nature in each reflection we receive, which is merely the 'greater self' responding to what we have been transmitting. Although much of this may be on a subconscious level in our desires or needs, as our awareness catches up to what is moving on our behalf, we will perceive our deepest longings being met as we call out to the universe; even in our lowest or most painful of circumstances, our highest vibrational frequency is at work with universal arrangement. Once we become aware this, and that these are some of our most powerful manifestations emerging from some of the unruliest places within or those parts that once we were afraid to acknowledge, they become our most sacred allies in life, or workhorses and friends. And even though we may feel we are alone at times, and that no one knows the ache we endure, these forces that move in and around us are consistently aware of our process— when one thread is broken or disturbed, the entire web is affected by it.

By Our Design

By Our Design

Chapter 2

Egoic Construction

Upon incarnation, newborns often reflect the intensity of infinite universal expression poured into a tiny, finite body. Innocence, surrender, humility, trust, and joy are a few of the characteristics we may witness when first looking into the eyes of those who have chosen to undertake this pilgrimage. Each soul entering the world does so for reasons vibrationally which both the individual and whole of the universe agree on in careful coordination for expansion. And even though the fabric of a three-dimensional reality will quickly overwhelm any awareness of the abstract nature of the eternal, with the flesh dimming the light of divinity as a covering over time, this process may seem unorthodox, but it is completely natural; because three-dimensional, conventional information is unreliable to one who has come from an abstract realm of existence, the infinite experiences the finite in form, which is precisely what is needed for expansion to occur for a being of immense vision.

The 'ego' has developed as a natural part of this process in the spiritual evolution of humanity, donning the role of 'protector' in order to cope with the overwhelming sensations of the nervous system. Once established, it will challenge any approach that destabilizes a reality grounded in the third dimension. Its role is three-fold in that it creates a buffer to the overwhelming stimulus felt in the body from an early age, which in turn allows for a gestational process of energies that will be utilized in any transformational process as we are ready, and thirdly the ego over time will create an alternate reality that stabilizes the uncertainty felt in our experience of the world. When egoic constructs begin to be built, they create an almost unshakable foundation in the third dimension for an illusionary reality, and once they have taken hold, will not collapse until they are no longer necessary. This cycle is commonly repeated throughout our lifetime here as needed to fulfill what we have pre-contracted in the soul before incarnating.

There are many layers to egoic construction in how it serves to fulfill its main mission as protector, from developing patterns of reaction in behaviors to filtering our thoughts with a more acceptable landscape in perception to quell the overstimulated nervous system. Many circumstances that unfold in our life might be too painful, traumatic, or difficult to integrate in the moment, so the ego as guardian will buffer them and potentially create an alternate reality as a living shield. For instance, when situations arise that trigger intense emotions or energies, as the nervous system becomes overwhelmed by what we feel, we will react strongly, but this is often the ego stepping in to intercede on our behalf until we are able to process at a later time. Although this may seem counter-productive to our evolutionary path, the ego really is working in coordination with our body, nervous system, and our vibrational field for wellbeing. It is both effective and efficient in protection and recycling of energy, doing so until we are ready to integrate the energies necessary for our transformation.

Every one of us will undertake this transformational passage, whether we do so in our time on pilgrimage here or at the moment of physical death, although physical death does not guarantee transformation. We may awaken to transformational potential in our afterlife, but not necessarily the fulfillment of what we have come to experience, which is why many of us choose to return to a state of resolving energies for expansion through incarnation.

What we may view as the afterlife, or an existence free of this body and its cares, will rather be a 'continuance' of who we are on a much deeper level, and depending on our vibrational frequency, will determine where our life path leads us eternally. For some, there is a sense that the 'truth' has been watered down in various religious or spiritual dogmas to comfort the conscience that is ill at ease about the proposition of continuing in the next life with similar issues coming forward, while others may only hear the aspects of hell, in which we may be left to fend for ourselves, only to await eternal damnation in a much larger picture by refusal to conform to religious teachings or worship in a savoir. Ironically, these beliefs are not far from the truth, although inaccurate in many understandings that are protected by ego— we may be caught in habitual patterns that feel like hell, even from life to life, but these patterns only serve to cultivate the debris necessary for us to address what we have desired to shift as we are ready, not because we have been condemned.

In a sense, our demons work for us; they are the fuel that charges us with the emotional intensity to bring awareness to those vibrations or patterns within us asking to be resolved. Egoic construction only serves as needed for our benefit, never as an adversary to be vanquished. This is most likely one of the most misunderstood teachings in spiritual warfare, in that there is *no* spiritual warfare. The struggle that is felt within the mind, emotions, and body are the communications of the soul working with universal arrangement— never against it.

Commonly, these energies are received with a view of pain or suffering because they are seen through the filter of ego until they have passed, whereas desire is purposefully mixed with temporal outcomes. This mixture provides a path we cannot think or reason our way out of, as the three-dimensional constructs that support it are necessary to draw our attention to the emotional debris that surface in our cellular memory (which are connected to desires in our vibrational field). So, while we may want clarity or reason to stand as our advocate in thought, the law of love will only provide whatever we need for what is desired in resolving our vibrational field. In other words, emotion trumps thought in that any unresolved vibration, exploration, or expression has precedence in our manifestations and will consistently appear as a part of our known reality to be seen, heard, and held by us in love until fulfilled. As we learn to love ourselves through any experience we have or feel in the third dimension, vibrationally we begin to shift higher in frequency, allowing our consciousness to expand to multi-dimensional living, or the divine. Self-love is paramount, whether to ease suffering or fulfill what we desire, and as we practice loving compassion, our heart opens in the safety we offer, even when we move through painful afflictive feelings.

Pain is a critical part of our learning to be compassionate with ourselves. On the one hand, it presents an obstacle that seems to prevent our happiness, steal our time, and incapacitate us. On the other, it is the great 'motivator', a part of being human that enhances the joy in life and brings with it deep transformational power. And at a certain point in each journey, we will receive glimpses into the patterns experienced when we are nearer or more likely to 'sit' with our pain, feeling into how we are interacting with its energy. Although in times past we may have viewed pain with negativity, or as something unproductive to be overcome, the key to any shift is in our response; as we explore the potential for compassion, we may offer ourselves in how we feel with what arises observing our interaction with pain, the relationship with the heart deepens. This may feel awful at first as emotions may overwhelm us, but with the ego as guardian, working in coordination with the soul and universe, only as we are ready to offer love will it permit entrance in deepening. This process is not one generally in which the walls come down overnight, but rather in degrees.

By observing the pain in attachment and the nature of egoic constructions in relationships, we may become aware of how we ground ourselves to earthly objects or circumstances for security. This will come naturally throughout life— as we sense deep insecurity rising in us, we also notice physical impermanency. Much of the affliction we feel is based in our three-dimensional existence, but once we are capable of viewing these attachments, we also become aware of another path which will bring us relief. In contemplation we may wonder, "how may I love, yet remain non-attached to this or that in a relationship?" This is where we might feel daunted by the nervous system, as it tends to become overwhelmed by the fabric of a three-dimensional reality, one in which we will feel the emotional energy of our investments, egoic patterns, and the interwoven strands of desire in our circumstances where we begin to see attachment.

A simple yet effective practice in trust that may also reveal and yield relief in our attachments is saying the phrase, "I will ground my divinity by the earthly possessions I have." This will often provoke a rebellious response within us that clearly feels aligned in truth, but also leads to what is in resonance within us. Although this may sound ridiculous, it is utilizing resistance as an admittance to a rather large step in the direction of consciousness to greater self as we are ready to receive it. 'Trust' may sound easy, like a handshake or a verbal agreement, but vibrationally it involves our ability to be sound or 'ring true' in our agreements, which many times are much deeper than what we can perceive from a solely three-dimensional point of view. The reason this seems more difficult as a teaching is because we commonly do not know what we trust or don't trust except on a three-dimensional level, hence we form bonds of trust and base security on physical things.

For example, when I was grieving my mother's passing, a large part of trust in the greater process was experienced by the embracing of her transition through death. This meant sitting next to her, looking in her eyes as tears welled in mine, holding her hand as she gasped for air, and speaking heartfelt words that were difficult to say in these moments— both doing my best to comfort her and myself, knowing her vessel was a shell that housed her essence, and being with her, abiding in the pain of death. After she had passed, my body, mind, and emotions continued to grieve the loss, as then it was losing the common reference of who she was in her vessel. Then came the grieving of her in relation to possessions as the family went through liquidating the estate and feeling all the feelings attached on a cellular level to memories associated with her. These life paths we go through can be very difficult, but if we allow ourselves to venture deeper into the soul, we find they not only serve our relationships outwardly with others, but they also cultivate an intimate relationship within ourselves— one whereas we allow ourselves to grieve, feel loss, and face our attachments, we experience a much more profound level of love we ever thought possible. Humanity struggles with this depth of intimacy, and trust, which is why grasping to possessions helps us to remember and connects us sentimentally or vibrationally in the heart to loved ones until we are ready to

21

experience the loss of physicality, but the gain of what we love in higher vibration, which is never lost.

Releasing ourselves is not an ascension of overcoming or letting go, but degrees of grieving, respect, and nurturing that support honoring that which has served us, even in egoic constructions. As we acknowledge emotions that have lodged themselves in cellular memory, whether it is a person, place, object, event, or circumstance we may find difficult in attachment, we honor those parts coming forth in us. In abiding with them, we offer the love necessary for coming to know ourselves; we not only resolve deep issues, but we give attention to what has been asking for love or expression, sending a clear message to the ego that we are ready for a higher vibrational life in meaning.

But the paradoxical nature of our relationship with the universe is such that what may appear as 'two steps back' is actually momentum towards what we desire in our soul, especially when what we see is through the filter of ego. Societal perception can also intensify confusion in that most if not all civilizations are formed on the basis of three-dimensional joint agreements, whereas the universe works from a much larger picture multi-dimensionally, moving at the request of each individual and the whole simultaneously. So, what we may view as a decline in the physical, mental, and emotional health of humanity is really the awakening call for a much more in-depth relationship with the self or soul universally. And the intensity of focus we commonly witness towards outer circumstances in ourselves, other people, and events around the world is really a preponderance for the relationship that is ached for within.

Much of the time, these painful indications are difficult to hear because they bring the focus back to a state of personal responsibility in each of us, even though they utter the necessary information we are seeking for relief. Although we may feel daunted by the task of abiding with the feelings that arise, they are working in conjunction with the higher self in process as they move in every aspect of our lives. When we feel the effects of our circumstances weighing heavily upon us, however they may appear, we will almost certainly question the means of our deliverance when unwanted, ugly, and seemingly unfortunate experiences are involved. And what may be the darkest embrace of all is when the infinity of who we are begins to come to realization, where we may feel even more alone due to the nature of the vast expanse within us that is emerging. But again, although these places may be perceived as painful, or that we have entered suffering for no apparent reason, they are purposeful for us to be with ourselves in the greater context of who we are as infinite beings of divinity. What may seem callous, uncaring, and even malicious paradoxically contains the seeds of the tender, caring, and benevolent.

Although we may not see or understand what is happening in the transformational process and we are quite like children, as we continue to hold offerings of love out and within, our vision will adjust in the deep. This may feel unsettling (which is an understatement) by any understanding in three-dimensional terms, but as we give ourselves over to uncertainty and abide with all that is felt, as each part comes forth to express what is needed, a new reality emerges— one where we move with egoic construction at a pace that is compassionate and nurturing to the heart in reassurance of any unfolding:

Failure may arise, but only as an indication of what we have come here to resolve in our view as success.

Doubt may encircle us, as if to pounce when we are at our weakest, yet only comes in love to strengthen as an emissary of faith.

Grasping may weigh upon us, whispering, "if there is surrender, surely that which is held will be lost," yet it reveals the desire to deepen our roots.

At some point we turn towards the door rather than running from it. We feel what seems like failure when it arises, but as we love the heart we are fulfilled. We may cringe at our truths but acknowledge them with the support of innocence. And with each ache in loss, the universe foretells the room being created for that which is coming.

One of the greatest tales of the East is that of the Ramayana, and the central figure of Hanuman, who represents our simian lower nature as a monkey god in service to higher self. A favorite quote from Hanuman to Ram the Divine prince is, "When I don't know who I am, I serve you. When I know who I am, you and I are one." Our daily relationship with the body, mind, and emotions is similar to that Hanuman, so much that even when we may doubt our circumstances, they continue to serve us, providing a vessel of transformative power for the soul. As we become more open to the potential arising from the depths of uncertainty, allowing ourselves to embrace what we feel as instability, our vessel works perfectly as an instrument in coordination with universal forces to communicate what is in need of attention, love, and healing. So, although we may struggle with our physical, mental, and emotional path, these are already on our side as agents of deliverance, forming paths that will shift vibrational fields to align with the love we are asking for.

As we awaken to the purpose of egoic construction and its working in coordination with the universe, we learn that love serves in every aspect of our life, not only those which feel pleasurable. And over time, we slowly develop a discourse with the vessel, and how a formerly unrealized language of our "lower nature" has been here along in service to us. This works in a two-fold benefit for our journey, the first being that as we develop our communication with the body, mind, and emotions not only is life enhanced by being more fully immersed in our experience, but second that we come to know previously unacknowledged places as we expand dimensionally in our divinity. In the saga of the Ramayana, Hanuman is not aware of all the power and might he contains. He has forgotten what he is capable of and is reminded of who and what he is. In the story, as he grows in stature, taking a "leap of faith" to Sri Lanka in service to his prince, he discovers his true nature.

Although our first priority is to the heart— holding ourselves with loving compassion, being gentle, and never forcing our way through— by allowing ourselves to observe how we treat ourselves while experiencing what we feel in our pain or struggle, we effectively create a space for our vibration to shift in expansion and widen what we are capable of feeling. Even though we may be unaware of our soul-contracts, an agreement or trust begins to develop between us and the universe where we realize we are healing at a pace that is based in loving compassion. This trust is further developed with the universe as we experience degrees of resolution, and our faith grows in the promise of what we see coming: a continued resolution of manifestational arrangement offered by greater self-love working on our behalf with the soul. Even though at times we will exhaust our every effort for a quickened recovery or awakening, this will fall away gently as we realize resolve takes place on a perfect timetable of universal consciousness, manifesting precisely what we need when we need it for wellbeing.

Suffering, however, may be eased by the love we give to the heart through the various circumstances that arise in our life path. Whether we realize what is happening or not, we can still ease suffering through love practices which will embolden the heart and forge a relationship between it and the nature of our divinity. We may experience this as a 'stretching' of the soul in a sense, not in a forceful way, but rather that the heart is ready to proceed in expansion in what is coming forth as who we already are. Even though there may be pain in our realizations as we expand, energy itself expands dimensionally by the love we offer, and we gain a wider body of potential in peace for what we encounter.

In ascension, we are no longer limited by a finite, illusionary wall of protection, but as we feel and open ourselves up to the care of love, we develop a much more substantial path of fulfillment to the soul. This might seem like we are painting a bigger bullseye for universal interaction on ourselves, and we are, but really the mark is for us, that we may more easily find the resolution to what we are desirous of. And because the ego's job is to protect us while we expand dimensionally, we may find ourselves frequently living from multiple points of view as we become more and more aware in the ascension process. This is where being gentle with ourselves is essential, because from an egoic frame of reference, anything that might create instability is seen as a challenge to egoic construction and will most likely become adversarial with the ego, tapping memories of life events, our surroundings, and timelines as key elements in creating stability. The ego can be very much like a parental figure in a sense, even in its most incredulous, defensive behaviors and accusations, and will draw upon life experiences to form conclusions that will either strengthen three-dimensional paradigms (keeping the child's energy in its care), or, once we begin to question the nature of our reality (as the child matures, becoming responsible for its energy), utilize the emotional debris that arise to build energetic fields for transformation as we are ready.

In our current society, the structure of the ego has done an excellent job in order to stabilize what may surface daily in emotional duress, both by the comforts offered as a distraction and to appease what arises. Television, internet, video games, food, sex, and a reliance on an income for living have all attempted to ground an already over-stimulated nervous system, rooting our sense of self firmly in three-dimensional constructs of grasping. Societal norms of accomplishment, health, and beauty further play a role in establishing the ego's description of identity, both providing the appearance of a world thriving in dynamic desire and one which will serve the energies in waiting when we move into transformation.

Even though the situation may seem dire at times, these distractions, appeasements, and appearances are utilized by the ego to stabilize our reality and create a means of gestation for unresolved energies in the vibrational field. Underneath many of these energies are the vibrational strands of unworthiness, inadequacy, and longing for fulfilment that have received the ego as a temporary benefactor in relief. But as the pain of humanity continues to increase exponentially with souls calling out for resolution, overstimulation, coupled with a lack of inspiration, moves us further inward as a species in preparation for an evolutionary shift dimensionally. What this means for those that are ready is, as we realize the nature of divinity at work with life in three-dimensional terms, even egoic construction, is that rather than attempting to overcome it, we can fully appreciate and embrace the transformational gestation produced as a part of our process. Although in recent history we haven't viewed egoic patterns as helpmates to our spiritual evolution, there is a growing awareness of their potential as advocates for divinity rather than adversaries that cannot be vanquished.

The perfection of all of this is that every one of us has entered this experience knowing full well what our soul has contracted us for and is slowly coming to terms with what we are here for. Not one of us will be lost to the choices of our life, no matter where or how we may find ourselves in the process of awakening. Once we become aware of our purpose in fulfilling all that we are as divine expressions, wellness becomes a matter of settling into who we are as divine explorers. And even though we may wonder why certain circumstances unfolded, or how we came to know the events of our life as we did, when we emerge through our transformational process, we begin to view our previous life in energetic terms as what was needed for us to evolve vibrationally, rather than on solely three-dimensional outcomes of impermanence.

But until we are ready and our awareness catches up to universal orchestration, self-honesty may be held captive for much of our lifetime through distraction, denial, and the limitless conversations the ego cultivates as a part of doing its best to protect us. Even so, it is in our nature to desire harmony as we are resonant beings, and in order to have any type of relationship that might be more in alignment with ourselves or bring relief, we require moments of solitary quietness where uncomfortable and comforting feelings may arise. When we do so, it is common in these moments for any relationship we have to be challenged by ego with what comes to surface— from family, pets, significant others, work, our body, or health —in a variety of ways; the divine that we are is also aware of this developing space where communications of the soul present our needs in the language of emotion. And as we allow ourselves to abide with these deep desires, any emotional debris lodged in our cellular memory will begin to surface for our acknowledgement, and slowly the process of ego deflation will occur.

When first approaching any shift in consciousness or reality, the mind tends to race, creating a state of anxiety or depression depending on overall health, the state of our nervous system, and our spiritual well-being. This is why developing practices of self-love is so important, because regardless of where we are at in our path, they will ground us in times of doubt, fear, and uncertainty as chaotic energies clear. Many times, this is a repetitive cycle we live in under egoic construction until we mature energetically to receive the resolution required in the soul. And there will be moments of euphoric release in the liberation of lodged emotional debris, but feeling positive or upbeat does not equate recovery of ourselves— rather that we are in process; if a habitual pattern continues to rise within us, until it is acknowledged on the level the soul is asking for, a karmic shift will not unfold. This is precisely why when we go into core codes of our vibrational existence, self-love becomes paramount— because without it we often become overwhelmingly critical, incapacitated, and potentially experience a break-down in our functional capacity to heal. But, as the universe is inclusive, this will ultimately work for our benefit, with the ego continuing to guard the gates, holding 'self-honesty' prisoner until we are ready to receive the truth of what we have come to shift in our soul. When this is the case, we may ask, "Why then would I be concerned with my process when eventually it will unfold as I am ready?"

If we are asking or exploring our process, chances are we are already hearing our soul, and we are in some stage of transformation. And as communication from the soul unfolds, it will feel very much like being in a dark room that comes to light slowly, where we begin to notice our surroundings or question what we see in the shadows that emerge into form. As we do, there is a growing opportunity to expand our vision by what we offer in acknowledgment. This is where emotional triggers may work for us in the liberation of self-honesty. Loss, grief, depression, and anxiety seem to be in the middle of the spectrum on an emotional scale of common feelings we may feel here, and if we abide with them in a practice of self-love, we are opened to greater awareness of what has been coming to surface for any potential shift requested of the soul. We may tend to view this shift with a still existent egoic filter of a 'goal oriented' consciousness as the reward for the love we offer, but the reality coming to light is really in our intimacy we are developing with the self as we realize the nature of life in who we are. This will most certainly impact our outer circumstances of reflection in manifestation, but as byproducts of the love offered as we embrace what is coming forth.

In the short term, we may seek something to feel a bit better or more comfortable in the familiarity of our past, or maybe even justify our actions at times— that's ok, if we desire temporary relief and we are gentle with ourselves. But as we continue to befriend honesty when it appears and embrace what it has to offer, a new reality will come to light. Agreements made of obligation, fear, scarcity, and coercion begin to fall away as unobstructed energy flows freely, no longer held in contempt when honesty was a captive. Likewise, how we have seen the world in the past will begin to shift as we shift in vibration, our perception becoming more open to the potential in uncertainty.

When expectation does arise, it is only the ego's attempt to ease the fear of living that we may feel in an uncertain reality. But the irony in embracing egoic construction as an advocate working for our divinity is that when we begin to embrace three-dimensional living, it often reveals three-dimensional truths: the fact that we may not know what is about to happen, where our next step will lead us, and that the egoic patterns of thinking that filter our beliefs will always eventually reveal the nature of who we are as energetic beings of faith. Meaning, as we face a reality constructed on time, impermanence, and illusion, we will begin to feel the weight of unmet expectations on a continual basis, which reveals the integrity of uncertainty. Although egoic construction will consistently try to change this in outcomes by blaming and attempts to control, what we feel in our experience is often the soul coming forward in communications such as anger, bewilderment, and despair, asking for resolution to uncertainty in the form of a faith. Although this is completely normal as a part of our spiritual evolutionary process, it may feel as if we are going backwards in embracing the truth of uncertainty. However, as we do so, this is a crucial step towards multi-dimensional living as "manifestors" of creation rather than victims of circumstance.

Simple truths, such as an uncertain reality, will most definitely be challenged by egoic constructions in order to maintain stability, but as they come under heavy scrutiny will often become clear in their intensity, revealing the nature of grounding in the third dimension. And although it may seem as though it's our natural tendency to want an understanding, the ego often implying, "if we can understand, we will feel safe," the heart is a feeling organ, and only feels safe by feeling safe— not by 'understanding'. This is why holding the heart becomes so important for our life path, because it is only through love that the heart field will open energetically to innocence, and through innocence gain trust and feel safe enough to expand in reception of otherwise difficult truths; our soul, body, and the universe will recognize this expansion, and as we hold to the practice of love, will always shift to our most receptive state.

As a practice in holding the heart, there's no need to psychoanalyze, read into, look for signs, or figure out; we simply welcome feelings as they come, abiding with truths as they arise for the heart to receive. We slow the breath, breathing deeply, allowing, and relaxing into the moment with each sensation, feeling what we feel as we acknowledge any uncertainty. It helps to place the hand upon the heart, recognizing the heart as a gateway to love, bearer of burdens, passions, and possibilities. By embracing what we feel, we move deeper into the depths of who we are, and the heart in turn begins to recognize that it will not be abandoned, that its deepest needs are being met, which opens us to clarity, intuition, and dimensional expansion. Expectations will slowly fall away in this practice, as they are no longer needed in a universe where there is no protection necessary. This one simple practice will be repeated throughout this book, as it is the cornerstone to any spiritual grounding wherever we may be in our journey and a priority in coming to know our soul.

By Our Design

Chapter 3

Discouragement, Depression, and Despair

Sometimes we may feel so far behind or out of touch with ourselves that it may seem as if we are awakening in the last stages of a marathon where we are running only to catch up. We may read material from those that have walked the path before us, or hear stories of significant wonder, and believe that somehow life has passed us by as we view it in a mix of emotions. And even if we are not the spiritual sort, or we are seeking some form of understanding as to our place here on Earth, when the three 'D's are activated, we may feel as if the bottom of the world has dropped out from us, leaving a veritable bog of drudgery. When discouragement, depression, and despair surface, they are possibly the most controversial, misunderstood, and demonized emotions in the energetic field. And while by societal standards of mental health they are commonly viewed in a category of sickness, they remain a cornerstone in the evolutionary passage of humanity.

So we may ask, "how do discouragement, depression, and despair serve our sense of wellbeing, and why are these energies often a necessary part of the transformational process?"

In a sense, if we view ourselves as seeds of divinity, planted in the earth, which have come to resolve, explore, or express vibrational threads through three-dimensional experience, then as a part of this process, the ego's role is to protect an overstimulated nervous system by constructing a reality that provides stability until we are ready to expand. What are commonly felt as afflictive emotions are these energies of vibration in process, which are eventually revealed as communications from the soul that often destabilize reality in order to draw our attention to desirous threads that are ready to shift. This can be confusing in that we tend to think of time and

33

matter as linear for resolve: for instance, "if I do this, I will get that" or "1 + 1 = 2." While these laws work very well in three-dimensional constructs, when we start to apply these to higher dimensions, or multiple dimensions, the context of this paradigm faints. Meaning, we may view 'one' in terms of a singular count from the perspective of the third dimension, but universally, or multi-dimensionally, 'one' can hold multiples concurrently. How this helps with an understanding of "the 3-D's" is that the soul is constantly aware of our purpose and the bigger picture here on Earth, and from a multi-dimensional view, is working in coordination with both the ego and vibrational shift simultaneously; contained within "the 3-D's" are the messages we hear throughout life associated with those desires that are coming forward to be fulfilled vibrationally, but if we are not ready to receive these communications, the soul allows egoic construction to gestate these energies as needed to become ready, as well as stabilizing reality. Even though we may not be aware of it, discouragement, depression, and despair are utilized in any number of arenas to satisfy our soul contracts of incarnation, whose integral energies are effective in moving us towards what we have desired to receive vibrationally in our experience here.

What may be one of the most frightening aspects in these energies is the acknowledgment of decay or death in the cycle of transformation. When we view our overall physical cycle here, birth, infancy, childhood, adulthood, and death, rarely do we move beyond what we perceive three-dimensionally as the end. But if we do, we glimpse a similar process unfolding in relation to it in our divine transformation. While we may view certain energies with revulsion and ugliness, dismissing them as unnecessary parts of the human experience or desiring to *overcome* them, the universe is aware that energy is neither wasted nor destroyed and that everything has a purpose, matter being transient in form; death or decay is only one part in a larger circle of life and is never an end where creation is concerned. It provides the transformational space and power necessary in rebirth as part of our spiritual evolution or self-realization— death of an illusionary reality, constructed in perceptions based on egoic logic of separateness in the third dimension. Although one would think any illusions would crumble automatically upon physical death (which they do, to a certain extent), the passage of physical death does not resolve the necessary shifts we desire in our soul that often are in need of unraveling (which is one of the reasons we incarnate three-dimensionally here). This is what many of the saviors, saints, angels, prophets, enlightened beings, and ascended masters have presented over human history as the death that is unavoidable as part of the ascension process: 'the first death', which is the death of the ego. And even though it can and most likely will be the most excruciating pain we will feel in our lifetime, one which we will inevitably be unprepared to face, unable to deter, and unwilling to go through, most of us will be unaware of when it is happening until we are in the thick of it. The question of sanity almost always comes to light, and the proposition of physical death surfaces as emotions intensify for many people, with the possibility of suicide offering relief, although only temporarily.

In mysticism, this is a very ancient journey, one where we enter the cave of our fears with discouragement, depression, and despair as servants of antagonism to reveal the path calling to us. We may try to comprehend the paintings on the wall or figures in the deep by the modern light of our understanding, but in the depth, these scenes upon the wall will only come to life in the presence that primordial fire provides. As humans we are made from the divine soup of chaos, and harmony only comes as we embrace this mixture of worldly and other-worldly energies in us, all of which work together as agents of love under the timing and care of universal orchestration.

Discouragement moves in this process in the form of uncertainty, failure, loss, rejection, abandonment, or unworthiness, either maintaining a reality of egoic construction in illusion, or breaking it down as we are ready for spiritual evolvement; the integrity of our truth is one of the identifying factors as a catalyst to the awakening process. Although it may feel unloving in allowing ourselves to feel deeply into these uncomfortable energies as they arise, often, in any practice of abiding, it is both the nature of what we desire in resolve and the compassion offered that illuminate any awareness in us. So when we abide with the energies of abandonment while not abandoning, rejection while not rejecting, and unworthiness while holding a space in worthiness, we offer a space which effectively adjusts the energetic field of the heart. And if we are not ready, we simply won't do the practice— it is neither good nor bad from any perspective; it just means it is not time yet.

Discouragement creates a space of potential in loss, although when experiencing emotional intensity, it is unlikely we will see it at first. It is the adage, "when one door closes, another opens in its wake." This is a law of universal creation, one which can be difficult to comprehend in three-dimensional suffering. But when we do allow a practice of abiding, even though we may frequently feel the sting of fear, doubt, and confusion as emotional debris surface, vibrational threads are given the necessary love that has been asked for by the soul and we will begin to see another purpose in our afflictions. Manifestation is always a response to our vibrational 'prayers' we have been issuing forth, whether we are aware of what we have been praying or not. And as we feel what we need to feel, allowing ourselves to love those places asking to be loved, emptiness cannot help but hear life being spoken into the void, which creation views as something not 'ending' but newly formed in this potential of love we have offered.

So we may ask, "what happens if I am not ready?"

The interesting thing about dimensional living is that everything still moves in accordance with what we have come to resolve, explore, or express vibrationally, even though it may not seem or feel like it at times. It's very much like looking at life through a multi-faceted diamond, seeing reflections that both mirror where we desire to go and what we already are as potential is embraced. From a divine perspective, nothing in life is ever disputed because every timeline serves a purpose from all points of view. What feels like resistance is the ego attempting to stabilize any aspect or facet of our reality which is overwhelmed, effectively creating a space of gestation for energy and awareness to meet when we enter the birthing process. So in one sense, we are never "not ready," only in a different state of abiding, where energies have the opportunity to gestate or ripen for the resolve, or any exploration, and expression we desire. This is not the 'aware abiding' referred to throughout this book, but rather one that the nature of our divinity has encoded within us, which knows precisely what we need and when we need it for any metamorphosis to occur.

The mind tends to complicate matters by trying to 'solve' energies that arise, and the ego attempts to stabilize our reality, both of which are based in three-dimensional understanding; although many of us are aware of the need for resolve, likely most of us are unaware of what we need for resolution. We may not even realize we are in this process, and it is common to view an emotional inventory from an egoic filter of three-dimensional stock, which is a very narrow vision of what this journey has offered us. Even if we deem that we have been 'successful' from this point of view— in our trade, education, or marriage —often there will still be unfulfilled desire in our vibrational strands which will eventually contribute to feeling like life has been for naught. This is the void of uncertainty, doubt, and darkness where, when approached, many of us feel deep sadness, unresolved discontent, and an unwillingness in our motivation, although unbeknown to us, is exactly where our soul has arranged that we belong.

If and when the opportunity arises, instead of asking what the point of discouragement is or trying to solve it, we may ask, "what if the point is to be with discouragement," and, "what if we practice embracing, not in a harmful way, but by allowing ourselves to be vulnerable in these moments of perplexity by offering love even in what may feel like failure?"

The universe works in terms which are difficult to understand when viewing spiritual power from only a three-dimensional point of reference, and it may quickly overwhelm the nervous system as we attempt to do so. As unlikely as it may sound, part of our journey is to underestimate the power of love in feeling where we are at and question the feelings that arise in coming to know the raw potential that surrender provides. As we integrate unresolved energies, our vibrational strands or frequencies will shift, which means that, even though we may be unaware of it, our divine nature is moving dimensionally on our behalf. So while we may be trying to 'fix' how we feel, how we feel is precisely what we have come to experience as a part of our process. The most loving thing we can do is be with, honor, and allow the feelings that surface, granting space for their energies. And although what we perceive three-dimensionally may not have the appearance of egoic fulfillment, as we trust in this process, we deepen our relationship with the soul, expanding in the simplicity of the heart where true potentiality meets us.

As a part of this process, it is common to move from discouragement into depression if energies remain unresolved. It is not necessary, but from an energetic place, if what surfaces for our attention is not offered the love it asks for, we will cycle further inward or deeper within these energies. Again, this is not necessarily to be viewed as a 'bad' or 'wrong' thing; it simply is a part of our personal evolutionary process. Many great teachers in human history have had their full run with the 'three D's, from the Buddha, to Jesus, to Muhammad, all of whom emerged by the practice of compassion. And although it may feel awkward by religious or theocratic standards to look at saviors or great prophets in their tribulations (or what we may view here as afflictive emotions), especially those parts that seem less than divine in our perception, they have walked the path before us and will bring ease to our experience if we are open to receive their experience of humanity.

One of the mysteries of incarnation is the mix of spirit and flesh working cohesively for our benefit even though it may feel oppressive at times. There's an uneasy truth that arises when depression surfaces that can be felt through this mix in the gentle sounds of nature, like when the waves of the ocean lap the seashore, or the wind lightly moves through the leaves of a tree. It is no coincidence in identification, as these are harbingers of unanswered calls which bring the subtle sensations of ache in the undertone of our life path to surface preceding, unexplored depths.

Although depression is an agent of the soul sent forth as an informant for some vibrational part in need, it can also work for the ego in any further gestation we may need. And for those in deep depression, it can feel as if any light of consciousness has faded or is slowly fading into the background of a shadowed existence of life. Most societal norms refrain from the type of interaction the soul is asking for, misunderstanding the forces at work, and labeling these energies as illnesses of the mind, abnormal genetics, chemistry, and addiction, among many other issues. But the resonating factor in any of our circumstances is why we have chosen to be born into a certain time, place, and purpose arranged by our soul. It is the root of our choice to incarnate into a finite experience from a much larger journey. And the uneasy truth that is so difficult for us as a species to address is that we _are_ more, much more, than we currently acknowledge.

Some years ago, there was a documentary on Buddhist monks that would go up on the hillside of a mountain in the cold of winter and, stripping down to only a damp linen sheet, would proceed to dry the sheets through meditation while keeping themselves warm in below freezing temperatures. Although this was called an extraordinary feat by those filming it, the thought occurred to me, "I could do this." Not in some vain arrogance, but simply knowing internally on some level that this was within my human potential. Although many of us may or may not realize what we are capable of when we encounter seemingly extraordinary or impossible circumstances, frequently what we feel are the energies of our own reflection in challenging us to look deeper— deeper into those portions of our life that desire to awaken, believe, and come to know the 'extraordinary' soul.

Some of the most basic energies in life are the ones that we experience every day but will only receive when we are ready to feel them. As we come to know ourselves, there will be more than a few characteristics that we wouldn't mind shedding in our life path, but in order for those parts of our self to be addressed, we must integrate them on a deeper level. We do so as we stop fighting and sit with ourselves, whether cold or warm, dark or light, comfortable or uncomfortable. We embrace all of what we feel through love. We come to find that those places begin to open themselves to us, that the 'impossibility' is only there to bring our attention to those parts that desire possibility. When reflecting on those monks' faces as they were being filmed, they weren't expressions of 'extraordinary'; they were more 'matter of fact', even curious as to why they were being filmed.

Although the prospect of divinity as our true nature may sound far-fetched through a three-dimensional lens, and even when we explore the process of 'ascension' itself we will find it feels more like we are 'descending', as we move into abiding with the parts that are insecure, desirous, or most likely expressing themselves as afflictive energies, we will find the paradoxical nature of our divinity is such that the seeds of light are sown in the darkness. And the choice to be incarnated was for this light to expand; what we may deem as unnecessary, evil, or ignorant in the world was formed by a choice of losing ourselves, or falling from the heavens, that we might be redeemed by the love of our divinity. We do not need to know the details of this expansion, only that it is for our personal benefit, and moving us further inward in relationship to all beings, especially the soul. And when we grant ourselves the space of actively sitting with what we feel, being immersed in our feelings, we are allowing ourselves to be with the energies themselves that arise for attention. This is where we begin to see divinity in a different light, one that is not afraid to engage chaos, that supports us in darkness, even when there is seemingly no way out or rescue at hand. In the moments that unfold before us, although we may feel we are confined to only one paradigm of thought, there is a much larger, longer life we are living as divine beings, where every relationship is valued as a deepening in the soul.

Throughout our process, there will be times when we find it difficult to love, challenging to abide, and we may succumb to deep sadness falling further into the pit of depression. Although this may seem like a set-back, it only means that who we are is much deeper in the soul, and what we have come to experience in our feelings is moving us along, stretching us in potential. These are only indications of, or petitions for, certain aspects of resolve, parts which desire to be acknowledged, healed, and listened to in a loving manner by us as no one else can. In short, depression is desire or anger (when intensified) turned inward, and when we begin to acknowledge these emotions, we are in effect validating the truth they present to us in energy. If we seek relief here, we may offer simple statements to the heart such as "I love you" and "even though what I am feeling may be difficult, I will not abandon you, you are not alone, I Am here." If we have not loved ourselves in this manner for some time, we may experience resistance, the skin may crawl, the mind may become rebellious in thought, and anger might surface. But eventually, the gentleness we offer in our surrender through compassion will affirm to the heart that this is what the soul has been asking for.

As we acknowledge our fears, desires, and aches, allowing grief for any loss we feel, we come to know places within ourselves that may have previously been unintentionally ignored or left to fend for themselves. A union or alignment begins to develop in our energy field as we explore these feelings, and we may experience a contentment here that we have never felt before. This is based in the core of who we are as eternal beings of a much larger whole, where recognition exists multi-dimensionally from any point of view, in which expansion is rooted. This may take us years, even lifetimes, in unfolding, but once we become aware, it will feel as if it happened in a blink of an eye, and any illusions of loss will begin to fall away to reveal a reality where manifestation is working on everyone's behalf in love. Even though it can be a horribly uncomfortable process, ugly at times, and incredibly painful as we proceed through it, no one is ever left behind, and we will all eventually experience this expansion which we previously thought impossible from a three-dimensional point of view.

This brings us to the final gatekeeper or key available in the three "D's." Despair arises in the matrix of emotions when we are on the edge of the precipice, the tipping point where we teeter, both reluctant to leap yet feeling no other option if we are to live. It is a sacred place in the landscape of consciousness where the infinite and the finite meet, and one of the highest signals that we are ready for a shift. Within despair are the necessary energies of urgency that move our experience into the void of uncertain surrender.

If we imagine purposefully placing ourselves in a stasis pod at some point in our past, where a cocoon of environment, relationships, and circumstances proceeds to envelope our journey over whatever time is necessary for the gestation of energies or vibrations we have come to resolve, despair is the culmination of this transformational process where we must choose to come forth or attempt to allow the ego to rebuild the layers of egoic construction. As the ego senses its death in this evolution, we sense it also in deep ache, extreme anxiety, and a profound sadness at the loss of our 'protector'. This may be a repeating pattern throughout our lifetime until either we, or the greater self that we are, decide that life here has served us as much as possible in our current reality, and it either shifts in the present timeline or we move on to the next. This only occurs when the walls of egoic construction crumble to a place where they cannot be rebuilt. This is the most powerful phase of transformation, and the most dangerous, in terms of our incarnation or life path that we will encounter. The loss that is felt when reality fractures can be devastating, traumatic, and completely disorienting to consciousness. But illusions must be shattered if we are to fulfill what we have come to experience, and despair provides the opening through the cracks where vibrational threads that are to be resolved may expand. It is an understatement to say these can be some of the most intense sensations one would ever feel, comparable to living through the energy of death itself.

When this process begins, the essence of who we are in three-dimensional terms will begin to slip from the body, and we will experience the utter and complete powerlessness associated with shifting vibrational frequency. And although the death/rebirth in transformation will come in a variety of ways, and most likely much of what we experience we will desire to avoid at any cost, it is an essential part of our metamorphosis. Although this is as natural as waking from sleep in the morning, or the cycles we witness in nature on earth, and is a normal part of divine nature in our spiritual evolution as a species, it is common to have thoughts of death as the sensations that are felt in the body are those of 'death'. In mental health terms, it can be observed as a deterioration into hopelessness, extreme substance abuse, rage, mood swings, self-harm, and thoughts of suicide when we are ripe for a shift of reality. It is a precarious place where love is much needed, and frequently misunderstood by society, in its revealing.

When in despair we may blame others and ourselves, or rail against life events that feel beyond our control, and angrily question how we came to be in this place or circumstances of our journey. Although this sounds unappealing and can be very exhausting to the body, the weight these emotions provide helps to create cracks in the egoic shell toward its eventual collapse. Desperation becomes an agent of acceleration to what we are feeling, prompting our eyes to open and integrate the truth of what is revealed. As this process unfolds, we are granted a reprieve from the protection of ego, which can be both terrifying and exhilarating as we explore the prospect of a potentially different reality. And even though this may be painful in that what we see is the loss of our former life, it is a place where innocence may come forth, within which, when the heart feels safe and vulnerable enough, our energetic field will expand to receive higher vibrations of love. The heart has a direct line to our soul and the deepest desires within us, working tirelessly with the soul to fulfill our most intimate longings. It listens closely and will reveal a great deal to us when it is approached with the innocence of child-like humility. In the twilight of despair, we receive insight into our core where innocence presides, frequently coaxing our awareness through the uncomfortable mix of flesh and spirit to an inner peace in surrender.

By Our Design

Chapter 4

The Innocent One

Innocence is one of the most powerful ointments for releasing rusted hinges; it is the cherub of possibility and faithful messenger of love's grace. It allows us to stand in the fire, free to express our desires, and gives us immunity when all seems lost. The wisdom of innocence speaks when nothing else will, sharing difficult truths with gentle ease. If we grasp at illusion, or feel the sting of it, innocence reveals that we are only abandoning ourselves. It works closely with all other emotions, content to remain in the background until we are ready to receive its purity. And the heart recognizes the 'innocent one', and it will never bow to any contrary notion of separation when in its presence. But when we incarnate and the nervous system becomes overwhelmed, the ego develops as protector, building walls in an effort to minimize the over-stimulated nervous system. Although this is a natural part of human development, and our innocence remains intact, its light will eventually fade, covered in the fray of egoic construction, buried deep in the recesses of a seemingly forced abdication, pending its season for emergence once more.

Life certainly has a way of returning, recycling, and bringing us back to those places that may be difficult to hear. We may wince, shiver, and pull our covers close in the night, but eventually the energies that are asking to be felt will surface in some form or another. With each feeling of discomfort in the smallness of a finite experience, our divine rooting takes place; it is a dance we will never forget in its melodious solace, and it will create a foundation of trust, even when we feel deep aloneness or despair. It may be, though, that we meet ourselves with an irreverent grace, defiantly asking "why?" with each unfolding, refusing the love that is needed. But the prospect of suffering to the attachments of a three-dimensional paradigm only creates a grasping which enhances the pain necessary for resolution, and will eventually reveal another path to take us into the depths. And even though many of us consciously call out daily for assistance in resolve, most of us are unaware of what is in need, or the necessary steps which we must take for resolve. This is where innocence works hand in hand with surrender, not from a place of mindfulness or thought, but energetically on a deeper level of what we feel, where our soul already knows what is in need. Innocence guides us by allowing the circumstances we are in, the sensations we feel, and the body we have incarnated in to explore unimpeded where we are at in life. We listen, we grant passage to our humanity, feeling into the mix of spiritual workings that present themselves to us, and from this place, even in the most uncomfortable of feelings, we receive an enlargement of who and what we are. This really is a process about coming to know ourselves intimately, all of who we are, even in those places that may seem separate.

Trees are an excellent example of this inner/outer interaction of intimacy, and will teach us to ground in overwhelming circumstances, or the most difficult of environments. Growing up in the heart of the Allegheny National Forest, frequently I would hike the many trails there, exploring nature. It was common to come across seeds that had fallen on great boulders and would seem to have a rough go of it, but there they were, of all sizes from saplings to full grown trees, on rocks, somehow managing to grow in difficult conditions. One day I came upon a small tree that had fallen over on one of these great rocks, and although mostly uprooted, one root held, and had seemingly stretched across a great expanse to ground, nourish itself, and survive, even *thrive* in its environment. The resilience and integrity it showed in difficult circumstances was a faithful transmission, especially in a time of life for me, personally, where it felt as if there was no ground to stand on.

When we consider nature, as humans we often attempt to set ourselves apart from its workings. We tend to think of ourselves as somehow above or unlike nature because of our reasoning capabilities, yet we find a balance of peace by immersing ourselves in it. This is one of the most perplexing perspectives of our journey, in

46

that we purposely allow ourselves as divinity to be swept away in darkness, that we might be enlarged from the point of view in coming to know the light. In parabolic terms, we are not unlike a seed, which comes to know itself in all forms as a tree through its development. Energetically we work in coordination with the universe to immerse ourselves vibrationally in an environment where we can explore what we experience as the one who is uncertain of outcomes, has doubts, and feels fear, all of which cultivate an expanding trust, love, and faith. But working with our environment and in connection to

Only through the lens of innocence can we come to know our true potentiality, see who in essence we are, and learn what we have freely lost that might be found. When we begin to embrace our circumstances, moving inward into the depths of our feelings and thoughts, it is common to try and 'figure it out' or force resolution within ourselves. As we do so, we fall into those most elaborate and beautiful traps which allow us to go deeper into the chaos and feel those parts most relevant to our healing. Though it may not feel like it at times or seem prosperous in the moment, the here and now has been orchestrated for our highest destiny to unfold. All that we feel, think, or react to is exactly what we need for experiencing ascension. Events, people, places, and things have moved and acted in a manner completely unique to us, being introduced to our life path in perfect coordination for well-being to come forth. Ironically, although it may seem narcissistic from an egoic point of view, each of us really is the center of the universe as a multi-dimensional being, and has a relationship to it experiencing everything on a personal level. This challenges other paradigms which suggest to be 'self-less', but the simplicity in this is that if we truly love ourselves in how we feel, what we think, and our actions, we automatically love others from a deeper sense of being. But from a starting point of awakening or opening our eyes in the dark, we will only come to know our light through the vulnerability of childlike faith, with innocence leading us into the bliss of our heart's desire. And with every surrender, slowly we begin to see the orchestration coming forth for our highest fulfillment. Even in the most afflictive of struggles, struggle itself becomes a road to walk upon if we allow ourselves to go into the pain knowing we are cared for in transformation, which is answering what we have long desired and who we are as divinity.

There are times, however, when we become too overwhelmed, or the weight of what we feel has broken us, and that innocence works with the universe and our soul to provide levity as is necessary that we may find relief in the struggle. Considered wise in mysticism, the Fool is an example of this, and often brings urgent counsel for the king's table that great sages would dare not mention. The Fool also knew when a situation needs levity and how to diffuse tension in those around him by his own blundering for the sake of the kingdom. The presence of his actions is shrouded in mystery, and he is frequently seen adorned in a colorful costume that messages might be received with ease. In tarot, the Fool is represented by the number zero, which is the symbol for infinity and represents faith or new beginnings and innocence. Reversed, it can be a sign of folly or chaos in one's life path.

In some traditions, such as the Native American or Norse Mythos, this is one of the purposes of the coyote, or Trickster. The nature of their spirit is such that it may seemingly circumvent the rules, even making light of them, crashing through the sacred in ceremony, reminding us that higher forces are always at work, guiding and holding all of creation in love. The trickster laughs in the face of the serious, urging us to embrace the silly side, and acknowledges the dark night of uncertainty with a childlike playfulness. And if there are a multitude of fears, the levity trickster brings will open forgotten doors by admonishing the way of balance with imbalance. This can be witnessed in almost any civilization or culture when we are superimposed with societal burdens and raised in ways that seemingly allow us to come together as a 'civilized' nation, but individual wellness suffers— which, when it does so for the sake of civilization, civilization is no measure of a healthy humanity. Sometimes, in order to be free, we just need to be free. Free from the constraints of our own judgements and opinions, free to share our innocence with those that it resonates with, and free to grant ourselves the same permissions we deeply desire from others.

Children often display the Fool's path as the opening to our greater self, where the imagination is unrestrained, and innocence runs freely in the form of exploration, possibility, and play. Although they may not recognize it as such, the Fool comes naturally to them in various energies. For instance, normally children are much quicker to forgive, to find the bright point of what may seem like a dark situation, and to share an innocent truth in what they see. And though the term has been greatly misunderstood, overused, and subjected to conventional wisdom the past few decades, each of us has an 'inner child' that desires simplicity of heart. In Matthew 18:3, Jesus said, "…Verily I say unto you, except ye be converted, and become as little children, ye shall not enter into the kingdom of heaven." Many teachers, prophets, mystics and saints have referred to this innocence, as it is rooted in the divine source code of humility that we are. Often the Fool will arise in our life through outer circumstances in order to take us deeper into our inner path of the infinite, where the eternal bliss of our child thrives. The Fool or Trickster will work with innocence in allowing us to bend the rules in pursuit of liberation; although chaos may seem to move us further away from what we perceive as our destination, inwardly it always leads us back to the road of surrender, trust, and faith. Once we begin to recognize this aspect of our being and learn to listen the child in our reflections, we begin to see a world of potential opening for us, if we allow ourselves the humility necessary for transformational growth in our pilgrimage.

So even in something that we think might be out of alignment, and in extreme cases, even if we believe we are outright living a lie, innocence serves our energy field by granting the forgiveness necessary to explore the feelings that are arising in us. Although outward circumstances may provide some insight, frequently the mind will want to resolve them with our focus drawn away by egoic construction to settle in energy rather than explore it. From a higher-dimensional point of view, the energies that arise in any interaction, regardless of the circumstances, are always for our benefit, even in traumatic or undesirable events. This does not grant us permission to harm or be harmed, but rather the space to genuinely sit with the feelings that surface in any situation we may or may not be ready to change, which is part of the reason we have come here as vibrational beings in the vessel we reside in. Everything from the friendships we cultivate to the family we were born into, to the clothes we wear, foods we eat, jobs we choose, and mates we are attracted to all provide stimulation for the inward election of what we desire most to address, heal, or express when attachments are formed.

And as we learn to allow what we need through an organic process of living, instead of forcing decisions based on old paradigms of "right" or "wrong," we heighten our sensitivity to what resonates with us as it unfolds. When we sit with what we feel, the true nature of these energies will eventually provide insight through the abiding of love. And sometimes, the surprising revelation in these energies is simply to sit with ourselves or the soul, which is asking for resolve in what we feel arising— not necessarily in relation to anything else, but simply us giving our time to love us as no one else can in acknowledgement; outer circumstances are merely triggers to draw us into a clearer communication or an intimacy that is being asked for within us vibrationally.

Although we may find ourselves in a situation time and again where we press upon the heart to give us the guidance into what is most in alignment for our wellbeing, comfortability tends to come to the forefront in a variety of any decision making, and with the egoic filter, often the mind will reason what the outcomes will look like based on how we feel. While this is indeed a practice in following our passions, the difference is in the abiding space that is being asked for by the energy. This is necessary for a variety of reasons, all of which may not be clear until a later time, but some of the most frequent are clearing cellular memory, deepening the relationship with the soul, healing or adjusting vibrational fields, and expanding who we are as divinity. When we find ourselves in a variety of circumstances that we may not feel are to our liking, yet we continue in them, whether we feel it is by choice or not, there is something in those circumstances that we need for wellbeing. Meaning, although comfortability is a two-sided coin, one which we commonly feel the sides are "good" or "bad," heads or tails isn't conducive to resolve if we become focused on the duality of what we feel for an interpretation of what the soul is communicating with our awareness. Both sides of the coin reveal energetically what is being asked for in resolve, so whether what we experience is felt as comfort or discomfort, either one when embraced will begin to resolve desire.

In any awakening process, developing self-honesty is crucial and can be very uncomfortable, even painful at times, but with the support of a childlike humility, allows innocence to form. Once we begin to acknowledge how we feel with honesty, integration provides an opportunity to acclimate our nervous system and increase our capacity for what we are able to feel. As we learn to trust our evolutionary process, not only do we feel more capable in what we are receiving energetically, but the heart continues to expand in the safety of love as we embrace what arises with honesty.

If we haven't developed a practice or daily ritual that we can rely on when we begin exploring deeper into the soul, it is paramount to do so to provide relief. On the other hand, if we have been too reliant on certain practices or routines, we may consider switching things up for a breath of fresh air as we may have been stagnating. In either case, the importance of this is that the body works in coordination with the universe and the soul towards clearing emotional debris and giving attention to areas in need as energies move to resolve any issues in our vibrational field. It is very common to have intense experiences, especially if we are unfamiliar with engaging these energies: tears, tightness of breath, exhaustion, lethargy, and extreme mood swings are just a few of the indications we are either in need of or already in deep integration. Healthy care of the body reinforces this process, which allows it to be a more effective conduit that we may fully embrace these energies. Listening to what the body needs in areas of nutrition, rest, quiet, and exercise will support our well-being and the space necessary for these energies that are attempting to resolve or adjust vibrational strands in our being.

But if there are certain things we are not ready to be honest about, love is always our first practice of embracing. Even though it may seem unproductive, there are times when it is completely natural to find ourselves walking away from honesty, even to the point of denial or downright refusal to look at something when our nervous system may feel too overwhelmed and physically incapable of doing so. This is also a universal wall we may encounter when going too deep when we are not ready, and the ego will work for us in providing another reality until such a time arises when we are. *It does not mean the process has stopped*, only that we are in preparation for what we will receive at a later date. We continue by listening to the body, developing a daily practice of self-care, and tenderly doing our best to hold the heart wherever we may be at. This is where innocence is often misunderstood in that it not only provides a support for our deepening exploration by allowing us to proceed into turbulent or intense energies, but it also stands in coordination with other forces universally to guard our perceptions if we are not ready to receive insight. In the world of 'right' and 'wrong', the mind views innocence as 'just' or 'unjust', but multi-dimensionally it is energetically viewed as an essence of faith, which works however is needed for divinity. An example of this might be when innocence intercedes as naivety as a traumatic situation unfolds, shifting our perception, perhaps seeing a riot as a parade, or an explosion as colorful fireworks, for example, if our nervous system is unable to process the emotions in relation to certain events.

Although a tendency may persist for us to will our way through circumstances in an effort to overcome what may be perceived as obstacles, or we may strive to view the sincerest form of truth available for a solution in our choices, the spiritual realm works from a place of paradox, dimensionally seeing obstacles as opportunities and uncertainty as the substance of hope in building faith or love. The spiritual realm exhibits patience, surrender, and an embracing of what arises as a part of our transformational divine nature; doubt and pain may seem like enemies emotionally, but they are actually emissaries of the ego working for the divine in coordination with our circumstances to take us deeper inward for transformation. Our part is simply to move through the process, allowing relief where we can in coming to know these energies and the one coming forth in them, being open to the messengers that arrive rather than viewing them as something to be overcome. This is where 'childlike faith' serves to open doors, and the universe meets us with an unraveling of fortune, even though we may see it as a possible unwanted outcome of unknowns.

As we allow ourselves to embrace the depth of our soul, innocence allows us to develop a unique relationship with the universe, one where 'reflections' begin to appear in connection with the innermost places of the heart, revealing both the confidence and insecurities at work in our vibrational field. Up until this point, the ego has done a wonderful job at structuring our universe for 'self-protective' purposes, building a wall of reality that served as an incubation chamber for the energies to gestate. But when the timing of perfection urges us, we begin to see the truth of ourselves mirrored in our relationships, as the essence of who we are begins to emerge from the intertwined nature of the fleshly and spiritual existence we have been living. Because we often don't recognize who or what we are in this emergence, we may rail against our circumstances, blaming the outer world for the afflictive emotions that are coming forward in us. These whisperings of our depth are the places in us that work tirelessly to manifest through our vibrational field what we are in need of; because they are often unrecognized and mostly unacknowledged, except when necessary, they appear as our demons. As they appear, they can be critical of us and others— not to stand in judgement, but rather to help raise our banners by the triggering of desires that are deep within us. This is the evolutionary process of the higher road of fulfillment, where we walk both on shifting sands and upon the solidarity of our making by the love we are willing to offer as an 'ease' to what arises for our benefit. It is the narrow road of our eternal path that can only be seen with the childlike humility of embracing the heart in innocence.

One of the most intricate workings in the universe is the divine nature of the heart in its reflective patterns of innocence as they appear— those people, places, and events that synchronistically vibrate with our energy field to reveal in their mirroring meaningful relationships to our awareness. Although it may not be obvious at first or will take time for our awareness to catch up to these relationships, on a deeper level of connection, our soul is always working with them. In hindsight, when we look back on these occurrences, in each circumstance that has arisen there will be a deeper understanding of who we are, what we have come here to explore, and how we are healing parts that have asked for these interactions. Through each conscious observation, we are offered the opportunity to feel into the reflections the world has provided, giving attention to the energies that arise as we allow ourselves to be vulnerable with innocence. This may cause some instability to our view of reality, and the ego will want to step in to provide support, but, if we are ready to claim responsibility for our life path through compassion, the ego will slowly step aside as 'protector', no longer needed when we are able to offer love.

Even if what we hear is hurtful at times, the heart knows it will not be abandoned by the abiding love we offer in what is felt, which also serves as an anchor to any turbulence we may experience in doubt. As we go deeper into this practice, the universe responds vibrationally by the arrangement of our circumstances to meet us where we are at, and with each polishing of the mirror by love, the reflections we see become clearer in the nature of any relationship we have universally. The love we offer and receive is a key to the relationship we are forming with our divinity and will provide us with an expanding vocabulary of communication as we come to know the one who is coming forth in us. We may find that old paradigms will begin to fall away, and who we once were was merely a shadow of the master that resides within us. In these times, it is not uncommon to feel hatred, anger, unworthiness, and a sense of betrayal to our former self, seeing them as ignorant participants of a former world we knew. The ego will move quickly in these intense energies to seek relief or provide protection through anything that may stabilize what we feel, so it is crucial that we learn to love the one who only did their best, *even if they knew better*, as it was what they were capable of at the time.

Each and every role that circumstances play in our life for revealing will often tempt the ego to grasp for an alternate reality if it senses instability. But as we learn to develop a practice of embracing rather than letting go, nurturing instead of blaming, the love we offer becomes a transforming agent of our reality, even in the midst of any hate that we might feel. And where time was once perceived as an enemy, we may begin to see it as an ally —the cocoon of our ego working masterfully as part of a greater equation— with each forming of barriers having served temporarily for protection and a reality that was built for a purposed gestation to hold the mystery of our incarnation until we were ready to receive it.

The humility of innocence grounds us in the heart of compassion by utilizing circumstances as a vehicle for our evolutionary process. By listening with love to those places within us that may feel agitated, triggered, or frustrated when we receive reflections, we only deepen in awareness to the divine dance we have chosen and open the road to further the intimate relationship we have come here for. Each piece of our life we may have thought was once lost begins to fit into a larger picture and yields a trust in how the universe works on a scale we never could have previously imagined. And even though we will still feel loss, loss also quickly becomes a space for what is coming on our behalf for a more fulfilling reality. Although it can be difficult to embrace our circumstances if we feel uncomfortable, finding simple truths in the face of uncertainty is precisely the point. And often the more confusing or overwhelming the circumstances are, the simpler the truth is in form of communication from the body and soul requesting attention. As we learn to hear the requests of our soul, giving audience to what we feel, insight becomes more apparent by the love we offer.

Years ago, I had an experience watching several training videos for work, one of which was on "shooters in the building and what to do." There were 5 other men in the room watching the videos with me, and suddenly I felt a deep sadness welling up within, and an ache for the portrayal of violence in these scenarios. Tears began to form in the corners of my eyes, and I remember turning away from the other men because of what they might think. Later that day when sitting with the feelings of that experience, the realization came that not only had I turned away from these other men, but from my heart as well. Innocence and my heart were working perfectly to reveal a part of me that was precious, that desires peace, non-harm, and a world in which men can freely share their emotions with one another without fear of judgement or condemnation. Whether we are aware of it or not, circumstances are always for our benefit, even if we may struggle with the outcomes three-dimensionally; what we feel in struggle is an inherent part of the process in coming to know compassion. Through it we welcome divinity, and what we perceive as a chain of bondage is released, not necessarily because it has been broken, but because we are no longer the same creation. So while we may rail upon our former life or express anger at the one who lived it, that one was and is a necessary step in our evolutionary path of ascension. Only through the love we offer ourselves, and where we have been as a version of our self may we come to know the new creation that desires to emerge.

As we develop compassion, we realize that inherent in everything there exists some form of what was, what could be, and what is. When our vision expands in seeing this potential that exists, we will first identify what is: our current circumstances, how we feel, and the nature of our mortality as living in a finite experience. But in coming to know what is, both in us and the outer world 'what is' no longer satisfies that part of ourselves that is triggered or activated in circumstances. Again, this journey is much like that of the seed, which, having the full potential of its nature contained within it, only needs the context of circumstances to activate it. Although humanity views its purpose here on Earth through the lens of egoic construction, until it is ready, once conditions are met and we know we are much more in potential, what we feel in questioning our reality is the unresolved energies to be that which we already are. Whether this is to shift vibrational strands as a part of our journey in evolvement or simply to express divinity, these energies, once activated, will be the driving force in our life path, even though we may be unaware of what is in process. The restlessness, irritability, and discontentment we may feel at times is an indication of our awareness being called by the soul as our divinity steps forward. And as we acknowledge these feelings, another reality is presented to us in awareness, one in which an invitation is sent by the universe sensing the transformational quality of our readiness. Each breath in observance and space created allows for reflection to cascade in the body emotionally. Over time, these energies are integrated through each abiding of compassion, and vibrational strands slowly shift to align with the soft ebullience of surrender.

The irony in this process is that although we are complete masters of our design and creators of reality, as multi-dimensional beings, we have allowed ourselves to become darkened in order to shift that which could only be transformed by a place of coming to know ourselves again. The space we are attempting to move through or into is both so small and yet infinitely vast that only the love of surrender will suffice to grant entrance. Once we begin to acknowledge the shadows of our resistance and the doubts we may have when in uncertainty, the energies that we perceive as inflammatory in our life path will begin to reveal a transformational quality of liberation we never thought possible through embracing them.

In the Yoga Sutras, the second of the Niyamas ('virtue') of Patanjali's Eight Limbs is called "Santosha," which is derived from the Sanskrit "sam," meaning "completely" or "absolutely," and "tosha," which closely translated is "contentment" or "acceptance." All together it may be rendered in interpretation as "complete contentment." Santosha may be realized in yoga through asana practice by accepting bodily limitations, creating intention, and expressing as we are rather than striving for achievement beyond the love we offer. This is both the path in the nature of surrender and the transformational qualities of embracing the energies of how we feel. And when we step forward to meet our process, divinity always steps forward to meet us as we meet ourselves.

As previously explored, the essence of who we are can be seen in the innocence of children as they reflect the 'complete contentment' of divine presence. Where we can become confused is in the egoic interpretation of our divinity experiencing complete contentment. Our divinity, like a seed in the earth, is at where it is at in each experience of relationships, environments, and circumstances in our journey. And although the energies of these may tend to overwhelm the nervous system at times, sending our thoughts in many directions and even causing the development of egoic patterns for protection, all of this is both witnessed and felt from a place of complete contentment from a divine point of view. It is frequently in our awareness that we are mostly trying to catch up with what and who we already are as the divine.

It may seem as if we are on a ride without our permission, but energetically, cellular memory, the environment we are in, and those we interact with have been prearranged by our soul or contracted with the universe as a necessary part of our experience in deepening. When we feel resistance and want to run, fight, or hide from what we feel, the resistance that is felt is an aspect in our energy field which we have incarnated to resolve. Even in the most traumatic of circumstances, these energies are asking for resolve, but depending upon where we are at in our journey, we may not be ready or able to address intense emotions or perceptions that challenge any egoic construction of protection.

When we are ready, we can begin by observing the immediate energies of our environment that are arising for attention in what we feel, such as an irritation with a coworker, the chill in the wind, or the uncomfortable state we may have in our finances. If more pressing matters come to light, we give attention starting from where we are at as we feel what we feel. This offering of love is substantial in that it honors the nature of the relationship we once may have resisted or perceived as an enemy, and, even if we still do so, the energetic implication in allowing ourselves to acknowledge or feel what we feel shifts our vibration from adversarial to harmonic. The universe not only responds in kind to this but does so at an astonishing rate and, in many cases, both reveals and resolves soul contracts simply through the acknowledgment we offer in observance. And once we give ourselves permission to feel whatever may be arising for our attention, we not only begin to resolve but find relief in our body as the energies in need freely flow.

Often these energies are intermingled with what we perceive as afflictive circumstances that challenge our reality in emotion, and we will not allow ourselves to explore how we truly feel because of egoic construction. Our ego will use tactics such as sarcasm, blame, and guilt to induce judgements of shame in order to turn on ourselves in fear, which will act like a fortress to keep us trapped behind the safety of egoic walls. Seeing through this veil can be difficult, if not impossible, when we are grasping our ridicule and holding on to any sense of stability the ego may have created, even if based in affliction. Although habitual patterns may feel like plagues railing upon us again and again in our daily walk, the stability they provide in recognition of emotional energy will frequently be more appealing than the prospect of an unknown future. Only the 'innocent one' may approach these constructs by the offering of love granted to the heart in surrender as the energies are felt. And as we go deeper into the pain through abiding in compassion, we find that the egoic patterns themselves provide the transformational power necessary for our resolution, which are only waiting for our readiness in coordination with the universe to abide in the depths of what we are feeling.

An effective practice in granting ourselves permission to feel is to go into our dreams, passions, and desires as we are ready, simply abiding with our 'likes' and 'dislikes', exploring the heart in what arises, whether it be inspirational or aching. When difficult emotions present themselves, we abide in what we feel, allowing the desires to emerge from them while holding the heart in loving compassion, breathing slowly, steadily, and deeply as we do so. These moments are closely related to eternal threads, and as they come forth to be acknowledged, resolution will appear in what we desire. Innocence will support us by setting aside beliefs of transgression, 'right and wrong', and 'good and bad', leaving room for our truth to present itself in the energy of what we feel. This is not an exercise in thought, but rather an allowance of energy where we take part through abiding, and in turn it begins to take part in us, revealing a much larger path of self which begins to fulfill previously unacknowledged desires. As we feel what we need to feel while holding the heart in compassion, we will find a greater sense of self emerging as the heart expands in safety, knowing that it will not be abandoned. This is our true power as divine beings, creators of the universe, and masters of manifestation: the love we show ourselves is the potential shift we may move in all things of matter, whether light or shadow, upon the earth in reflection. We trust in the process, that the universe is watching over us, working with us, and moving on our behalf to provide what we need. Where once we saw only impassible barriers, innocence reveals the weight of this illusion which must crumble any former reality unable to stand in love.

By Our Design

By Our Design

Chapter 5

Pain

Growing up in the sixties and seventies was a rather chaotic time, where wars, protests, pollution, poverty, and politics loomed over our home. There were no video games, cell phones, or internet, so frequently families gathered nightly around the television set for news and some semblance of connection to the world. Everyone seemed to have a thought, opinion, or feeling on current affairs, and often people felt strangely engulfed in their views yet still searched for some evidence of truth that might support their beliefs. Humanity's fixation with industry and understanding its role in the coming technological age of pre-twenty first century circumstances was obsessive, even compulsory at times, as frustration, anxiety, and fear played out in acts of escalation.

One of my earliest memories as a small boy in the sixties is of sitting on the front steps of our house, about two or three years of age, sipping a vanilla milkshake through a straw. It isn't a particularly happy memory, or one that stands out because of anything extraordinary, exciting, or special; it was just a boy enjoying a milkshake, sitting on the steps when the world was in a state of very intense, often confused energy. The war in Vietnam was graphically violent on the nightly news, and while society seemed to rage, looking for answers or voicing opinions on the television, inherently there was a part of that child that knew deeper roots of existence within himself. And although the nervous system would eventually succumb to the overwhelming sensations it was immersed in, with egoic patterns forming in an attempt to build a reality that was protective and functional, the soul would continue to advocate through every experience, even though I may have been unaware of it growing up. What we often ask as humans, though, is why is love not apparent or revealing when we are hurting? Where is our

63

advocate in deep loneliness, and how could certain circumstances come to pass to begin with when a benevolent being or God of compassion is witness to our pain?

Although some of the most intense sensations of pain we may ever feel in our lifetime are associated with love, the deep wounds we may have harbored as 'loss' along the way were not purposed in vain by it; we may not recognize love working in our circumstances, but everything we encounter in our journey, however we may view it, is moving on our behalf as we spiritually evolve.

It may be difficult to accept the arrangement of some fears, as they strike with such manifestational precision and depth that it feels as though our heart has been squeezed by an unseen hand. When they are accompanied by feelings of 'not being good enough', or that we have somehow done something 'wrong' and deserve our perceived misfortune, they can often leave us cowering in a corner, bruised, bullied, and utterly oppressed. Frequently they arrive with expressions of anger, hatred, and accusations of taunting until we fold inward, sinking into depression. And when they rear their head again, they will often lash out with such ferocity that it will feel as if the whole world has ganged up upon us, leaving any sense of life overwhelmed in the wake of their energy. But as we learn about the nature of bullies, we find that most of their lives, they themselves have been bullied, receiving little to no acknowledgement, their only desire to be heard, seen, and shown the attention or love they have needed. Once we begin to ask the difficult questions when we are hurting, even though we may seemingly provoke a giant and slip deeper into despair, the energies we are addressing give themselves to us in a different light if we meet them with love.

Opening the door of pain is no easy task and inviting it inward with innocence of heart for as long as it desires to stay can be one of the most difficult surrenders we will ever experience as human beings, especially in the deepest emotional traumas of the body where there is the belief that we have done something wrong, or that someone else has wronged us, and that our life path has been altered in occurrence from what would have been 'right'. The mind will work in conjunction with the ego, telling us that if we were born into different circumstances, had made better choices, or knew the outcomes of them, we would feel differently. 'Wrong' assumes a great deal of blame for how we feel, and when we are inclined to beat ourselves up by it, we effectively suffocate ourselves in our own judgements and opinions about how many possible variations of reality 'could've, should've, or would've' taken place if only we knew better. The egoic mind can easily perpetuate what we feel, running each scenario we could have chosen by the screen of scrutiny, forming deep resentments of anger and fear that seek only to punish for some sense of justice from what may be viewed as a burning house of derision. And not only will it destroy until it has achieved complete devastation, but a belief system of 'wrong' will continue to build walls of protection, influencing any future decisions of potential as it shifts our vibrational frequency, often staying in journey with us for many years, spanning dimensionally across mortal boundaries into lifetimes rippling back in reflection from the cosmos.

When we condemn ourselves or judge someone else to be 'wrong', we close the door on that part within us which desires to be healed. But, ironically, the universe is made in such a way that no energy is ever wasted. Even when we close one door, the universe will recycle the pain of our judgements to create or open another avenue to those parts in need of acknowledgement. As emotions surge forward to be embraced by our innocence, what we may feel as depression, anxiety, loneliness, and ache are the agency for the energy in resolve as it works in coordination with divinity to grant latitude in our vibration for healing; what we often see as devastation, the universe views as a new beginning or place of expansion. Just as that little boy knew the simplicity of sitting with himself on the steps, enjoying a milkshake when the world was crumbling about him in confusion, our soul knows what we are in need of for acknowledgment, feeling into both our past, present, and future as a multidimensional being, seeing pain as an ally for our spiritual evolvement.

Although the chaotic moments may seem like they need solved, in retrospect, much of what we entertain as a species in life circumstances serves to educate us in who we are. This may feel unfair or without balance of justice at times, but this is only from a perspective of egoic introspection three-dimensionally. The soul allows us to undertake certain aspects of our journey that we may come to know both the darkness and the light of who we are; it is only through the various facets of our incarnation that we may fully embrace the transformational energies necessary for spiritual evolution.

Some of the most heart-wrenching experiences we will live through and potent words we may ever hear in our life are those that trigger the deepest fears of potential loss, abandonment, unworthiness, rejection, and separation. When life partners, lovers, and friends give attention to their own needs, the egoic tendency is to receive such news as a personal assault on our character. We may wonder what we have done wrong, or how we could have avoided such hurt, and as the ache of our circumstances intensifies, the ego will grasp for any saving voice that might appear. We will want answers to the broken pieces we begin to suffer as our heart shatters in response to all that we feel when hurting, and it is not uncommon to accuse, blame, and become indignant as our emotional investments or beliefs begin to unravel. When the nervous system becomes overwhelmed, desperation will enter in any way it can to press deliverance: we may act out, say things we regret, and lose ourselves entirely to the reality shifting under our feet. And if we feel deep emotional trauma, our only initiative is to survive the strong waves of energy that engulf us and love our heart as best we can in difficult times.

The ego will want to protect us, searching for anything as an emotional life raft when we feel overwhelmed, especially if the rational mind is beyond reach. So when we are deeply engaged in transformative energies, our only mission is to survive; we may not know how we will emerge when we are overwhelmed, or what new reality may be, but life is at the root of who we are— both as a species and as divine beings who view survival as a step in our evolutionary process. Godly, or divine, presence doesn't mean we will not hate, dislike, or rail against what we experience or witness, but rather that as we evolve, we will come to know these energies as parts that are in need of love, attention, and healing in our humanity.

As we awaken we will encounter glimpses of our divine essence, which will inspire us to move further inward, investigating the integrity of what we are experiencing. This is paramount in our manifestational process in that the trust we cultivate through the hope we receive in surrender allows us to unfold our divinity and opens the heart to the realization that nothing is ever without purpose, whether in expression or as a part of healing. We may be flooded with emotion or find ourselves strangely immersed in calm, but by abiding with what arises in compassion, our heart knows safety and that it is watched over, secure even though we may feel turbulence in our circumstances. Thoughts may come and go incessantly, and we may be triggered by past memories of joy or pain, but our only duty when overwhelmed is to survive, to breathe, and to receive the here and now as it is. There is more than enough material for our attention when we are able to heal those parts in need, but when we are 'in it', we simply abide with who we are, where we are, and what we feel by acknowledging the waves of energy in our experience, even though we may not understand the 'why' until later.

As a practice, we may develop a relationship with pain, or befriend it, so to say, in our conversation when we abide with its strong energies. Utilizing the imagination, our breath, and our senses and slowing down, we are capable of an intimacy with ourselves that many of us as human beings may have never experienced. And although this is a very ancient method of communion and is a natural part of our evolutionary process, practices like this may be heavily opposed because they challenge egoic constructions and undermine the status quo of the world. But when we are ready, we may simply say to pain, "Come in, I will not abandon me nor resist you, but will love my heart in your presence and acknowledge, feel, and hear you in all that you offer."

When we listen to pain on this level, the integrity, confidence, or insecurity in our vibrational thread shares itself intimately, and what we say to ourselves or others becomes apparent in revealing those parts that the soul has been asking for us to love in acknowledgement. We may become aware at times that the entirety of the universe is observing us, just as we would draw our attention to some part of the body that is in healing. Moving inward, we allow that which is arising to come forth by embracing, feeling all that we feel as an offering of love to the one we are here in journey with. Although we may feel anxious, uncomfortable, and distressed at what may surface at times, we practice slowing down, being with our body, and ensuring the safety to the heart, which in turn will calm the nervous system. If we feel resistance, we acknowledge those parts by placing the hand on the heart, feeling what we feel, and again offering love to the one feeling what is necessary.

Pain may have many more friends that arrive once we open the door, such as Self Pity, Poverty, Cruelty, and Ugliness, which are a hard-looking bunch, mostly from many years of living on the fringe of existence. Often, they lounge wherever they please, mostly choosing to sprawl across the heart as it opens to receive them. But as they do, we do not oppose their energy, but rather divine a way less seen or offered to them. We sit with them as they gather, holding our heart in the midst of their chattering, and allow tears to fall upon the cheeks if they come, gravity guiding them down well-known paths as they flow.

Abandonment, Rejection, and Unworthiness will usually complete the crowd gathered, a full house, yet still we hold true to love, being with strong energy and holding the heart as each of them comes forth to be felt, listened to, and seen by us as no one else can. Breath by breath we feel intimately those that arise for acknowledgement, that healing may occur as needed with each truth that presents itself. We continue by gently setting aside judgements and opinions about the circumstances of each arising, simply feeling, allowing passage for cellular debris to release as they will; just as a sliver works its way out of the body, so too the creation serves us even amid the most difficult of circumstances.

Over time, each of our guests will slowly depart, moving on as we sit in a place of compassion with our heart through every truth that arises. And although the room may feel empty or lighter as our guests leave at first, 'lighter' may feel foreign, or cold, even unrecognizable as resolve in the beginning. But soon we may notice that somehow we fill more of the room; as we come know the parts that are hurting, so too we are coming to know ourselves and the one coming forth in us by the love we offer. In each holding of space for pain in all its various forms, we befriend our inner chambers, breathe easier, and deepen in relief. Vibrational beliefs such as 'wrong' become not a prison cell for us to be abandoned in, but rather feelings to be felt for the greater self to come forth in loving compassion, sharing with us the necessary paths we have incarnated to experience and explore.

Holding space is one of the most powerful energetic bridges of intimacy we can provide for ourselves and others in pain, struggle, or transition. Too often we desire to move past our pain or that of another because of the uncomfortable feelings we may feel. Egoic tendency is to make things better, comforting for the sake of being comfortable, rather than creating a space for resolution to occur; healing requires room for the acknowledgment of feelings which must be felt in order for resolve to manifest. If we allow ourselves to feel deeply into the moments asking to be heard and desire to be held in painful circumstances, we discover those places that share connection. We may find no words when strong energies arise and may be unsure of how to approach a situation, but by allowing ourselves to feel with compassion, we are developing a practice of self-love that will provide relief in times of distress.

When we hold space, it not only roots us deeper within ourselves as human beings, but with those we care about, providing tangible evidence in the form of fulfilment, as energy is acknowledged with love as its agency. Pain is merely a part of the process, an indication of our transformation, and an awakening to those parts that have needed to be fulfilled for our self-realization to come forth. When we come to know love, we come to know that everything has its purpose, all things serve for highest destiny, nothing is without merit, and to respect another's path in that there are no wrong choices. All things flow for our unfolding —every irritation, judgement, and feeling that we feel— and have light within them, carrying a vibration to the universe for our most prevalent desires. Life provides the raw material for the soul to delve into the places within us that desire to come forth, that we may come to know ourselves more intimately as parts surface vibrationally when we are ready to provide an acknowledgment of love.

As the outer and inner converge in synergy, this draws up waves of emotion where the ego will grasp to hold fast to known realities and former relationships, anything familiar, but this will only serve to spark resentment which kindles the fire of divine passion further. We may view our circumstances as walls to our progress and feel blockages as to where we wish to go or who we want to be, but this is only a part of a universal ruse built into our humanity that we may go deeper into the energies arising for transformative power; the energies that arise in deep loss feel like they will end you, that your very essence and body are being torn apart as emotional debris surface and often leave no sign of reconciliation, but this is precisely the point of them.

In 2014, my life path was filled with incredible pain: the passing of my mother shortly after going into the hospital on Christmas Eve, a divorce after a partnership of 17 years, one of my closest friends eaten away by cancer, a dog who was both confidante and teacher euthanized after a prolonged struggle, sale of our property as part of the divorce settlement, loss of job, and complete abandonment by most family and friends. I must have looked like a walking plague, and many people kept their distance just in case circumstances might be contagious. But in that pit of darkness, each of us comes to know only two choices set before us: reset, start over, and experience all the pain, bewilderment, and difficulty again in another life, or feel.

When someone is in extreme pain, whether physically, mentally, or emotionally, feeling is not arrived at lightly. We may share here about these practices as a way of alleviating or releasing the pressure by acknowledgment of what we feel towards resolution, but if our former reality was built on denial, opening the door to previously ignored or resisted energies that have been crying out for attention for years or lifetimes can capsize any sanity we think we have. Paradoxically, though, the universe works in such a way that when we lose our sanity or resist what we feel, this only creates a parallel opposite for potential in alignment or resonance that builds in energy. In other words, faith works by the energetic circumstances of uncertainty, and what we perceive as loss by the universe is really the space created by our greater mind or consciousness to fulfill what we desire. So while we may perceive circumstances as hurt or 'wrongs' by ourselves or another in action, our universal reflection is attempting to tune the heart field that we may see beyond those circumstances of any trauma or suffering, moving deeper into the layers of who we are as love vibrationally, which allows us to embrace life abundantly and live more clearly than we ever thought possible. It's easy to become confused, as the egoic mind will attempt to build conclusions about the circumstances of what we are feeling, but as energy beings, this is why our resolution rests in what we feel.

So as I sat in extreme pain, loss, and bewilderment, one of the most prevalent realizations to arise, surprisingly, was the sensation of 'arrangement'. That circumstances, people, relationships, and patterns had all been wonderfully, maybe ominously, orchestrated for on purpose. The feeling was so strong and overwhelming that it felt as if all choice had been removed from me. For someone who believed that they lived in a universe of free accord, although this was disturbing, to say the least, somehow it felt very comforting. My world became much smaller in a blink of an eye, but also much vaster in the perspective of who I am. And although there was utter aloneness in this, there was also a 'knowing' of being held by the whole universe, divine nature being my closest friend.

A profound sense of living holds us when we are in metamorphosis, where if we lean into the temptation to run, we no longer run. As we observe our fears, we no longer freeze in them. And as we surrender to love, the need to resist dissipates; every demonic appearance we perceive as nightmarishly tormenting is only so because it must be in order to be most effective. The circumstances we experience as potent emotional trauma, suffering, or pain are not only *NOT* in vain, but they are highly valued as commodities or vehicles of transformative power in their energetic potentials. Some of them we were born with or into, others we have incarnated specifically to experience through soul contracts. Although we may do our best to consciously equip ourselves in preparedness, even if we *are* aware of what may be unfolding, the transformational energies that shift frequency on a vibrational level are so strong that a life path can easily be overwhelmed and utilized for their purpose. An example would be that we are aware of an addictive behavior, but the energies of obsession and compulsion are so intense that they still easily overtake any effort based in resistance. But, when we embrace, or "lean into," the desires arising in these energies on a heart level, an admission or acknowledgment occurs which provides relief for them to flow, and we discover parts of the self, hidden within the layers, only waiting for the attention and love we have provided.

Many of our most basic feelings arise from places within us that have a need for connection or acknowledgement and will manifest in ways we might not suspect. It's only natural for the ego to seek security from the relationships around us, especially as comfort, in all its various forms, portends how real this sense experience is. But in all that we build three-dimensionally, eventually cracks develop in our reality where distinguished whisperings of light reveal a much larger picture than the shadows we have found comfort in. Ironically, this is where we begin to take notice of our surroundings as teachers, first noticing fourth-dimensional aspects of something greater at work, and an underlying current moving in circumstances. From the oldest of times, humanity has been connected to the earth in a myriad of ways, both from our reliance and interactive relationship with it to the principles of spirit which nature teaches us: how to flow, patience in creative life force, and manifestational energies within and around us. As divine beings, we have come to experience, adjust, and express a mixture of these energies on a level in human consciousness we are frequently unaware of, but not by mistake or misfortune. The soul, as a mystical agent in disguise, has universally agreed to allow parts of our journey to be withheld from our awareness until we are ready and will align for us what we need that we may receive the frequencies necessary for our vibration to shift as we have desired. As multi-dimensional beings, this works best in exploration when our experiences have significant personal meaning for each of us, that we may interact with our environment energetically in a pure state of 'unknowing', seeing our relationships as 'others' in our life path. Basically, we have purposefully lost ourselves that we may face or encounter ourselves in relationship, coming to know love like we have never known in depth before. As the seers of ancient times have said, "if you cannot find God in a blade of grass, surely you will not find love in the holy texts." Meaning everything has its place in our dogma, all environments contribute to our evolution, and even though some manifestations arrive with strikingly uncomfortable circumstances dependent upon what we need, all turmoil, trouble, and afflictive tides that disturb the waters of life are a part of the key energies needed for alignment, expression, and exploration.

Even so, sometimes we may we feel like retreating, pulling back, building walls, and going into familiar patterns of energy, but as we do, the heart feels all of this, as if the heart is being pulled away from us and walled in, and it will ache for affection. This is where the ego will step in to recycle rising energy, often in obsessive thought and compulsive behavior with old wounds of unworthiness, rejection, and loss, manifesting in storylines of victimization. Although these patterns may seem aggressively defeating to us as we ascend, in each life path there are elements of attention that must be brought to fruition in order for the heart to be fulfilled.

As we become ready, frequently these energies will manifest in appearance as 'empathy', being triggered as we identify with suffering, our own pain rising in connection to them. When we have unresolved issues, what we tend to feel are the vibrational strands within us being 'plucked' like strings on a musical instrument, activated by circumstances as cellular memory recalls emotional distress. This may be in relation to something we have experienced in this timeline or a previous incarnation, or that we have desired to explore through a finite experience here on Earth. It is also one of the reasons why 12-step or self-help programs work so well in that the starting common denominator is a place of identification in these wounds. These energies must first be acknowledged before any further revelation, and it is very difficult to do so when the ego stands at the doorway of their release; the deflation of ego is necessary before any relief or clarity in awareness can come forth. Pain works as both an arrow of direction in drawing our attention to what area is in need and as a communication when complacency or stagnation have begun to corrode our life path.

When we feel challenged in our perception of reality, especially concerning "old wounds" that resurface, it is really the soul working in conjunction with the universe to resolve vibrational threads that we feel are in need of love. As this arrangement of circumstances occurs, the pain we may experience is both for our benefit in allowing us to clear emotional debris and for us to go further into the depths of intimacy we have desired in self-exploration on pilgrimage here; no wound is ever without purposeful existence in serving the soul. Every reflection we are touched by in our life path is beneficial in some way. And although we may not understand what we feel, our capacity for feeling what we feel is rooted deeply in the love that we are. So while at times we may be overwhelmed with the emotions that arise in us for our attention, it is not the 'understanding' that we have which will bring relief to what we feel, but the love we offer as we feel what we feel. The 'empathy of old wounds' is a part of our spiritual nature and is a process for revealing those places that are difficult to visit alone, providing a connection with others through the identification of sharing our pain. As we learn to listen to the vessel we are in journey with here and observe what triggers the body emotionally, we intuitively develop a sense awareness for the love necessary in furthering our evolution. Although some decisions are made for us universally in what we have been asking for vibrationally, others gain momentum as insights become clear into why we are choosing them. Life has a funny way of working things out, revealing places, and shifting the tide to journey us to the shores necessary for our experience.

Even if we feel the weight of indecision in difficult choices, although the ego may seek the path most familiar or comfortable as a means of alleviating suffering, if we allow ourselves to embrace our experience, regardless of which choice we choose, we open the energy of transformation to move on our behalf for the desires of the heart to gain traction. Regardless of outcomes, when we offer self-compassion in this way, we encounter a fulfillment we never could have imagined possible. For some, this might be a career choice, considering marriage, parenthood, or a financial decision of importance, for others it could mean infidelity to be with a lover, walking away from a family, or rebellion against the system. But in each case, the point is that as we come to know our passions, inspirations, and attractions, they are not wrong; they are simply a communication of the soul. Yes, there may be consequences, even devastation as we follow the desires of our heart, but if we do so with love for the heart, no matter what we choose we always grow closer with ourselves.

This is a difficult teaching because it appears as a loose cannon, that we may fire at will upon what we will. While this is not far from the truth, it is only a part of the resolve. The other part is that we listen to our reflections, taking heed of our guidance in greater self, and build integrity with the soul who knows us better than we know ourselves for what we truly desire. In each life path, we have all longed to be here exactly in the capacity that we are, not necessarily to stay with or in a particular situation of pain, but to embrace and own our choices as a part of higher destiny. And as we learn to honor ourselves in the roles we play, paying attention to the feelings that arise as divinity comes forth, we begin to honor others, seeing a kaleidoscope of theater in everything, where everyone is here living out their soul contracts. Ultimately, we come to trust, knowing that the same forces at work in the heavenly bodies of the moon, stars, and planets are also at work within us as divine masters.

We may weep in the darkness of uncertainty, sometimes uncontrollably, fiercely even, when feeling the pain of doubt arising, but as we do so we find an inextricable bond to the dark in its offering of faith available to us in the love that we are. And though it may seem long in its approach, when we are ready, everything comes to light as we open ourselves to the love we have desired. Often, at first our reflections are not without pain, especially if we have ignored parts that have persistently come forth time and again to be heard, but when we say to ourselves or another, "I acknowledge your pain, the frustration, ache, and deep feelings arising within you," we are opening a door energetically for emotional debris to be heard and integrated in resolve. We may dislike what we feel, hate ourselves or another at times, and resist what comes up in us or them, but the body, mind, and emotions work in coordination with our reflections, empowering us as agents of healing. This exchange of information in our vibrational field is a normal part of the celestial organism of creation, moving in harmony for our benefit. As we become more aware of our divinity, we will begin to experience less and less resistance as "agents of healing" through our own embrace of that which has surfaced for our attention.

Many of us may have experienced these energies throughout much of our lifetime but were unaware of the exchange that was taking place. When we give our attention to something, we are forming an invisible thread of connection, whether we realize it or not, to that which we focus on, even on a subconscious level. Most of us have had experiences where we have been walking down the street and we look at someone in front of us on the road, and they suddenly turn to look at us as if they had eyes in the back of their head. Or an old friend may come to mind, and as we ponder our acquaintance, we promptly receive a phone call from them. Although we may not be aware of what we are projecting or receiving in our energetic field, nonetheless it emanates from us. These natural phenomena, coupled with a sensitive nature which is often darkened in an understanding clouded by ego, can be quite intrusive, pre-awakening to our divine potential. Sometimes this journey in itself can last years or many lifetimes, but the universe knows precisely when we are ready to receive certain insights and patiently awaits the love necessary for those deep places in us to be revealed. Our mind may do its best to try and figure things out, but if we let it run its course until exhausted, we find even exhaustion working for us to a greater depth of surrender in returning to simplicity, making us more malleable to vibrational 'tuning'.

This process can be incredibly painful, but as emotional debris surface to be cleared, we begin to see how the simplicity of acknowledgement creates an energetic bridge for relief to occur. Some of us may be new to pain, others may have felt burdened for much of their life, and a few sense eternally a vibrational thread of longing that has stretched across many lifetimes. But regardless of what we believe, science says energy continues and that it cannot be destroyed, only transferred or transformed. Events, people, and circumstances that trigger strong energy in us that are difficult to acknowledge serve us specifically as manifestations to expanding consciousness. Although we commonly think in a linear timeline from a three-dimensional point of view, and most times are unaware of the role that pain plays as a part of the healing process, as humans, we are the perfect nesting ground for an incubation of divine consciousness.

In any case, whether the pain we feel is fresh or we have experienced it from our youth and possibly longer, the fact that we are aware of a potential path of resolve is an indication we are being readied to receive it. As we become open to who we are and what is available to us, an awareness arises within us that we are effectively here as a part of a social contract with every soul we encounter, and that we have come willingly to explore in our pilgrimage.

Chapter 6

Soul Contracts

I incarnated in a time of great emotional upheaval, when the Catholic Church condemned divorce, people of color were striving for civil rights, and if you were gay it wasn't disclosed for fear of retribution. The Vietnam War was raging in the late sixties, peace protestors had been shot at Kent State, pollution was at an all-time high, and the Cold War was still simmering with the threat of a nuclear holocaust across the globe. The energy in the world was very chaotic, full of emotional charge, and many people were learning the power of their voice, with the media outlets of newspaper, radio, and television carrying exploding passions. It seemed as if the whole world was teetering on the edge, and everyone had something extreme to say about it.

Although humanity can feel dark sometimes when observing society, as though we have lost our way as a species, there is also great potential in the shadows of derision that the ego presents in the mind. On a deeper level, the soul always works as a modem with the universe for the orchestration of emotional debris to be carefully woven into the circumstances around us to address vibrational fissures of desire. Discovering these truths in the undertone of suffering we view in the world can feel disconcerting, confusing, and without merit to the uninitiated, especially when life opportunities are perceived as obstacles. But while we might doubt our conditions, looking for some answer among the chaos, the very circumstances we often seek to overcome are of our own making in the soul, which has heard vibrational pleas that have asked for resolve. We may resist transformation, even rail against it as it approaches in the form it chooses, but the universe works with such precise movements that our denial, struggle, and exhaustion will coincide with when we are ready to begin an exploration of what is presented for wellbeing.

Soul contracts are one of the avenues we proceed with, both in previous agreements we have made with ourselves or other souls in an effort to express, heal, or adjust vibrational threads. As humans, much of our process begins with external circumstances but will always lead to deeper issues that we were previously unaware of, hidden vibrationally beneath the surface, especially concerning wounds we have experienced. It's hard to imagine a path of any inner work without a curriculum of suffering, not that we seek suffering, but that it is an inevitable part of our grieving as we acknowledge the disappointments which have formed in our beliefs, the losses generated by them, and a reality that shifts in the wake of becoming consciously aware of how the universe works. And where healing is desired, the depth that is revealed is always in relation to what we are ready for, working with such perfection that its synchronicity challenges our reality in order to adjust, aligning both body and spirit in sense experience for the most effective shift to occur. This can prove to be frustrating in our day-to-day life in a world or society built upon egoic construction, which, although may seem to impede us, actually moves us closer to evolution as energy gestates within us. Although as humans we live in 3-D reality, we are multi-dimensional beings existing on many planes simultaneously, and what appears physically in our circumstances is only one aspect of our journey, which is much vaster than we are consciously aware of in experience. It may be difficult to accept or comprehend, but there is another layer to some of the most painful traumas in many life paths, such as childhood abuse, neglect, or environments we have incarnated into. And in the undertone of these events are the necessary energies for healing, or a shift on a vibrational level which is eternal in nature, one we have deeply desired, more so than we will ever understand from any logical point of view in which we try to comprehend three-dimensionally.

Part of the process in our soul contracts is to be unaware on some level of what is happening that we may fully engage in sense experiences. Although as we explore our relationships in the sensations we feel physically and emotionally, there is a tendency for the ego to react to any discomfort or instability that is felt (which in turn will create a series of potential timelines and outcomes in an effort to ease emotional upheaval). Egoic construction works in conjunction with our soul contracts to provide the context for emotional energies to be intensified, never wasted. So while we may feel the nervous system of our body becoming overwhelmed as circumstances unfold that we are incapable of processing in the moment, when the ego and body step in to create a barrier, these events are stored in our cellular memory until we are able to process the charged energy of what has happened at a later time. So even in unawareness, we are consistently working with our life path in all situations, although at times it may not seem so. As infinite beings, this finite experience in our incarnation affords us the opportunity of an eternal adjustment in vibration, but only as we are ready for it, and is metaphorically the 'caterpillar' moving inward into the 'cocoon', eventually emerging as the 'butterfly' in rebirth. This is found throughout most, if not all, spiritualties, religions, and mythos as the 'hero's journey'. As we explore our life path, although we may be unaware of the soul contracts we have, they are in essence the delivery system of this journey.

Three of the most common questions in human experience that arise in relation to them are:

"I'm in such deep physical or emotional pain; what can I do for relief or healing?"

"Do I have a soulmate, and if so, when or how will I find them?"

"How do I create or attract abundance?"

These questions are very similar to each other in the nature of their substance or energy as they all constitute a resolve of who we are through personal desire. The soul works in coordination with the universe by our circumstances to provide the necessary steps we must fulfill as these energies reveal themselves for integration. And although it may seem unlikely, often paradox is a how soul contracts move in any adjustment process. So even in that which feels lacking, afflictive, or unfair, all forms of suffering present themselves as a deeper level of intimacy within ourselves. Once we begin to recognize this relationship with what we feel as illumination, not as right or wrong, good or bad, or any dualistic notion, it supports us as a component in compassion.

These questions or energies always appear as we are ready and will reveal the one common thread within each which is ourselves: how we vibrate, what we are willing to feel
(or not), and what depths are arising in connection with our sensory experience. Whether we feel the deep ache in the wanting of a soulmate, a desire to be healed of a condition, or the craving for more abundance in life, these each start with the acknowledgment of energy swelling within us; every question has the desire of its fulfillment in its own asking and the transformational power in its ache for the one listening. So as we begin observing, listening, and feeling into those parts that provoke the questions we ask, as we learn to hold the heart in loving compassion, we grant passage for the energy to move as necessary in our soul contracts to meet our desires. When we honor the one coming forth, in whatever energy they may appear, we begin the process of fulfilling our soul contracts:

The healing we have longed for has been longing to heal our heart.

The soulmate we have been asking for has been asking for us.

The abundance we have greatly desired has been desiring us.

As we acknowledge, so we are acknowledged, and with the love that we meet, we are met.

In the yoga sutras there is a practice which will help us to explore these energies while holding the heart, receiving them on a much deeper level of intimacy. If we are willing or desirous of relief, surrender allows us to receive what is in need of being felt for resolution with the soul. This sutra does not promote resistance or suppression of any sort but instead faces pain or desire with nonviolent thoughts and actions, doing no harm from a proactive stance.

'Tapas', or 'tapa' as a verb, like many Sanskrit words, has various meanings by its context, but generally means to heat, shine, purify, shift or change, and to transform. In older scriptures, tapas are translated as the "burning off of impurities," but in many schools of thought this implies a rejection, or 'getting rid of' something which, from an inclusive point of view, suffers universally by design. This encourages us to look deeper into the mystery of its meaning and how it could be applied. Although feeling into the void of pain could easily overwhelm the nervous system, the difference when we do so consciously with love, and not as a reaction or because we are fighting against it, creates a vacuum of space for observation and potential resolve. Heat is generated by the embracing of our conditioning and the patterns that arise from the time of gestation in the cocoon ego has formed for us, which enables malleability. This kind of heat is not the violent struggle of rejection, which takes us further inward into the gestation period, but rather the creative power, which is released in the raw energies in process through our surrender. The 'burning' or purification we may feel is the power of transformation shifting vibrational frequencies in the space which has been offered by the love of abiding with strong energies while holding the heart in compassion.

Each of our soul contracts serve in purpose for our highest reflection in energy beneficially. Even when we are unaware of what is happening, our soul has already worked out many of the details in coordination with universal nature for any vibrational shift or sharing. Although this may sound somewhat as if we are locked into predestined outcomes, this is only so from a view within the matrix of three-dimensional living. Many dispositions we hold on to such as expectation, projection, resistance to surrender, or desire for control from a divine perception are energies calling out for expansion. Although we can become accustomed to our afflictions as they seemingly materialize chains of bondage, and we may even begin to feel safe in their familiarity, the divine spark in us will always ignite the suspecting notion of something other than their reality. Being 'open' might sound easy, but it can be incredibly difficult when our known reality is challenged, resulting in fear, confusion, and deep pain.

Some of us may remember our first science class, where we were introduced to other worlds as we placed a glass slide on a microscope and peered through the tiny hole with one eye in anticipation of what wonders we might behold. And depending upon where we were at in our journey, this prospect may have triggered terrible anxiety or an exciting possibility filled with exploration. Once discovered though, these worlds within worlds would forever change how we viewed reality and often opened the imagination to other wonders which might exist beyond what we had previously known. We may have cowered a little deeper under the bedsheets at night, afraid of what may lay hidden within and without, or dreamed further into these fantastic worlds, but in either case, once these places were revealed they moved in our subconscious, indicative of an awakening to a much larger universe (*or smaller one*) that we live in.

Ironically, some of the most prevalent worlds we are desirous of participation in seem unopened to us, shrouded in obscurity, and when we feel they are out of reach from us, quickly fall prey to dismissal. In this dismissal, though, are the keys to their uncovering, those moments we may pass by that are awkward, overwhelming, or unaligned with our current reality. In these places are the vibrational frequencies that have surfaced, working closely with the soul, that hint at our deepest desires and other worlds that exist beyond the walls of egoic construction. On a quantum level, this opens us to a vast array of potential that cannot solely be determined by cause and effect, but rather what will most serve us multi-dimensionally in manifestation. This alignment is where the soul, universe, body, and all that we feel work in coordination for who we are as multi-dimensional beings, rather than an existence based solely in the third dimension. However, these doors will not be opened until all is fulfilled energetically within the scope of our current reality, which is why the simplicity of starting where we are at, with mindfulness and allowance being key in compassionate practice. We can utilize the third dimension to work for us, rather than attempting to move beyond it, in unlocking awareness of other worlds simply by being with the body. This is one of the most basic soul contracts we have signed, in that we have chosen our specific incarnation purposefully with the intention to express, heal, or resolve vibrational frequencies on a much deeper level.

As humans, we tend to view soul contracts only outwardly with others as a result of egoic construction or three-dimensional focus. But as we awaken to the nature of our existence, a quickening unravels the sleep of limitation to reveal that we are much more than we can possibly comprehend from this one point of view, and an exploration of our relationship with the body alone will inform us of multiple contracts, which immediately begin to open new doors beyond previous human experience. Regardless of where we start, if are testing the waters, *we are in process* and awakened to untapped realms of divinity in our current life path.

One of the most profound challenges of our current age is learning the language of our soul and effectively engaging manifestational forces available to us. As humans, we will naturally develop a narrative in relation to this timeline but will struggle with the simple communications contained within it. Finding meaning or purpose to our existence is no coincidence in the feelings that will consistently arise throughout our lifetime, and listening to the body is a practice that must be adhered to if we are to learn the language of the soul. Creating a space for abiding with what we feel in the sensations of the vessel allows us not only quality time with the soul but inherently will deepen our relationship with the nature of energy: how it moves, its reflective qualities, and its 'non-attachment' to desire.

A relationship with the body becomes a part of our healing, and as we spend time with ourselves, offering the listening required for any potential shift, egoic constructs of comfortability will be challenged under the weight of the raw energies that surface. Often, many of us will experience distraction, with the mind telling us, "But we have to go here, there, do this, and that— what about friends, work, and family?" This is where the real initiative of our contract with the vessel becomes apparent over time, in that when it is unacknowledged either intentionally or unintentionally, our physical health, mental state and emotions become overwhelmed in a plea for attention. If we view the relationship between our awareness and the body as a symbiotic one, frequently a solution is already there just waiting for us to catch up with the 'body of information' being shared with us. And even though much of what arises may seem confusing, it isn't that we don't understand or need to 'figure things out' but that what we hear is so simplistic of a solution for resolve that our reality becomes unstable (which is the beginning of any shift), and the filter of the ego will step in to provide something else if we are not ready for what is coming.

Developing self-love with the body will open the doors of communication with the soul and reveal contracts, even if we are unwilling or feel unworthy of approaching them in fulfillment. Learning to love ourselves in these energies is precisely the point of much of what we experience in humanity. Although with the filter of ego we may view 'unwillingness', 'incapable', or 'not ready' as terms of failure, the universe sees these as a part of our depth in coming to know love through them, rather than something to be overcome. Many of us have chosen to incarnate into vessels specific for this purpose, facing difficulties of the body as experiences that trigger energies we have come to resolve through the love we offer in them. The soul contract with the body while in pilgrimage here is one of the most sacred agreements we have entered into, and it is an essential key to the language of reflection through which the universe communicates to our awareness.

To develop or deepen communication with the universe, we start by simply offering love in relationship to the body we have incarnated into. One of the most powerful forms of this is through the setting of an intention, verbally affirming love in relation to the body. An intention we voice may sound something like this:

"May we eat well, feeling into the foods we chose and the body's response to them.

May we feel the clothes we wear, their texture, colors, and fit to the body as it whispers what resonates with us.

May we nurture the body with movement, feeling the oxygenation of the cells, refreshing of energy, and flowing of blood in the veins.

May we balance the body in nature, feeling the healing capacity in all things natural, acknowledging the harmonizing power in creation.

May we allow love as attentive listening, feeling all things working in coordination with the body, that we may honor the one coming forth in us in benefit of all beings.

May it be so, so it is."

When we allow a space of awareness to develop such as in the preparation of a simple meal, we cultivate intimacy on an energetic level beyond any egoic constructional view of reality. By feeling the movement of our hands over the food, the texture, smell, and sight of it, we engage our senses with nurturing attentiveness that not only resonates with the body, but pierces the veil of any solitary three-dimensional paradigm of living. And by receiving food into the mouth, tasting it, the body itself acknowledges the nourishment of life-force as a unique relationship in energy, where we come to know ourselves as a whole in wellbeing. We can expand on this awareness in any interaction we have, from the clothes we wear to the moments of rest we provide, that each and every engagement in the body may teach us the language of the soul. Because of these interactions, even though we may be unaware of who or what we are, we still receive glimpses beyond the three-dimensional in our day-to-day experiences.

Anxiety, depression, abandonment, and rejection are all significant emotional indicators that our soul is awakening us to unfulfilled contracts that we are in exploration of here. Even though getting to know our body can be overwhelming at first, as we learn to hear the language of the soul, our physical, emotional, and mental processes help us to form a relationship like no other in depth; we practice being our best friend, advocate, and partner when afflictive patterns emerge by simply allowing space for and loving the one feeling them. The human body is very much like an 'avatar', in a sense, or a musical instrument in terms of its interplay with the world of our circumstances. Emotionally, when we are triggered, it works in conjunction with the soul to communicate vibrational 'chords' and what is in need of tuning or alignment in relation to our deepest desires. Often what appears as affliction through egoic filtering are these strands being 'plucked' for what resonates within us and to gain our attention in love. And because we live three-dimensionally incarnate with the ego frequently filtering experience, as humans we tend to focus on circumstances rather than what arises in us asking for care; it is common to develop attachments when we are in need, which in turn create feelings of loss associated with the world. But again, these emotions only appear to us as agents of information to us of what the soul is shifting vibrationally, or as reminders of who we are once a shift has occurred.

Loving the heart through our contracts is crucial as the heart generates the most powerful human magnetic field. This may be seen as a 'back door' of sorts to a very complex maze in resolution, because as humans we tend to focus on outer circumstances for any vibrational shift in perception rather than what arises from our energetic field within. So as the heart is loved through what we feel, a measure of safety is received, which enables a shift in our energy field. This vibrational shift is one of the keys to the kingdom of heaven, as many great teachers have alluded to, and in it we are afforded the opportunity to expand consciousness beyond the linear or three-dimensional paradigm of living. This practice expands our communication with the soul as we hear our needs and desires, granting us insight into the infinite self where we receive the comfort of our well-being, even in times that previously may have felt despondent.

If we allow ourselves to listen with an open heart, we discover a myriad of bodily reactions to what we hear, from disgust to elation and everything in between. Many of these feelings may have been secluded behind the wall of egoic construction for many years, and most extend beyond this realm into deeper vibrational issues we are desirous to resolve. When holding the heart in loving compassion while feeling what we feel, we create a sacred space of observance and allowance for these energies to shift vibrational fields in the vessel. It may sound a little simple, but this process is very much like tuning a stringed instrument; what we perceive as a loss of harmony is neither good nor bad, it is merely an indication of where we are at vibrationally and of what feels in tune for us. When something 'rings true', it doesn't necessarily mean it is the absolute truth as defined by egoic logic, but rather it is in alignment for us as an experience which is part of our evolutionary process. Our soul contracts with the body, environment, and others support us in this process of alignment, or 'tuning', helping us in reflection as to what we are in need of.

As we become more familiar with the vessel that carries our soul and continue to learn the language available to us, we will also expand in awareness to the universal reflections and contracts that have been coordinated for our benefit. Energy is observable in its various forms, and how we interact with it determines the level of intimacy we develop within ourselves. A mindful conversation with a friend when allowing room for observance can become a very flexible practice: what we hear in tone, see in gesture, and how energy flows between people can reveal a great deal vibrationally in being. How we treat ourselves and one another in the context of our humanity determines our spiritual evolution, and even the inner conversations we have in thought ripple vibrationally across one another's realities. Once we are ready to acknowledge these energies, we can go further inward by opening a dialogue of nurturing affirmation with the heart. Some of the most precious words we will ever hear are those that we say to ourselves while holding the heart in times of distress, when we are hurting or uncertain of our circumstances, and feeling alone. And as we learn to utilize our imagination, we can respond to previously unknown areas in need with a whole new level of embrace by acknowledging them with our own personal creative touch.

One of my favorite forms of acknowledgement to difficult feelings was imagining my needs revealing themselves in the form of old black and white cinema horror characters such as: Frankenstein's monster, the Wolf Man, Count Dracula, and Creature from the Black Lagoon. By sitting with the look on their faces, the low groans or mumbles they voiced, and even imagining the possible smells that accompanied each character, this practice allowed me to be with what felt like intrusive or afflictive energies in a somewhat comical way of love. Although the feelings still felt intense, there was relief in the seriousness of the mind, which also supported the heart as a form of love. Some vibrational threads are in great need, which can be very overwhelming to the nervous system, but as we learn to work with our contracts instead of resisting them, even difficult energies can coarse through us creatively. This same practice can be utilized in various forms as we engage the mind, body, and emotions, allowing ourselves to express, heal, and explore what the soul is asking for in each of us. Some of us are more prone to preparing meals, playing music, or painting pictures, but each of us has our own way of saying the words we desire to hear, and granting the relief necessary for the heart to expand in nurturing. Whether the words we desire to hear are from someone in our past or have longed for in the future, by allowing ourselves to hear them, we shift our vibrational field of potential to receive what we have needed or desired universally.

Although hearing or seeing this potential in our soul contracts may evoke deep feelings of ache, this is only from a point of view where the ego has filtered what we experience as loss. This becomes apparent when we explore two of the most common contract archetypes we will fulfill while in pilgrimage here.

The first is very difficult to endure and has been greatly misunderstood throughout the spiritual community in energetic terms but works tirelessly and intensely to shift our vibrational field. Twin Flames are those contracts which challenge us in a chaotic, addictive manner, turning our world upside-down and inside-out as they reveal parts within us that are aching for love. The nature of these agreements is in the similarity of their fiery passions and will often inspire, provoke, or activate us by enticing a wide range of emotional, mental, and physical desires. They are so incredibly disarming, seductive, exotic, and pleasurable, yet destructive, painful, ruthless, and ripe with potential that they will completely shatter our known reality. Often, the overwhelming energies felt in them are the chords of our vibration shifting in frequency if we survive their fulfilment. Specifically, the contract we have with a twin flame is nothing more than the awakening of our inner confrontation, or mirror parallel opposite, where duality brings to surface parts of the self that we've ignored, treated poorly, and wished to be resolved.

This contract can be very disturbing when we begin to see the patterns, and the ego will do its best in order to shield our awareness from any truth, or cover over what was once hidden to avoid the pain we may experience in this relationship. Eventually, though, any avoidance will be overwhelmed by the needle of desire, surfacing and resurfacing in mental, physical, and emotional energies until we are moved towards transformation, resolve, and self-realization. Even if we are unaware of the burning within us, or those places which desire acknowledgement, once the Twin Flame has occurred, the vibrational threads within us will never be the same, and how we proceed with our life path will depend upon the love we are willing to offer ourselves in relief.

The second type and more common in contracts is the Soul Mate. Although this too has been greatly exaggerated or misunderstood in energy, ironically the notion of "one soul that is perfect for us as a mate" is not that far from the actual purpose in pre-agreement. The Soul Mate consists of those that enter our lives in a much more harmonious manner, providing support, insight, and periods of growth, even in times that prove difficult. This contract is often nurturing, wise, and will work in coordination with universal surroundings, openly transparent to the light of love.

Either of these contracts may appear in various forms, from a pet to an employer, family member, or a lover, even our relationship to situational experiences. The main differences between Twin Flame and Soul Mate contracts are in the intensity, resolve, and egoic deconstruction —both will have synchronicity, manifestational power, and transformational qualities, but the energies activated within the Twin Flame move with an emotional investment on such a deep level, in a very short span of time, that the combination rearranges reality so fiercely it can be strenuous to accept; some truths are so difficult to be with that we must go to great lengths before we may be willing to see them. We may view our circumstances as the enemy, feeling confrontation within us, and act out in various behaviors, but our true nature is only coming forth in these energies to acknowledge those parts that burn for resolve. If we attempt to deny, ignore, or slay the demons that plague us in *any relationship*, they only steep further, becoming more a potent concoction perfecting their effect. For many of us, the Twin Flame will bring us to brink of death, possibly suicide, or other violent behaviors in attempts to control a shifting reality, but when an unraveling occurs to this magnitude, it parallels the egoic death of constructions which have been built to function or survive up to this point. The tragedy we may feel is in the misunderstanding of these energies, what their purpose is, and how we may walk through them as divine beings in mortal experience.

Every life path becomes a potential shift, exploration, and expression as we are ready. What may seemingly goad us into retribution or reaction is only there to bring our attention back to that which is in resolve. And although certain events in life are tragic, they mark specific points of revelation and rebirth in our life path. Some places are only accessible by these contracts, which activate or trigger energies in relation to the realization of what we desire. We may rail against any new reality, or what we have known previously, despising what was or has been created in our need, but if we are to allow resolve, it is only through the embracing of these aspects in our life path. Both the dark and light come together in resonance of arrangement, and though they are an unlikely pair in seemingly opposite form, they move in conjunction with love, complementing each other as one. Any person, society, or world view which feels unbalanced in the nature of its life force only does so to unlock or trigger the chaos that ensues as the necessary material for spiritual evolution. Each of us has our soul contracts and reasons for coming here, and although every one of us is experiencing a finite path unique to us, we are all infinite source creators working in coordination as love.

In every situation, we are presented with an opportunity to acknowledge what we feel with love, and as we do so, we dimensionally begin to ascend beyond boundaries of previous limitation; once egoic constructions begin to crumble, we awaken to the expansion of potential alignment where we may receive what we have desired to fulfill. Clarity comes, but only with the integrity we offer in viewing our 'reflections' as we feel into each experience and love those parts within us that are asking for attention. And any being we interact with has chosen to be here simultaneously with us to fulfill agreements which are mutually beneficial. In other words, it really is all about you, but also others, where each center of the universe has come together as collective consciousness moving as 'one' in the creative process.

As we learn to trust in the space created for us, we open ourselves to the bridges being built in the void of what we may feel we have lost. Whether we perceive loss as a surprise or we knew on some level that it was coming, we never experience a hollow unless we are ready to fulfill some contract our soul has made. And the most intense contracts are those where our deepest desires reside, which allow us to fully embrace what we feel in connection with what we experience. Although emotional turbulence may not look like resolve, resolution is precisely the point of the intensity we may feel. Whether this comes in the form of healing, expression, or exploration, life provides a pathway for us to both feel and integrate through the body what we are experiencing. Whenever a disturbance enters our energetic field, as a practice we may develop our listening by acknowledging the reflections which have manifested. Whether we perceive any manifestation as 'negative' or 'positive' in occurrence, the simplicity of acknowledgment opens a dialogue for communication to become possible in a larger perspective. From this eternal or vibrational point of view, everything, all energy, is working in coordination for the benefit of love, and dualism is only one perception among many in the multi-verse. So as we come to know ourselves as multi-dimensional beings, we expand our ability to respond from a larger paradigm of love. From a linear perspective of the unknown, there may always be fear in our experience for the potential of what we feel as loss beginning to manifest. But as we shift or ascend vibrationally, abiding practices help to transmute these energies where nothing is ever truly separated; we are only limited, pending what we are ready to receive in love for resolve. Soul contracts are an integral part of the evolutionary process because they open us to the potential resolution available through the experience of relationships, without which there would be nothing to activate or move us energetically into the resolve of our desires. What we like or dislike not only supports us in this process, but helps to develop intuition and deepens our relationship with the soul, granting us fulfilment on a level we never could have previously imagined.

Although the journey itself becomes broad in multi-dimensional terms, with a new sense of freedom in the expansion we have found in relationship among universal forces, the road we walk will feel as if it has narrowed at times. As we encounter our reflections in soul contracts, the uninitiated may experience common symptoms of anxiety, depression, and grasping prevalent in the body, or even a feeling of complete digression. We may question if the path we are on holds significance, or if we have lost our way, with surreal moments of seeming insanity. But this is exactly what occurs as a natural progression when areas are challenged by new realities or perceptions, and only as these energies are embraced will the one attempting to come forth in us be revealed.

As we walk through life, we begin to realize that we cannot escape fate, and despite our best attempts to fend off affliction, suffering will arise. Although adversity, conflict, and devastation may be unavoidable, our vibration and point of view will shift as we offer abiding space for the emotional turbulence we feel. This offering of love may seem unfamiliar to the body, even uncomfortable or void of compassion at times, but the heart will recognize the attention, support, and nurturing it is receiving. And as we continue to practice a view of childlike simplicity, we will begin to see that the most precious things we can provide when we are deeply troubled are not new toys or temporary fascinations to hold us in distraction, but acknowledgement on a ground level of what is being felt. Ascension is a process of developing a deep connection to places that may have been closed off for years, lifetimes even, and any suffering we move through will ease as those energies become integrated, receiving the love necessary for healing. This in turn sends a clear message to the universe that our needs are shifting, that parts which once felt 'abandoned' in our vibration are being held with the care they have been asking for, and that the creative life force of potential may flow as we desire. In response, the universe coordinates with us in an ever deepening communication with the soul, meeting desires at an unprecedented rate in our life path.

What we experience while focusing outward on our circumstances is necessary to bring us inward for our wellbeing. The emotions that arise within us due to our outer environment and relationships not only tend to carry debris for clearing as a part of the healing process, but also information about what feels in alignment for a deepening in the soul. As we look closer at our pilgrimage, the potential reasons for coming here, and what we are in need of vibrationally, we will begin to become aware of our divine nature as the mystery that has persuaded us to be born into 'mortal' circumstances, which are often confusing, but provoke the very patterns that are a part of the shifting process. And by honoring our soul contracts that arise, we honor the one coming forth in us that desires to fulfill our deepest desires.

Chapter 7

Reflections

As we evolve spiritually, we will become aware of how the universe works through reflection, as it is a fundamental foundation for any self-realization. Whether viewed as karma, good works, or measurement in some degree, once we begin to notice a greater world of interaction, questioning will arise in us is in direct relation to the possibilities desirable to us. This 'mirror' consciousness allows us to engage life on an ever-deepening level, beyond surface cause and effect, where our journey expands in existence as we awaken to multiple dimensions working in coordination with our soul. Whether this is for our benefit or what we perceive as someone or something else's, from a larger point of view the whole of who we are is always served.

The illumination of reflection is often first noticed spiritually as something greater in perspective than the egoic constructs which have developed to solidify a life based solely in the third dimension (as we remember from previous chapters, the ego is a part of our process, and develops in order to stabilize our reality as a 'protector' until we are ready for evolution, that we may fully engage in the attachment of sense experience). Although each dimension holds reflective qualities, higher dimensions have expansion beyond previously formed boundaries in sense perception, which many of us experience throughout life, though mostly unaware of any context they hold in reflection. Depending upon where each of us resides in our journey (the body, environment, and circumstances), other dimensions may be felt differently according to our personal needs in what we have chosen to come heal, explore, or express. It is common, though, when awakening from a linear path of the third dimension to move into fourth dimension experiences such as meaningful coincidence or synchronicity, the sensation of 'something more' in the universe (beyond solely third-dimensional living), and God or spirituality as a higher power moving in our lives. Humanity is not new to fourth dimension experiences, in fact whole religions and spiritual belief systems have been built around them, but rarely has it gone further inward into the fifth dimensional transformation of energy integration.

This energy integration is what many of the saints, prophets, mystics, and seers have alluded to as *the transformation* which shifts vibrational fields for the ascension process. Again, like reflective qualities, energy integration is not exclusive to any one dimension, but higher dimensions have an expanse in depth and connection that allow much more flexibility in spirit. This is the freedom many great teachers have shared of love, such as Jesus did in John 8:31: "...If ye continue in my word, then are ye my disciples indeed; And ye shall know the truth, and the truth shall make you free." The "truth" eluded to here is our infinite divine nature— the being that exists on the currents of eternity, and is aware of love as the vehicle within which we are and travel dimensionally.

To be very clear about this process before proceeding further, each of us arrives precisely as we are intended or ready to receive what we have desired; there is no wrong or right way to approach enlightenment; simply, when it is our time, we become willing to see. And even though what we see can be quite intense or challenging to feel as we begin to awaken, the events that come into our lives are in perfect correlation to the heart field we are vibrating. As with all things in nature, our human body, spirit, or energy field is heard by creation, and in turn responds to our needs for wellbeing in balancing our life path.

A friend of mine once taught a foraging workshop at a small intentional community where several people including myself lived. As we walked, he gave instruction in foraging, using old shamanistic ways of 'reading' what nature has to offer and how to harvest with loving respect for what the earth provides. Our group came upon one of the small community cabins, and he remarked at the massive amount of yellow dock (Rumex crispus) that had engulfed the structure. He asked who stayed there, and if they had any health issues. One of our members came forward and shared she had been on a high dosage of iron supplement, due to iron deficiency with an issue in her blood. My foraging friend smiled and said, "Yellow dock has one of the highest concentrations of iron in the plant kingdom, and is excellent for cleaning the blood."

What we experience in our reflections are the "listenings" of our higher nature surfacing in response to our needs as it feels those parts within us that vibrate desire. Whether for expression, exploration, or healing, we are a part of the creation, and as divine beings incarnate we have come to fulfill desire vibrationally; we just experience this energy in an arrangement of matter three-dimensionally. In order to better understand our reflections, it will help to form a picture in the imagination of what this looks like in 3-D.

Imagine our essence in human form encapsulated in a sphere of fluid, similar to a droplet of water, where we may move about freely upon the earth. Even though we are in this sphere, it is in no way inhibiting— we may completely engage the world, its inhabitants, and all we experience through our incarnation. In our interactions with the creation, as we look closer to the world around us, the environment we live in, things we encounter, our circumstances, and what is felt, we develop an understanding of *cause and effect* in relationship with what we are in sense experience with. Often from an early age this relationship becomes intermingled with egoic construction, where how we live with others and our environment is based on cultural, societal, and family specific norms, which leads to a moral code of agreement in our humanity. However, at some point we begin to suspect "something more" in the course of human development, and we will question our bubble as we experience its reflective qualities on a deeper level in personal meaning, which up until this time, the outer world has mostly provided a set of laws that align with cause and effect, egoic construction, and the third dimension for some sense of stability. But once this line of questioning begins in our reality, it will never end until it is resolved.

Within our vibrational field of incarnation, we are very much like a seed awaiting to be awakened to who we are as divine nature. Although many of us will live somewhere in between the third and fourth dimension with seemingly very few of us expanding to the fifth, as infinite beings, time is a construct which works for our evolvement, never against it (from an eternal perspective what we as humans view as a 'lifetime' is one very brief span of our journey in a much larger existence). The importance of this to us in this life or any other of incarnation is that any act of love we offer moves us further inward, closer to our divinity, whether we are aware of who we are or not; resolve is the spark within us that beckons us as multi-dimensional beings of love to evolve. One of the reasons reflections are so important to us both in this evolvement process and as multi-dimensional beings is that what we think we understand in definitive terms of time, environment, or language as humans is really refined in communication through energy, which can be applied to a myriad of interpretations personally —such as healing, exploration, or expression— all of which fit resolve. And the doors to perception cannot be opened by anything other than love, because the egoic construction stands as guardian to the inner chambers of evolvement, which can only be accessed through the heart field. Thought, in a sense, is held captive by what we feel in unresolved energies, purposefully imprisoned by our greater self until we are capable of embracing higher realities of who we are as divinity.

Once we are ready though, it is common for the world, or what we perceive as reality from within our sphere, to become unstable (remember, for most of us, up until this point reflections were only seen as 'other' interactions we had in relationship to the outer world and very rarely as reflections inside our 'bubble'). Most of us will begin an exploration of some sort to what is felt in these experiences, and can easily become overwhelmed, often plummeting any journey into a vast array of emotional, physical, and mental health concerns. As a society, what we view as obsessive/compulsive disorders, disease, and even criminal behaviors are frequently this instability coming forth as unresolved energy. Tribally, many indigenous cultures saw these energies as 'other realms', or 'spirits' in communication with those that our current world views as 'afflicted' through the filter of egoic construction. But each journey is carefully crafted, although it may seem otherwise, and much of the suffering we may feel is contrary to divine purpose is taking us as a species deeper inward for transformation.

There is frequently a gestation period when we are somewhere between the third and fourth dimension of evolvement, where our vibrational field adjusts in potential to any new reality or consciousness of expanding dimensionally. From a worldly perspective, often as humans we will grasp at religion, spirituality, or some belief system which exhibits or aligns with the experiences of meaningful coincidence, higher power, or afterlife in worship (which are fourth dimension traits). These experiences may become so intense that even in extreme suffering we will find ease or comfort through what we may feel. This allows the space for energies to travel as needed, gestate, and come to fruition for any eventual shift to reality. What we view in reflection moves us closer to the 'interior' perception of our droplet, rather than solely exterior in circumstances. Many religious practices are designed specifically to raise our consciousness in awareness to divinity, or the self-realization of who we are, but until we are fully ready to embrace that reality, God or higher power is viewed as 'other' by egoic construction. And although the fourth dimension opens us to power beyond the confines of solitary three-dimensional existence, it is a bridge of potential, not a destination of living.

Something that frequently occurs within us as a species which is quickly dismissed due to the egoic constructions we live in is the self-centered nature of who we are. Society, or the agreements we have come to know as a moral code of behaviors, limit evolvement in the sense that we can only move beyond them with self-love. When we begin to see our reflections on the interior surface or our sphere (meaning we are at the center of all that is in experience by us), rather than the exterior as circumstances unfold in the outer world, the ego will challenge this perception as 'self-centered' in relation to others. A simple translation in perception to this experience is "love your enemies." While most faiths indoctrinate through egoic principles of love in those new to understanding, with a focus on the outer only in others, those that have an inner well of stability know that when this teaching is applied inward, what we may perceive as the outer "enemy" is resolved. In other words, when we shift our perception from circumstances existing outside our sphere and what we interact with as 'other' to viewing all circumstances as here, inside, to serve us as the central focal point, we expand dimensionally, opening ourselves to manifestation on a level of awareness in which we truly are the masters of our universe or have the keys to the kingdom of heaven. This is an incredibly difficult perception to receive because it means we are taking full ownership for our circumstances, that even the most hated, vile, ugly situations which we have experienced in life are somehow serving us as divinity. Once we begin to explore this notion (that we are truly the center of our universe, and so is everyone else in reflection), we will either find relief beyond measure in universal arrangement, or if we are incapable of this shift in perception to our reality, we will grasp at any egoic construction available until such a time that we are able to receive this view.

Our droplet remains our droplet, regardless of what we perceive, whether outer or inner in reflection, and everything is here as an agent of help to us. But the reflective power in our integrity will always ring true once we begin to shift vibrationally; we cannot stop being who we are as divinity— we can only do our best to prolong the inevitability of love. This process may be layered many thousands of times, or lifetimes, as it requires a level of trust, vulnerability, and surrender that will only manifest when we are vibrationally ready for our reality to unravel. We witness this in material form frequently, as energy can never be created nor destroyed, only transferred in form. And although some matter may seem unfamiliar in circumstances, the energy of form will always reflect manifestationally what the inner journey requires vibrationally. The importance of this, once we become aware, is in the recognition of universal arrangement, where we transcend the cause and effect in material form, moving deeper into the layers of the energy itself which is in resolve.

Whether we view these energies as afflictive or pleasurable in appearance, the issue of resolve is always in allowing ourselves to feel while exhibiting compassion. When we are exposed to principles of compassion, such as empathy, mercy, forgiveness, and patience, this compounds any reasoning solely based in the third dimension, opening our awareness beyond physical circumstances. Even though three-dimensionally our view is obscured as to the nature of our connection or depth with the universe, on an energetic level we are not separate but whole in cooperation with our surroundings. Just as my friend had taught in his foraging class, the earth energetically knew what was needed for resolve, and created the form for healing, even though at the time the person was consciously unaware of it. This energetic fabric of reality permeates everything and is always moving on our behalf for wellbeing.

Although reading the reflections of our reality can be one of the most challenging propositions to any egoic construction and the ego will desire an end to the uncomfortable emotions we may experience, this is only a characterization of moments necessary for the transformation within the psychological cocoon to come forth to fruition. We may not understand, but once we become aware of our reflections on some level, how we abide with these energies can be one of the most powerful elevations of the heart, both in coming to know higher destiny as a possibility of hope, as well as receiving the universal cheerleaders that whisper glimmerings of support to us.

As we feel into each sadness, doubt, and darkness that arises, moving gently down into the depths, it might be the hundredth or even thousandth time that we step back, and say "hmmm..." In this pause, we see our life from a different angle as energies align in convergence, allowing illumination. We begin to understand that who we are is much greater in 'self' dimensionally, often appearing in the reflections seen, even in the most traumatic of circumstances. It is common when these doors are opened within our sphere, for the ego to immediately shut them in denial. *This shift in our reflective process of viewing reality is so intense, abrupt, and overwhelming, it can easily shatter the mind, and is rarely approached unless we are ushered in.* This is the realization of our focus moving from the external circumstances of what we perceive as the outside of our sphere to the interior walls of our droplet, that everything in the universe is a reflection in some way to us, *of us*, and we within it are the center.

Often this realm will be tested repeatedly by the ego and egoic constructs as a safety measure to ensure we are ready to come forth in it, the ego standing as guardian to affirm we are ready for transition, which must be made by the integration of those parts which are in need of love. This process is in the divine nature of us as spiritual or multi-dimensional beings and works with the universe manifestationally for any self-realization. These doors cannot be opened but by love, as at our center this is who we are in essence. Through the simplicity of love, our actions are magnified universally, and as such, manifest the keys to any door in the depths we have desired. This is precisely why many great teachers refer to this journey as the "road less traveled" or "the eye of the needle," because it can only be approached with the humility of childlike innocence, surrender, and openness.

Often in the spiritual community, we may hear terms like, "go with the flow," or "let go and let God," but in the universal realm these are already in existence naturally— it is only in our state of perception we may be unaware of them. And although these teachings are excellent for a fourth-dimensional paradigm, our soul will not rest until we embrace the necessary steps in resolve for spiritual evolution, as they can be limiting when we become inadvertently comfortable with them. Eventually this will lead to feelings of frustration, which often is an indication of our soul communicating that we are no longer fulfilled fourth-dimensionally, and expansion is coming as we experience higher vibrations in process. This whole process within our sphere of reflection may be repeated again and again in preparation for ascension. And as we ascend, the inherent quality of flow within us will begin to break down our reliance on God if we continue to see God as 'other', meaning that as we shift into higher vibrational frequencies, we become aware that we are responsible for our reflections beyond the veil of synchronicity or coincidence as intervention, and that our soul is directly working in coordination with the universe in every dimension beneficially.

Regardless of where we are in the evolvement process, if we continue with the practice of abiding with what we feel while holding the heart in loving compassion, the senses expand by the infinite potential in exploration of manifestational energies moving on our behalf. Whether we realize it or not, this 'flow' is always with us on deeper levels, but our awareness either needs time to process it or we are unable/not ready to receive the higher frequencies of transmission. In shamanism, this 'flow' can be observed through many of the earth's intuitive responses by nature as mentioned earlier. In all things there rests a resonance of being, but without reflections there would be no vibrational awareness. We each add to the world around us as well as receive from it, and how we receive works in cooperation with our heart field, not only for our own benefit, but for the benefit of all. As we awaken to the potential coming forth and learn of ourselves in reflection vibrationally, we begin to recognize truths, which are those places deep within us that have been manifesting as outer circumstances in our humanity to spirituality evolve. And although it may seem strange for teachings to develop on 'tapping into' the flow when it really resides within us, what we are doing is becoming better listeners in awareness to the communications that we feel reflectively from the soul.

Even in circumstances that might be seen as deconstructive in our lives, it is merely the flow of arrangement reforming pathways in an effort for us to evolve through what we feel. Once we make a decision with the heart that we will not abandon, reject, or suffer alone, although we may feel all of these energies, we grant ourselves the space of loving compassion to abide with truths as they arise. By this one practice, we evolve exponentially as the universe begins to construct a new reality, one in which the outer world responds to reflect the love shifting our vibrational field. As we nurture this relationship with ourselves, life no longer is a wall to be overcome or figured out— it simply becomes what it was all along: the measure of love we meet it with. When we acknowledge the desires within us and realize that they are here to serve us, we allow our innocence to guide into the flow of our divine nature.

A simple yet revealing exercise in working with reflection is to hike along a trail in nature, allowing a pace or rhythm to develop in our walk upon the earth. If our mind wanders when we are hiking along a particularly challenging trail, we will find ourselves slipping, bumping, and stumbling along the path. Although there are many practices in mindfulness and being present, many times the simplicity of what, or rather *who*, we are being present with lies inadvertently undiscovered. And often, the more challenging the situation, the more uncomfortable we may feel, and the ego will quickly step in to stabilize our reality. But our environment, relationships, and body consistently provide the terrain for our reflections, where we may learn to love ourselves by allowing the flow or rhythm that naturally exists within us to arise. When we are hiking along a difficult trail, we quickly realize our attention is drawn to where it needs to be, and if we surrender, we observe this natural rhythm come to the surface in our pace —over stumps, roots, and rocks which are not seen as obstacles, but merely a part of nature and the trail— where a flow naturally develops with the terrain as we are walking.

Some days we may wake up, look in the mirror, and find this extraordinary life staring back at us, even in difficult circumstances, and we wonder, "Who are you?!" In these moments it's easy to become dismissive from the feelings that may begin to surface, and often the things that we allow ourselves to see are only in order to preserve our reality. But as we learn to love and acknowledge on a heart level, deep within each of us is a relationship we have come to explore, and there comes a point where we all find ourselves looking in the mirror asking questions. These moments are not by mistake, and if we are asking the questions, we are nearing a place where what is arising will not be easily dismissed. The desires we have longed for will not leave us, but will only expand, either in the gestation of the ego, or as we acknowledge each truth by the innocence of love. This is the great challenge in each of us in coming to know the places that are a delight or that appear darkened in our being. Passion proceeds at the behest of the heart, and those fires we might sometimes deem as destroyers are only burning as they do because of our heart's desire — if it burns within us, there is some truth we must embrace in order for resolve.

Reflections are universal transmissions in manifestational energy and provide the ways, means, and approach in which we may heal, explore, and express who we are. But we are purposefully limited to them both in what we allow ourselves to see and by what we are capable of receiving. Our ability to be open and to view life from different perspectives comes from an equanimity in grounding by loving compassion; universal self orchestrates circumstances for us that we may more fully learn to allow the love that we are, and when old paradigms no longer serve us, they will begin to fall away, vibrationally altering our reality.

Even in behaviors which may seem unproductive, self-centered, or otherwise harmful, love is always moving on our behalf, although it may seem unlikely. These energies are the communications which have manifested as part of our internal process of the soul and are the experiences necessary for eventual evolvement, or any awareness to come forward in recognition; struggle is a part of the ache in loss, but the space created is a sacred path, one that always leads deeper into our cocoon of transformation. When we are ready to receive resolve, obstruction may even feel like bliss at times as we realize the universe is working with and for our benefit in everything, never against it. Where once we saw only pain and may have identified ourselves as a "victim of circumstance," we begin to see that encoded within every experience there is a reflection for furthering our connection with the soul. This is the empowerment many human beings seek in a vast variety of three-dimensional experiences, and often do connect with at times, but are unaware of the potential that exists beyond resonant feelings. And although a state of dormancy may preside for years, or even lifetimes, for each soul this may be exactly what was requested in sense experience for the cultivation of love. When we move away from linear timelines to the multi-dimensional realm of living, the reasoning, productivity, and goal orientation we frequently stand on for stability in 3-D become very limiting in perspective, which is why as we evolve, agitation, frustration, and irritation become more prevalent (as the soul knows who we are, and what we are capable of).

As we evolve, we may find ourselves amazed at the nature of the universe and all the various parts moving in intricate perfection. What is destructive at one turn in the next will yield beauty as life unfolds. And where there was loss, we may realize the creation of space for something pleasantly unexpected in return. We see only a little until we are ready, building upon the sacred trust in both our soul, and in the universal forces that arrange on our behalf. Even in the most difficult of circumstances, we will find this movement relentlessly at work for our benefit that we may expand in relation to who we are and what we desire on a deeper level. So as our life unfolds, although we may experience afflictive emotions coming to surface, these feelings are really transmitting for our benefit vibrationally in what we desire to manifest. For example, if we feel we deserve better in a relationship, often feeling uncomfortable, irritated, and resistant, we are communicating to the universe that we need love in more meaningful way. The message heard universally is, "I Am deserving to be loved, content, and at peace." Often when these vibrations return to us in reflection, they may manifest as emotionally challenging circumstances in order to draw our attention to those places within us that are asking for love. And as we offer love in the form of acknowledgment, abiding, and self-care, innocence begins to guide us into our bliss or what we truly desire in the heart.

The deeper understanding in this is that the infinite multi-dimensional universe sees us as itself, which is already deserving, and it is only helping to reveal the higher frequencies of love that we already are; on a finite level we will never change what we feel in our vibrational thread by attempting to arrange outer circumstances, as those circumstances are manifested energetically for us as reflections of what we desire in healing, exploration, and expression. So even in our dislike of something, in an inclusive universe we are still communicating to our universal self vibrationally what our needs and desires are, which responds energetically with the reflections we receive in answer to our prayers. The only resistance we feel in life are the communications of the soul fulfilling what we are asking for, by drawing our attention to those places wanting love within us or asking for a shift in vibration.

One of the most common issues arising throughout humanity in this current age is the self-talk of "I deserve better," or "I don't deserve this." Again, if we look at this vibrationally from a point of universal recognition, the universe hears and manifests on our behalf circumstances that often challenge or trigger these feelings, because on an energetic level it knows we are love. The aches, pains, and disturbances are only calling out for our bliss to be realized, and the love we offer as we interact with our reflections provides the raw material for what we desire manifestationally. When we begin to acknowledge the energies of, "I deserve better," or "I don't deserve this" with compassion, the love of "I Am deserving" is revealed.

It's in these places when we allow ourselves to feel, deep in the crags of earthy depression, that bring forth the most substantial of awakenings. Many times, they come to us at the most auspicious of moments, wearing the garments of difficult circumstances as messengers in foray for our benefit, although we may resist their healings. Just as the surgeon meticulously makes his incision, so too the demons of our enlightenment are sent with precision. And as we open our heart to receive all that has been arranged, we are granted passage into our truths, which only arise within us asking to be met by our loving kindness.

As we love, so we are loved.

Sometimes, "when life gives you lemons," it's not about making lemonade. And because we can become so accustomed to our reflections from an egoic perspective, there is an attempt try to view them in an untruthful way. The deeper teaching in this is to allow ourselves to go into the natural state of what is arising for us to experience, or explore, and to be with the lemons, abiding in how we feel with their texture, smell, and taste. This yields not only the love we give our heart through what we are feeling as we abide but allows us to explore under the surface of once darkened places that may have been previously sweetened by the ego to suit our tastes. Frequently, there is another layer beyond comfort that allows us to see from a different perspective, and our space is enlarged for the infinite self to enter as the heart is nurtured through all that we feel. As we offer loving compassion while feeling what arises, we discover new doors and depths that once upon a time uttered, "impossible, impassable, and inconceivable," but are now released to the potential that awaits us.

We start where we are at.

We start with the circumstances we find ourselves in: where we live, our job, no job, relationship, no relationship, however we may feel, whatever we may think— we begin where we are at. The universe has a way of reflecting what we need for our journey, even in the most difficult of experiences, where parts of the 'self' step forward to be acknowledged by us as no one else can. What we may be supported in here is that there are no wrong choices; everything is a part of the equation in our life, and the deepest mysteries are unfolding as needed to help us for our highest evolutionary path to come forth.

As we explore, loving ourselves through what arises in feeling, we practice a form of karma yoga by tying the past and future in this present moment, by abiding with our circumstances in loving compassion. This creates a fluid avenue through which energy can flow, mend, and resolve vibrational threads that we desire to shift or that have become stagnate in potential. In a sense, this returns obscure parts of the self that may have been previously alienated or unrealized to their former potential state of creative power, giving us the opportunity to expand awareness in our vibrational field. We witness this cycle in nature as it consistently restores balance, or a state of harmony by utilizing the whole as a reference point for wellness.

'Dharma', or 'cosmic law and order' may be viewed as the code contained within everything in the universe that moves on our behalf, and it is the current upon which every transmission of love travels as well as the inescapable conclusion to every potential outcome in creation. Karma is the reflective process in nature that allows us to glimpse time and space as relevant source material for shifting vibrational fields with love. As we observe our karma and come to know our most intimate desires by the love we offer, our vision expands to receive dharma's invitation to the one we already are. Reflections form as an expression of the soul meeting our desire to shift these vibrational patterns in order to open the way for divinity to expand by the love we offer. In a sense, "our karma is our dharma," as the rich, experiential ground in every circumstance we encounter, ripe with vibrational insight and universal order for the most beneficial path in fulfilment; all things work together for us in both chaotic and harmonic fashion, resonating an ever-evolving divine state of love. Although dharma and karma may seem separate in their workings, upon introspection they reveal a working relationship in coordination as one on a higher plane of consciousness dimensionally.

The challenge, once we begin to become aware of how the universe works, is to the nature of egoic construction as it unravels. When we are in transition, the world will feel as if it is falling away beneath our feet, and instinctively as humans we will grasp for habitual patterns which once served to stabilize our reality. But once we are opened to the potential of who we are and how reflection is utilized universally for our expansion, egoic constructions which once served to stabilize our reality begin to crumble in this light. This place will often feel terrifying, as the very landscape we had previously come to know and trust disintegrates around us; when our bank account is waning, a relationship is crushed, or we suffer in the same job day after day, the emotions that arise can relinquish any merit of faith in love. But paradoxically, this intensity in what we feel allows us to move further inward into the depths of who we are, where an unexpected ground may be found in uncertainty as we trust in the form of surrender to how the universe works. This is where there is a more potent sense of awareness, or 'hearing', available to us, one which, if approached with compassion, legitimizes any transition.

If the mind still asks, "How do I shift my existing vibration to garner experiences more to my liking?" then the bigger 'I', or 'us' as 'universal self', always knows the deeper truth to our circumstances. As multi-dimensional beings, we are capable of communication with this expanded view, and our present self may be reasoned with, which we have incarnated to embrace. When we occasion hindsight in our life path, applying integrity in viewing previous events with an observation of love, even the most heinous of situations will show a larger picture in transformative power for well-being; our walk here is but a blink of an eye in eternal terms, and what we have asked for, what we really want to manifest, are the vibrational shifts for a much larger sense of wellbeing in our ongoing journey.

At first when these shifts happen, we may not be aware of them due to the overwhelming nature of their energy on the nervous system and the egoic patterns that have intertwined themselves karmically to our life path. But as we continue abiding and embracing what we feel in the simplicity of love practices, the truth of an inclusive universe will prove itself in reflection —often in meaningful coincidence— until we are ready to receive a deeper understanding in awareness to the transformational power available to us manifestationally. This may feel both frightfully ominous and joyfully exhilarating as we realize the infinite depth we are capable of in relationship to universal forces. This is where any shift has the potential of expansion dimensionally, depending upon what our soul has arranged with us vibrationally (some life paths have specific contracts of fulfilment, while others are here as an exploration or expression reflectively in desire). Many circumstances that unfold are meant to bring us closer to parts of the self which previously have been darkened, ignored, or purposely buried, and as we feel into them with compassion as our agency, we fulfill *destiny*, developing a unique relationship with future, past, and present awareness. But because many of us are in process and awakening to multiple dimensions that coexist, frequently when in transition there will be a feeling of profound aloneness, which is the vast space of expansion we are encountering. That said, whether we experience joy, pleasure, or even the shadows of pain, all are precious expressions of humanity and resonate deeply with our divinity.

But in any case, if we find ourselves in a situation where the circumstances feel intolerable, the road we are walking has potential for growth as we embrace it; whether we desire to resolve emotional congestion or spiritually evolve in exploration, the reflections of our world work with us as we are ready. The communications we receive in the form of emotional energy are merely the potential realities available to us other than the timeline we are currently living in. When we are open to this shift, the universe will begin to unravel egoic constructions in coordination with the soul, which often means we move deeper into the circumstances we are currently in. Although this may seem contradictory, the universe frequently works paradoxically when in expansion, so when we don't feel like going to work and call off, crawling back into our bed, this is where the space is being created to explore difficult questions often accompanied by difficult feelings. When we begin to choose unseemly choices in our circumstances and grant ourselves space as no one else can, as each distance is felt, we slowly come to realize the only distance we feel is the space that is in need of us being with us. The universe patiently waits for our readiness, and although days may seem to blend into weeks, months, or longer if necessary, it is only so in order that we are given the time to explore the energies of any perceived separation that we might feel, which are those parts of the self that are desirous of attention.

As we allow for listening, and feel what arises in us, the universe works in coordination with every circumstance of reflection for continued self-realization. Even the night grants permission in our dreams to reflect emotional threads, bringing to light faraway places near for the possibility of resolve; in the recesses where we may have felt stuck, peering over high walls of imperial three-dimensional understanding, is the one who has come to experience every choice we could ever possibly make from our birth. The reflections that we are aware of are evolutionary in our experience, and as we are ready to embrace life in the trust that we both offer and receive, we proceed with love into uncertain places where we find our most stable footing. It is in the darkness we come to know our light, and as we explore where we feel lost, alone, vulnerable, and unsure, we deepen our roots in the love that we already are. Once we learn how the universe works in reflection, the next step is abiding with what we feel in compassion and is the *art of integration*.

Chapter 8

The Art of Integration

Each day may bring a myriad of challenges to the human nervous system, some pleasant, others more difficult to abide with. Either way, when we find ourselves overwhelmed, love will ask for us to slow down. Energies of restlessness, irritability, and frustration are often communications of the soul asking for this. For the ego, though, it's easy to focus on the behaviors of others when these strong energies arise; we may blame, feel resentful, and disrespect those around us in our words or actions because of our own inner needs not being met. In the current social-political climate, we see this as an erroneous challenge to the inequality of civil rights, income, disease, standardized education, and a rising number of mental health issues in the world, where it is virtually impossible to see beyond these forms energetically. But as we move through our life, whether we have been overwhelmed from an early age or find ourselves in the circumstances which have arisen recently, once this line of questioning begins, however it appears, we have been awakened to opportunities of transformative power.

Although affliction is often viewed as something to overcome, these energies are really here for our benefit and can be persistent when asking for what we need through habitual behaviors. As we move deeper into our reflections, feeling those places within us that arise for love, the more we will begin to understand the necessity of spending quality time with ourselves; whether we sit by a grey window as the rain comes, listening to the drip, drip, drip upon the gutters, or soak in the sun's brilliant radiance, our soul resonates with the development of space we are allowing in relationship to the self. Through the process of surrender, we move into the depths of what we feel, and it is here that an evidentiary connection unfolds, fulfilling what we have genuinely desired manifestationally for love to close the gap between us and ourselves. We begin to sense that any grey area is not mundane or purposeless, but in fact energies we need time with. And when feelings of loneliness, loss, or ache arise, energetically, what we are missing knows this and acknowledges finite experience as precisely what we need for love to expand.

Frequently, the mind may attempt to seize what we feel by problem solving but will steadily be worn down by our evolvement as energetic beings. Any hurt that has been manifesting as frustration, anger, or injustice has only done so lashing out in an attempt to gain attention for love. Once we begin to embrace these feelings with compassion, we also realize their depth and the room required for the integration of them. As we learn about our complexities, we also learn the nature of resolve in simplicity. But this process only comes to light as we are ready to know ourselves through the incarnation we have contracted. Even a body's physiognomy is a wonderful work of manifestational mastery, one in which our ethnic origins or character run much deeper than our circumstances, eventually revealing the relational, vibrational nature we have come to experience in our pilgrimage here.

Although as humans we have similar journeys in the earthen vessel, we will find that each of us has a body unique to our soul that requires special attention only we may be aware of, everything from what we eat to the texture of the clothes we wear, the climate we live in, our activities, and the amount of rest we need becomes a part of the integration process. To the uninitiated, especially in the early stages of awakening, this not only serves as a buffering layer of assuring we are ready for continued expansion but becomes a practice in self-loving exploration to the vessel that carries us. Ironically, the kindness we show ourselves physically, mentally, and emotionally secures the ground for further introspection as dimensional beings outside any solitary three-dimensional existence. In other words, until we are capable of absorbing our circumstances energetically in reflection by the process of integration, there remains a distance dimensionally to who we are as divine beings. The art of integration is really a dance in relation to the partnership with the self and learning who we are through sense experience on an energetic level.

While on the surface level our careers, food, relationships, home, and belongings may seem only preferential in the choices that we make, they are also a part of an informed evolutionary process, serving as an energetically charged wealth of insight in transformative power. And as we awaken, we may find ourselves questioning every aspect of our life, but especially those areas where income is a concern. Questions may arise such as, "How do we earn an income in a way that both supports us financially and resonates with us spiritually in the heart?" or, "How do we create the hallowed work-life balance that offers us plenty of time to integrate?" Once we are aware of our universal potential and a much larger 'us' as we expand, we may feel unsettled three-dimensionally, even confined. Although we may have chosen our field of work and even enjoy it, if we feel overwhelmed, frustrated, and unsettled, this is a clear indication of the need for integration space, and we may consider exploring other options. When this happens, it is common for the ego to quickly move in on our behalf to stabilize any uncomfortable or unfamiliar feelings associated with unknown territory. Even if these explorations might bring us fulfilment, the ego will often move to intercept in reaction to the energies felt with replies like, "Oh, *you* couldn't do that," or, "Maybe someday, but not now." This is where we may find ourselves repeating patterns until there is enough unsettled energy to propel us deeper into the passions of what we desire. Although these energies seem contradictory to the evolutionary process while in conflict, where voices will speak loudly on both sides, this is precisely the point in order to upset any current reality for other potentials we desire. What we perceive as obstacles are really the fire of our baptism, working as both guardians of our path, making sure we are ready to transform, and providing the necessary energies to fuel the desired shifts within us. While we may feel overwhelmed at the intricacies, depth, and infinite possibilities we are awakening to, once we begin to question what we feel and abide with it, universal arrangement is only awaiting integration of what is already manifesting in coordination with our deepest desires.

With each encounter, we are measured universally by the ripples in our vibrational field with certain sounds, colors, smells, tastes, and touch, whether it's the foods we eat, who we are in a relationship with, the environment we live in, or our employment. And as we follow our natural desires that arise, these will lead us like a trail of breadcrumbs from one to another, and then another, and so on. The deeper we move into this relationship with the heart, body, and soul, the more we will require integration in what is revealed. The only seeming complication here is that as humans, we tend to make this communication about permanency, focusing on three-dimensional circumstances of familiarity and comfortability instead of abiding with sense experience in reflection. Again, this is not a set-back, but merely a part of the process, as some energies are in a form of gestation until we are ripe for expansion. Regardless of where we are at in our process, we may embrace practices that will help the integration of sense experience.

Although we may not consider waking up in the morning as a need for integration space, the body is already aware of this and begins the process an hour or so before we wake up. The temperature of our body begins to rise, blood pressure increases, and as serotonin and cortisol flood the brain, neurons start to fire. Everyone goes through the transition of "sleep inertia," where impaired performance, vigilance, and a common desire of going back to sleep is experienced, which can last several minutes to hours. And depending on the conditions of our sleep and how we awaken (abruptly or naturally, and our environment), we may feel groggy or refreshed. But none of us hits the ground running ready for the day; there is always a period of transition. And if we are woken up from a particularly charged dream, this process may carry on into our day with an overflow of residual energy in our affairs.

A few simple practices that we may develop in our morning routine will help here, first, a simple space of stillness upon waking. Although some of us may utilize alarms to be up by a certain time, depending on the type of sound, quality, and volume of these, each can have an impact on our morning time of stillness. Many of us remember the alarms from our youth or college with loud, blaring

118

beeps and flashing lights that could easily induce anxiety or panic upon waking (which may have been the soul asking for love and nurturing to the awakening process). But today, as we are becoming more aware of our choices, we can learn better self-care of our bodies, even tuning into our own internal clock, reducing any 'alarm' whatsoever to awakening. The body is far more capable than we often know, and we can simply communicate our desire with it as to what time we would like to awaken through intention. This may take some time, faith, and practice, but the space we are creating is in self-love, and the "stillness upon waking" allows the integration of energies we experienced while dreaming or resting.

Another simple practice for the morning is to greet the day. Whatever we may believe in spiritual terms can be applied to this, whether God, future self, or the sky and Earth, a greeting of, "Good morning, ____," spoken softly in compassion, can be applied here. This not only acknowledges the universe we have incarnated into, but us as beings in it, participating willingly in loving expansion. In reflection, if we ever doubt the love in this, when we ourselves are greeted with a smile, a handshake, or hug, we may have felt these actions completely shift our vibrational field, feeling refreshed in the body.

At first glance, two other practices that may not seem as integrative, but if developed will actually help set the tone for integration throughout the day, are intention setting and meditation. We can move further into grounding for the reception of energy by setting intentions for the day aligned with a practice of meditation.

Intentions are nothing more than what they sound like but contain an undercurrent of surrender to universal orchestration in them. They are a formal issuance of prayer to the universal self, both requesting and acknowledging permission of arrangement for our benefit. A simple intention is, "May I be more loving of myself and others, then I have ever been before, allowing compassion, encouragement, and wisdom to flow freely as deeply desired in all that I Am."

Although intentions are best equipped as generalizations which allow a vast flexibility in fulfillment, they may be expanded upon if we feel inspired. One of the most profound actions we contribute in life through intention setting is to give love permission to work, however necessary, on our behalf. When we surrender through intention, we are sending a clear signal to the heart, soul, and universal forces of manifestation that we are ready to receive what we have been desirous of. A more detailed form of intention may look something like this:

"May I give love permission for the arrangement of life as is necessary, through every feeling that is felt.

May integrity work through each pain to reveal the depths of what I desire that are only asking to be heard, acknowledged, and held by me as no one else can.

May I welcome the innocent one in me, who has only acted out for the attention, love, and friendship that each of us is worthy of.

May every reflection be an indication of what is coming forth for my benefit, and as each is embraced while holding the heart through all that is felt, may the growing sensation of safety comfort me.

Even though doubt or fear may arise, may I fall deeply in love, feeling the fall of love, trusting in each leap of faith with surrender.

And as intentioned surrender moves the universe in fulfilment of everything working together, may the veil of illusion be integrated, that I may come to know the one I have been waiting for, that I already am, in benefit of all beings.

May it be so, so it is, as love is."

Many of us will find that intentions work very well together with meditation. Whether we are a novice to meditation or a lifelong practitioner, as we expand, we realize meditation is vital to the wellness of the heart, our spiritual condition, and health of the nervous system. And if we view the body as a conduit for expanding consciousness, the necessary energies we integrate in this process are more likely to do so with ease as we develop a practice of meditation.

My first introduction to meditation might sound a little funny, but it's not so far-fetched given the time and environment of my youth of being raised in the West. It was around the age of twelve watching the series Kung Fu on TV, where the young monk called "Grasshopper" was raised in a Shaolin temple. Among other disciplines, he was taught meditation by his master, and with the priestly guidance of a loving mentor, found a quality of life that saw the value in everything he did. Other movies such as *Star Wars* and *The Karate Kid* resonated with a side of many souls that wanted to be heard, but very little was known about the mysterious practices that were involved (such as meditation). Personally, I remember walking out of the theater after seeing *Star Wars* for the first time, trying to grasp for some footing on what had just happened and how it had changed me. Fortunately for me, growing up in an age with no cell phones, internet, or video games, when you experienced something, you had to abide with it on some level, and it sank deep into the subconscious. Although meditation wasn't seriously pursued right away, there were reflective moments in nature when going for a walk or sitting by a stream, closing my eyes, that something began to shift and the body felt different, as though it was tuning into the rhythm of life.

When first starting to meditate, there can be looonnnggg tick tocks of the clock, seemingly endless minutes, eyes opening and shutting with everything in between coming to mind. I remember thinking, "How do people do this? What is the point of this? I could be doing something else...I could be doing something productive, something fun even. I'm bored. Why am I doing this again? Someone suggested meditating...Ok...meditating, ho hum, meditating...is it time to stop yet?" Over and over sitting in some uncomfortable posture, back hurting, eyes opening to look at the clock, closing them to soon wonder how many minutes had gone by. In the beginning it wasn't easy, especially when it was a relatively new concept in the West, and the few books that were out there back then didn't seem that helpful, weren't inspiring to read, and commonly left the student more than disappointed about *any* sort of real practice.

Over the years, there have been many descriptions on how to mediate, what it is, and the 'goal' of meditation, but really it is about spending time with us and the relationship we have with the vessel, our self, and the universe. And even when we may feel as if we are failing or not doing something right, the practice of meditation on a daily basis improves overall awareness, essentially giving results that at first we may not notice. Mentally, physically, and emotionally we will feel better, gaining clarity and proceeding in life from a place of being rather than doing. Doors will open through this one practice of being with ourselves (which may be a little uncomfortable at first as we experience the vast emptiness in the acknowledgment of uncertainty), but over time we will discover it is really about abiding with the energy of creative potential. Yoga International describes meditation as "…the means for fathoming all the levels of ourselves and finally experiencing the center of consciousness within." And if that center is love, if that's what or who 'I Am' is, who we all are at the core of being, well, that sounds like a pretty delightful place.

Although there are a wide variety of meditation teachings to choose from, it will be helpful to simply start or return to a practice of focusing on the breath. One such practice that is incredibly nurturing is to find a quiet place to sit, placing the hands on the knees with the feet flat on the floor and closing the eyes. Allow a few slow, deep breaths, and listen to the body while focusing on the breath. The body is a wonderful gift for the cultivation of awareness, allowing us a glimpse into those parts that feel uneasy, that we may be with them tenderly in compassion as we relax. Although thoughts may come and go, we bring attention back to the breath. At some point we may release this focus and simply be with the space we have created. This is a basic practice allowing energy passage by being with ourselves. It also provides a pathway for love to flourish in the essence of the soul, with healing as a byproduct in the stillness of peaceful connection. If inspired, there are several meditation apps available with timers that provide a background of sound which may be helpful. Ten to twenty minutes of meditation added to the morning routine is an excellent ground for supporting the integration of energies that may arise throughout the day.

These morning practices may be applied throughout other times in the day, but many of us find they are helpful in preparation for the day. Much, if not all, of what we experience is in terms of energy, regardless of the interpretation, and as we learn more about ourselves, the more we realize the need for integration space. Integration is merely the process which allows us to fully embrace any experience, validating energies on a deep transformative level, which expands our consciousness in the divine nature of who we are. If we struggle with any aspect of integration, nature is an excellent teacher and source of support that will help with this process.

There is an eternal 'knowing' in nature, where frequencies always return to a natural rhythm of harmony which resides in all things. Although much of what we understand three-dimensionally is darkened in our circumstances by design, beneath the surface of any understanding this same 'knowing' resides within us. What we may view as tragic, chaotic, or even violent at times the universe sees as an arrangement, fulfillment, and acknowledgment of desire. Nature teaches us to see every aspect of this process, even in what we may deem its most ugly forms. This perfection exists in everything, from the choices we make to the response of the universe, but it is especially noticeable as a help for integration in the simplicity of nature. This may not be apparent at first, but nature has a way of opening us to the current that moves beneath the surface over time and experience.

There's a scene in one of my favorite movies, *The Last Samurai*, where a great warrior struggles to find the perfect cherry blossom on a tree. This becomes a much larger life lesson nearing the end of the movie, when he is gravely wounded and, looking into the distance, seeing a field of blossoming cherry trees, remarks to a friend with his dying breath, "They are all perfect."

It's very easy to become so involved with what we think that "we can't see the forest for the trees," and the details of our circumstances actually hold our senses hostage from what we feel. But the body works in coordination with our awareness, which is especially clear when we allow ourselves to be immersed in nature and often loosens the threads of tension the mind provides for a sense of stability or comfortability. Nature is an excellent reflection of divinity, supporting us in grounding those areas of the mind that may challenge simplicity within us. And as 'perfection', it is an agency unparalleled in relief, unimpeded by egoic constructs of reasoning. When we create the space for a simple walk on a local trail, listening to birdsong in the morning, or sitting by a river, the lucidity of nature provides a force of energetic rebalancing which allows us to more fully integrate any experience in feeling.

At first glance, practices of integration, exploration, or healing established in nature may not seem like much, mostly because much of the energy work we require is done by an already existing field in its natural state, but there are a vast number of testimonials showering results nothing short of miraculous, if not laughable, in their simplicity as to the physical, emotional, and mental health received by them in wellbeing. To be clear, though, at our source or core, we already are a part of this existing field, and in a larger sense of understanding have only lost ourselves to be found for expansion in love. Also, by way of our incarnation, often in youth we are incapable of integration, and the experiences we feel overwhelm the nervous system, which is why the ego arises as protector/helper to stabilize our reality. And what we view as behavioral patterns of affliction are really unintegrated energies that are repetitive in our life path, until we are ready for the vibrational shift they carry with them upon integration. But, as with most evolutionary or healing modalities, frequently each is discovered while in a place of great need when the teachings are receivable. Commonly these teachings are unexpected, even unwanted in appearance, and can carry with them a general feeling of exhaustion, illness, or ache so unbearable that the thought of approaching them in embrace is revolting. My own personal 'teachers' in nature found me doubled over in a heap on the living room floor, crying so hard it felt as if my ribs were breaking, utterly crushed by the weight of a former reality collapsing. If an overall voice could speak for the waves of sensation rippling through my body, it would say "too much."

Where I lived through this period of life was in the Allegheny forest hills of Pennsylvania, in a cabin surrounded by nature. The nearest road was about a quarter of a mile away, and there was little traffic on it, if ever. It was common to leave the windows open as the fresh air always felt soothing, and during those difficult times of devastation, when painful truths surfaced in moments of intensity on the floor, I would hear the sounds of nature: the birds, chipmunks, crickets, and the leaves rustling in the wind. After a round of exhaust emptying, an awareness would come over me with the simplicity of nature. Eventually, this turned into a practice of sitting in a chair or laying on the bed and being with the feeling of a light breeze, watching the tops of trees slowly rock back and forth where there was a communion of energy. Although this seems like a fairly simple shift in perspective, the profound difference in being is one in a former reality that observed nature to one that realizes we are a part of it. What came to mind frequently in these times was an old Hebrew word utilized for a musical pause at the end of a verse: "Selah," meaning 'forever'.

Throughout life, there will be a space required when we need to integrate strong energies or refresh the conduit of the body for the purpose of receiving them. Jesus frequently allowed space for this where he would go into the hills or on the water, far away from the crowds. Muhammad was illuminated in the quiet of a cave where he received sacred teachings. And Siddhartha sat under a Bodhi tree where he was enlightened and renamed the Buddha, or "awakened one."

But for some, spiritual growth may look like an awkward assessment of character, where there is a stock-in-trade accounting of impulses, behaviors, and patterns that may or may not serve in functionality. Through this analysis, egoic logic will do its best to protect from afflictive emotions that arise by exploring alternate realities that no longer exist for the current timeline with ponderings of 'would have', 'could have', or 'should have' in thought. Although this approach may seem too involved with the mind, any nurturing of the relationship with the self on a more personal level reveals innocence and a connection beneath the surface of thought rooted in the depths of the heart, where every desire serves as an emissary of communication in coordination with the soul. The beautiful complexity or simplicity of spiritual evolvement in this is that it is precisely what it needs to be as it is, and even those dynamics we may want to change in our past serve as purposeful recordings that may be viewed at a later date, arising specifically when needed for our continued process of divinity emerging. Awakening comes when it comes— just as we don't force ourselves to awaken in the morning, we simply open our eyes, and say, "Oh, I'm awake now," so the universe moves in perfect cooperation with our destiny. Regardless of which road we choose, every path leads back to divine potential. Some choices may seem unlikely to benefit, even counterintuitive, but in an inclusive universe, everything is moving along a grid of perfection for resolve in wellbeing. And once we begin to explore the inner chambers of our most heartfelt desires, meeting the depths with a measure of love and integrating the energies felt, we may wonder how we or anyone could have lived with themselves so estranged. Often hindsight sees this force of loving universal arrangement, and what we could, should, or would have done becomes less important than who or what we are in essence of being now.

There is abundance in this expansion, and even though we have the universe at our fingertips, this space can be a little overwhelming, which is why we require a pace where integration is possible in receiving the energies that we have been desirous of in love. Very basic practices work best when in transition as they allow the nervous system to process, our awareness to catch up, and the energies we feel to shift our reality in a less painful manner. As we allow ourselves to acknowledge each ache, fear, and uncomfortable feeling with the simplicity of compassion, what we view as outer manifestations or changes in reflection are really our vibrational field adjusting to a potential alternative timeline; essentially, we begin to transmit an alternate frequency through each abiding of love, where we are capable of not only *viewing* potentials manifestationally but *creating* them. And because of the nature of an inclusive universe or what we may view as a law of attraction, the universe measures and meets our every desire energetically.

Acknowledging this new world can take time, and we only do so as we are able, especially if we've lived under the umbrella of egoic protection. Sometimes we're afraid of what will happen if we are honest, as if it might let the genie out of the bottle should we sit with the truth of what we feel, but really honesty is contingent on our wellness, and our wellness emerges by loving compassion. To be very clear here, we receive deeper truths as we are ready to love, not because we have earned them; any former life we may have lived or understanding we may have had of our actions or behaviors will be completely integrated as necessary for evolvement. Some of the most devastating circumstances we have experienced in our past are energetically charged with emotional debris specifically for this process, which will adjust our vibrational field as we love ourselves through what we feel. But when we first approach these energies (or more likely they approach us), it is common to meet a wall of reactionary defenses which ensures the loving compassion necessary for integration. These walls are made of the very substances which trigger deep emotional energies in relation to our beliefs, patterns, and vibrational threads many of us have come here to heal. When embraced, they release our most profound desires and those places within us that have longed for this journey of ascension.

As we venture inward, the mind will want to solve any unsettled areas that arise in emotion. Self-honesty may come to question, especially since any known reality has the potential to shift, and although the brain is a wonderful tool, capable of great reasoning power, anything we may perceive as a blockage to honesty comes from emotional debris, not from a lack of knowledge or understanding. There are parts relating to the self that we simply need to feel in order for well-being to occur, which will come forward in an attempt to reveal and release what we have been storing emotionally in the cellular recordings of our memories. What we have been learning in practices of self-love and how the universe works in reflection are for the integration process. And although we may want to do our best to help this process along, the more that is revealed, the more we begin to see that the honesty which serves us best is in the nature or quality of our surrender; as we surrender to what we feel while loving ourselves in compassion, well-being unfolds in the nature of what we already are as divinity.

So when we long for rest or solitude and a space with ourselves, we listen; what may seem like a waste of time to egoic constructions of the world are moments necessary for integration. As we allow transit to emotions emerging to be felt in the light, we may wince at what we feel, but the emotional debris that are passing carry with them clearing properties that work in conjunction with transformation or healing. And as they do so, we realize through the nurturing we offer that sight is being restored to our divinity.

Holding the heart tenderly, we remind it, "I will not abandon you nor reject you, even though I may feel abandonment, rejection, and unworthiness at times. All that comes to surface is a necessary part for the healing, transformation, and integration of energies being felt."

When we begin to explore our inner chambers, we find we have a friend we never thought possible that shines in the most difficult of circumstances. Dreams we once pondered and mused upon begin to reform from the depths of the heart, vibrating with potential as the universe reflects all of love's expression. And through each embrace, we come to know the one we have been looking for, that we already are, as divinity knows no other, but that which comes forth as itself.

By Our Design

Chapter 9

Shadow Work

My mother and I had a very unique relationship, very youthful in its nature where we would often play jokes on each other, pushing the limits of our humor, but still somehow recognizing just how far we could go. One Halloween we had made an effigy dressed up in old farm clothes with a skeleton mask for a face and sat it out front on the porch to scare trick-or-treaters who had come for their goodies (yes, our playfulness extended to others)! All night long there were little shrieks of terror followed by laughing delight at our prank. Some families approached the porch cautiously, expecting a person to jump up and grab them, but it silently sat and did its job effectively in everyone's mind.

After Hallows' Eve we left Fred (yes, we named him too) up for the fall weather, as winter moved closer with colder winds picking up, threatening of snow. Mother would go to bingo a couple of times a week, and my impish side got the better of me one night while she was away. I moved Fred inside the front door to a recliner, where mom would conveniently have to lean over to turn the lamp on. I fell asleep before she got home that night, but the next morning she exclaimed, "You scared the dickens out of me last night!" Now, Mother wasn't one to let a little payback fester, and soon enough, one weekend when I was out with friends, Fred got moved. After a long night and expecting to come home for some much-needed rest upstairs, while reaching over the bed to turn the lamp on, I found myself face to face with Fred! I'm not sure what Mom's reaction to Fred was when he was in the recliner, but I about peed my pants, half in fear, half I-couldn't-believe-she-dragged-that-thing-upstairs-and-put-it-in-my-bed laughing!

It was beautifully perfect and a wonderful relationship that I'm so grateful to have had. For years after I moved out of the house, usually around ten o'clock the phone would ring, and upon answering I would hear Mom exclaim, "It's me!" And with a chuckle I would reply, "Hello, me!" Although I miss that unique expression of "me" dearly, in the larger picture of things I Am still visited from time to time. Often, we never fully understand the embrace we give ourselves as divinity until our world is turned upside-down, and we experience our uniqueness from multiple perspectives in relationship.

Back in January of 2015, some of my deepest fears began to manifest. Mother was dying, and my sisters and I spent the night with her in the room at the hospital as she drifted into the shadows, becoming unconscious at dusk. The days before this, she began nervously questioning what I thought would happen in death, "Where do people go?" as if she could see her final hours approaching. Not long after, her mouth became very dry, she lost the ability to speak, and her breath became labored as she slowly slipped somewhere between this world and the next. Although her eyes were open, we could see she was in a journey of transition. We would frequently wet her mouth, and as we held Mom's hand we would say, "It's ok mom, we're here, we love you." As I laid my head next to hers, looking into her eyes, the little boy in me who she watched over for so many years wished he could reach her one last time, give her some ease in her passing, and tell her he knew of some place we could meet soon. But in those last few hours, I couldn't help but question my own transience, consider the places within that labor to breathe, or ask for help to be loved when there is such uncertainty of what we traverse.

We all did our best to be with our mom, to love her, and each other, in life as well as in her final moments. But whether we said silent prayers, or out loud "I love you's," ultimately each of us walks the details of our life path alone to some degree, under the shroud of mortality's embrace; the emotions that we feel, the desires that we have, and how we integrate experience are a personal journey with the soul. Although we are intimately connected with the universe, much of who and what we are lies hidden in the shadows until we are ready to enter the darkness.

But the universe has a way of connecting with us through the shadows where doubt, fear, and questions reside. My mother passed at 6:01 in the morning. I hadn't received a text or interruption of any kind all that night, but not one minute after her passing, my phone vibrated. At the time in my grief I didn't look, but simply sat with my mother's body, tears rolling down the cheeks as I stared at the shell of her incarnation. Death of any sort is nothing less than traumatic, but the universe recognizes our struggle in the darkness, and although at times we may feel alone, devastated, and limited in understanding, greater self always views our grappling with compassion; love will not leave us long in mortality's embrace. Later that morning in the hallway outside her room, as we were making the final preparations for the body, I glanced down at the phone to read a very simple text: "I love you."

It's difficult to articulate the sensation of overwhelming grief accompanied by a 'knowing' or faith in love; loss is hardly reasonable, let alone understood, when we are in deep emotional trauma, but the universe knows the depth of shadows that appear in our journey and will always support love further than any realm of egoic construction. And what may seem like the demons to our devastation are often our liberators in disguise. In the places we fear to tread are the shadows of our derision, but not to our demise— *for our benefit*. The death of my mother was one of my deepest fears, but in reflection, the years, weeks, and days preceding it in its approach mirrored the undeniable places within that longed for resolve. Rarely do we as humans understand death as a part of life, but we just accept it, and even more so, how often do we consider life as a part of death?

When we face circumstances of intense pain, loss, tragedy, or grief, the ego will always grasp for some rational form of justification in order to process what we feel. But what we feel is beyond egoic construction or solely based in this reality three-dimensionally, which is why we struggle to come to terms with any resolve. Frequently as

133

humans we view loss or pain with an ugliness of disdain and direct our attention in an effort to overcome rather than embrace it. To be clear, though, when we are in the experience of loss, grief, or any other intense emotion, our first priority is to simply survive what we feel. At the time of my mother's death, there was only a space of being with her, in thought, emotion, and body of grieving. But after, even though the void of her absence was unmistakable, it was also somehow revealing in that the energies of her presence I had come to know and love for so many years beckoned me to look further.

When any afflictive circumstance challenges our belief system, it will always be accompanied by this calling. In moments of intense emotion, though, rarely will we hear or recognize these communications, mostly because of the overwhelming nature of them, but also because our reality is often based in egoic constructions of thought for stability. But when our reality begins to unravel, it creates an opening for potential expansion in awareness. Any resolve always begins with a larger space of reflection, where previous understandings, paradigms, and constructs are challenged by the intensity of what we feel. As much as many of us would prefer to avoid the pain of loss, grief, and death in any form it manifests, these energies always work with higher purpose as servants to the divine nature of who we are. But the body will regularly record traumatic events in our cellular memory until we are ready to proceed into the shadows of our experiences. Over time, these recordings will form patterns, replaying the stored energies in our body both as a reminder of unresolved issues and as agents of communication, coaxing us to look beyond any known reality. And although healing is often a part of the process and manifests for us in a variety of ways, never does it arrive solely as the 'answer' to our life path, as it is only one facet to a much larger reality of who we are as divinity.

When intense energies arise, it's easy to become dissuaded from holding the heart, especially if they are associated with feelings of deep loss, grief, or death. What we perceive as an end in any form, whether a career, relationship, or even moving to a different apartment, can trigger unrecognizable feelings of abandonment, rejection, betrayal, and unworthiness which are closely related to loss. Ironically though, these are the very indications of shadow work, where the love of who we are is moving to connect the experiences we have in relation to our deepest fears and most prevalent desires. Whether we feel the passing of a loved one, the loss of a relationship, or any circumstance in life where pain enters our path, these places are transformative in power by their very nature. But in order to do so, their energies must pass through the gate of the heart.

Often in shadow work, what we think we know is preventive for our benefit or protection until we are ready to proceed into uncertainty. Coming to terms with this in itself is a process of purposeful struggle, which assures any entrance of energies to the heart the necessary surrender required for their passage. This process may well feel like standing in a dimly lit room where the eyes will attempt to adjust; when there is uncertainty, the shadows can take on an overwhelming persona of monstrous proportions in the mind, seemingly stalking from the void in an effort to fill in the blanks. But as we abide with our circumstances, giving credence to the heart in loving compassion, we present ourselves with an opportunity to be with the one having this experience. At first, we may be startled by the uncertainty in the shadows, and often the mind will frantically search out this space, desirous to find any sign of clarity or stability. But as we continue to be with the one in experience, focusing on the body, breath, and our position of self-love, the shadows reveal a story: one full of patterns, seeking, and purpose in energy. Our practice here is not to overcome nor escape what is felt or revealed, but simply to feel what is felt in whatever darkness we perceive while offering love to the one having this experience. As we build this intimate relationship, we will begin to observe the shadows in a play of sorts, moving with us as circumstances in a variety of shapes and sizes, with some being very familiar while others may seem foreign to us. Many enter and leave our life path, jobs, friends, pets, lovers, and health, like wisps of smoke dancing upon the walls of our room then fading into the darkness. This may be frightening to the uninitiated, as the ego will always grasp for memories of pain or pleasure, looking for some stability to ground on. But in this place of darkness, we come to know that part of us which is light, which almost never occurs to us when we seek to understand the shadows; it is only by the love we abide with in the dark that the brilliance of our divine nature is revealed in contrast.

There are many practices from different cultures around the world in relation to shadow work, but indigenous peoples and certain spiritual disciplines have developed rituals as guides that may be helpful when moving into these explorations. One such ritual is a 'Vision Quest' which is offered locally by Native Americans in Northwestern Pennsylvania for those on the 'Red Road' of enlightenment, prayer, and healing. It involves deep preparation with elders, attending regular sweat lodges, and honoring the traditions of those who have walked the path before us in communion with the earth. There is a strong bond that forms in nature that often we may overlook, fear, or even criticize in civilized society, one in which, when we embrace all parts as pieces to the greater whole, we acknowledge well-being as a source which flows with the soul. It is only through abiding with these various aspects— especially in nature —that we come to realize the creative life force in our infinite being and the will of incarnation to fulfill our soul's highest destiny.

One of the local Vision Quests involves a deep pit where the practitioner is led underground and then the entrance is covered for three days with the person being immersed in darkness. Every few hours, encouragement is offered by drums beating in the distance as prayers are sung in support for those in deep exploration. Shadow work can be an overwhelming experience of emotion, as the body, mind, and spirit are challenged in the depths of self-abiding. The physical representation of going into the darkness supports this work where questions that may arise in day-to-day living may be held in distraction, and the soul seizes the opportunity in the void to expose them. Egoic constructions become transparent when stripped of grasping, where nothing is left of preferences or discomfort, and we become open to the essence of who we are.

Each of us has shadow work to embrace as we are ready, our own Vision Quest, where we come to know the parts we may have avoided or were unseen in the light of day. And if we find ourselves in the shadows, we hold to the continuing practice of compassion we have been offering, allowing the dark immersion to wash over us for the benefit of love. We acknowledge those parts we may despise or deem 'weak', the ones who have cried out to be heard, longed to be held, and enter the darkness with them, loving the one in this experience of abiding. Paradoxically, the shadows work in coordination to reveal the truth, which often in the deeper recesses may lie hidden in the light. Shadow work can be one of the most poignant forms of surrender, as aspects of the 'self' come forward which once may have felt foreign or separated to us, but when we recognize these needs, and those parts asking for reconciliation, even in the most difficult of circumstances well-being begins to flow. To those that have experienced these depths, even in the most pitch black or dark night of the soul, the light of who we are begins to illuminate our reality in coordination with them. One of the most interesting comments my friend made upon sharing after his vision quest that I have found true in my own experience also was, "...even in the darkness, I found over time there was a light that was with me, where I could see the roots in the earth."

We don't always realize this in the intensity of the day, and often we can experience a state of being so overwhelmed in sensation that the feeling of being carried away by our circumstances will arise. Although this may seem unorthodox in spiritual methods of awakening, it is the natural current of flow which exists underneath any three-dimensional construction, which works in coordination with divine desire by provoking or triggering those parts within us that feel lost. In an inclusive universe, the words 'loss' or 'lost' signal that we are ready to be found, and the egoic mind will intensify experience in an attempt to draw us either deeper into stable ego constructions, or it will force our hand if we are ready to awaken. When close to these doors of shadow work, it is common for cellular recordings to play over and over again, creating an obsessive, compulsive search for the key to what is felt. Resentments may form where questions surface, such as, "Why did events unfold in the manner they did?" or, "What could I have done to prevent this or that and have a better outcome?" But again, this is part of the process where we are introduced to energetic threads or habitual patterns of karma which we have desired to shift in the soul, and we have contracted every circumstance as means to do so in our life path. They are the necessary traps we must fall into as our manifestational cocoon is weaved for transformation.

Whether the shadows we experience are a deep sleep of unknowing or else a darkness that comes upon us suddenly, if we find ourselves in them, it is a necessary part in our process. We may grasp for familiarity, looking for any recognizable ground and become stifled or increased in movement depending on how we react to uncertainty. Even routines we once knew well might feel distant, and friends may become estranged. Sinking feelings of despair will have a tendency to form depression, and as we feel what we once identified as 'self' slipping away, although this may seem as though it is working against us, this is not our end, but rather a shedding as we move from one room to the next in a great house of possibilities. The purpose in the unknown world is not to hold onto our sense of self, but to experience the expansion of who we are in the potential of it.

The ego will do its best to fix instability by coming at us from every side, but when we are engaged in the shadows, this is in an effort based on its own identity and those parts sensing inevitable death. When we are in this place, we are meant to feel what we feel: the experience of being set apart from others, different from the world, and lost— which will feel emotionally unstable, mentally unwell, and physically painful at times because it is supposed to. It is not unlike the birthing process, where the world we have come to know, trust, find comfort in, or become accustomed to is shattered by the entrance into an overwhelming one. The shadows work in coordination with the soul to reveal our faith, ground us in love, and provide hope in the surrender we experience beyond conventional means. Paradoxically, doubt, fear or grieving energetically afford us the opportunity of embracing, where we may explore that which is coming forth in the space they are creating. And if we are ready to abide with simple truths of self-love, we reinforce trust in the universe, creating a wellspring among experiences we perceive as loss.

Throughout our journey of incarnation, we will encounter many such opportunities, but perhaps the most profound are those which we perceive as death. The revelation of impermanence often carries with it a cascade of emotion, which can be very difficult to process and will easily overwhelm the nervous system. In the West, death is possibly one of the least discussed topics in our current society and carries with it a stigma of avoidance. But in many older cultures and traditions, it is viewed as a part of life and was addressed with such texts and rituals as the Book of the Dead (ancient Egyptian funerary script), *Antyesti* (rite of passage) in ancient literature of Hinduism (which is centered around the teaching that the microcosm of life is a macro reflection of the universe), and the more recent *Ars moriendi* from the early 1400's (Art of Dying). When we move into shadow work, whether we find ourselves in sudden darkness or see its approach, eventually we will come across the shade of death, and learning to love ourselves while intense energies flow is paramount as we deepen.

In Buddhism there is a specific practice of abiding with death where one sits among the dead at graveyards, seeing the physical and uncomfortable feelings arise for attention. In Tibet, this teaching can feel incredibly overwhelming in regions where "sky burial" is performed for the decomposition of the body. This entails loved ones who have passed being cut up and placed among the rocks for the birds to come and pick away the flesh until only the bones are left. Although a practice such as this may sound morbid, there is no doubt as to what becomes of the vessel. By allowing ourselves to go into the places that scare us, we may consciously cultivate a response of love as emotional debris surface and egoic constructions of fear present themselves in association with death. In western culture, the spiritual tendency is to want to overcome the ego, extinguish it, or 'let go' through rigorous self-discipline, which often has no long-term avail in an inclusive universe where it must be integrated. As we have chosen to incarnate in a life path where mortality looms in some future for us, one of the most elegant ways we may embrace our current life is to befriend our physical end.

Shamanic journeying is a wonderful way of introspection into this moment, where, as we abide with the body in death, we gain insight to the love we are capable of offering in life. In this next practice we learn to sit with the final moments of life, where just as the sun warms the body, giving contentment to the heart in the lit hours of the day, when night comes with all its hues upon the sky, we may embrace the contrast with our presence. Although this may seem difficult in comprehension to our physical reality, who we are as beings of love does not fade with the passing of the day; by learning to abide with the strong energies, we allow ourselves to fully embrace experience and integrate in any transition. As a reminder for the journey mentioned below, thoughts are only utilized as a guiding tool to our feelings; once we are present with what we feel, we simply allow ourselves to be with what arises while holding the heart.

When we are ready, we find a quiet place where we may meditate, nature being optimum in setting if we have access, sitting under a tree or in a field where we may be with the body. If we can lay down comfortably, we do so, as this will help us to relax more fully in our engagement of what we feel for this particular journey:

We begin by settling into our breathing, filling our lungs from the belly first then allowing the chest to rise, and exhaling in reverse. This will feel like a slow wave of water bringing in the tide, and back out to sea. If we are in nature during this meditation, this only adds to our experience, as we may feel the earth rebalancing our energies by its magnetic field. *We continue by simply focusing on our breath, allowing ourselves to be in the body, relaxing any tense parts that we feel. We notice the colors, smells, and sounds of the earth, gently reminding ourselves that it's ok, trusting in the love that we are as we gently hold the heart. We feel ourselves breathing, being immersed in our surroundings, and we observe the sky briefly before closing our eyes.*

We imagine passing through death, and how we would like our corpse treated: would we like it washed, or held, the hair combed, or viewed by others? How would we like our body taken care of as it begins to decompose? Would we like to

140

be buried in the earth? In a mausoleum? Set afire? Or maybe placed on a pier to decompose under the sky? We imagine what we would prefer, and we allow ourselves to be with that experience, remembering this is our vessel, and it has served us well in journey. We then move on in a timeline fifty years or so into the future and feel the remains of our corpse: What do our hands feel like? Do we still have eyes to see with? Has all our skin rotted away? What does our chest feel like absent breathing? Once we have sat with our body and experienced energy in transition, we gently bring ourselves back to now, feeling what we feel from this experience, but doing so with compassion in the heart. We breathe in the rising motion of belly first, then up into the chest, filling our lungs, and exhaling in reverse, envisioning the tides of an ocean. We acknowledge the preciousness of this moment, the gift of our body, and the experience of being incarnated here to explore.

Whatever we may have felt through this journey, we are gentle with ourselves, and focus on the gift of this moment now. We grant ourselves reprieve from any intensity we may have felt, and simply being with the breath we open our eyes and receive the world we are now living in.

As we are opened to higher-dimensional living, we become more familiar with our evolutionary process, and a natural grieving will take place as egoic constructs begin to fall away, which will feel like death. This is why abiding with strong energies in loving compassion is so important, because as we ascend, these energies both fuel our transformative process and clear emotional debris in passing. When the habitual patterns of ego that once served us in protection are no longer needed, they will begin to die a natural death, but it will feel like death physically, mentally, and emotionally. In some cases, this may be a very long painful process as we learn to abide the uncomfortable emotions, or universal arrangement may suddenly thrust us into the intense heat of a fiery baptism (as we are ready). More likely, though, there will be an experience of both, where there is a culmination of circumstances to fulfill certain facets of death. As humans, we tend to think linearly and along dualistic lines of progress; universally though, or as 'multi-dimensional beings', death is witnessed many times throughout each life path. The more intense experiences are rare, while the integration of small shifts in vibration are more frequent. Developing a sound routine of setting loving intentions for the day, meditating, caring for the vessel, and honoring the sacred supports this space in our process. Much like any relationship, the depth we are willing to go and the risk of vulnerability we allow even in the perception of potential loss is where the real beauty of love comes forth to shine. The most rewarding days where we feel a sense of contentment, wholeness, and fulfillment can also be some of the most challenging, but in hindsight we wouldn't trade them for anything. How we greet what is seemingly defeat, ruin, devastation, and death is how we will meet the most auspicious moments of the soul, where we come to know the parts that we have long desired to connect with. And by moving further into these energies with compassion, some of my most intimate moments with my mother have taken on new life after her passing that ironically might never have manifested while she was alive.

As we explore further into the potential of our species as multi-dimensional beings, what may have seemed impossible from a linear perspective unfolds to reveal an infinite wealth of possibility in our relationships. Often in the awakening process, this is the revelation that may elude us for some time, which is why providence supplies an abundance of faith for our journey.

A few years ago, my travel companion and I had the pleasure of visiting Kartchner Caverns in Arizona. From an outer perspective, when approaching the limestone hills containing the now well-maintained, manmade entrance to the caverns, we had no idea what we were in store for. The hills themselves do not sit that far from the highway and leave little to be awed by from an outward view; to the untrained eye there is nothing above ground that gives any indication to the incredible beauty that awaits discovery below the surface. Once inside though, the cavern opens to another world of mind-boggling wonder, one in which the dark recesses only awaited the light of exploration.

It's difficult to believe when looking at the original entrance, which is hardly noticeable among the rocky hillside, that a small, dark hole in the earth escorted the two explorers (Gary Tenen and Randy

Tufts, who found the inner chambers) into the extensive cave of such magnificent beauty beneath the surface. The park takes great lengths in precaution to preserve the still actively growing cave, which has taken hundreds of thousands of years to form. We passed through long tunnels, painstakingly made for easier access and preservation of the caves, entering a total of three large metal doors for temperature and debris regulation. But the dark hole first explored at the eastern base of the Whetstone Mountains was a tight crawl, painstakingly traversed in care, until eventually leading to what the two men described as the "blowhole." It was through this that they made a small entrance, barely fitting through, to the remarkable discovery of the untouched depths.

Caverns are a rare place on Earth that bring our awareness to a sacred depth within the self, one where it's not difficult to be awed by the amount of time, pressure, and gravity of circumstances some creations must have to reveal their beauty. And although caverns are unparalleled in their stunning landscape, the more you learn the truth about how they were created and the process of their discovery, they only become more extraordinary. The ranger guiding us turned and remarked, "It's hard to believe this much beauty formed over so much time in such darkness."

In our own journey, we may not view darkness with such reverence, mostly *because of* the tight places, crawling, grasping for openings, and trying to reason our way through what we perceive as limitations. But being human really is about feeling those spaces and allowing ourselves to abide with the dark, seeing beyond the uncomfortable circumstances into our desire of something much more than we could ever have hoped for.

Every basic need comes from a wanton urge to be fulfilled, and if not addressed will manifest demons for our initiation. Hunger, sex, power, health, security, and more all bear signs of our human condition at work for eternal well-being. Learning to be with these while holding the heart in the longing of our urges, even in the most loving of practices, can be challenging as the emptiness we feel is creating the space for something beautiful forming in the dark.

143

Although it is our physical instinct to react as we are triggered by our needs, if we allow a space for our emptiness to breathe, offering compassion in place of comfortability, we will come to find that the void serves as a blank slate for creation. By no means am I suggesting hunger, mistreatment of the body (in ourselves or another), or any sort of activity purposed with pain is the answer, rather to allow ourselves the truth in what arises energetically for acknowledgment in the creation process.

Peering into each darkness with the ground of love as we are ready, we come to realize the feelings that are arising are only there as unmet allies, parts of our infinite self that have longed to be acknowledged in us. Even though there are basic sustainable needs of the body, the drive underneath these needs is divine inspiration of something further, beyond the waves of instinctual reaction. Through each desire and every ache in the most difficult of moments, as we allow ourselves to explore any emptiness we feel, we begin to find pure creative life force ready to engage us as every emptiness contains an infinite abundance of potential hidden in the depths of its space. Practices such as meditation, intention setting, walking in nature, and a green diet will help in establishing a connection both physically and spiritually with our divinity. Although when we explore emptiness, we may feel distant, alone, and cold at times, this is only those areas of emotional debris assisting with their transformative power and coming forward to be cleared. The objective is not to relieve the pain, but to be with it as love. When we sit in the chambers of our innermost self honestly, with all that we feel in loving compassion, we will begin to feel the warmth of being alone and our true nature in connection with everything. By giving ourselves this time and space, we have stepped into a much larger room where the pure potential of divine expression may come forward as we spiritually evolve as dimensional beings.

But the most difficult part in coming to terms with our shadow work is that we have agreed to them in journeying here. Any demons, tribulation, or plagues that have been cast upon us are in response to our groans, as the universe grants exploration to our summoning requests we have been uttering vibrationally. The reflections of our outer circumstances move for us to draw attention to our desires, the soul working with universal consciousness arranging on our behalf, each path presented to deepen for infinite wellbeing as we abide with loving compassion. Loss is designed to move us into attachment, not to vanquish or conquer, that we may come to know ourselves intimately. Pain is not a ruthless adversary but a revealer of higher-self, and when we allow circumstances to unfold as the universe sees fit, we embolden our trust in the evolutionary process of working with uncertainty.

A helpful practice in shadow work for this is to simply look up at the greater picture of the sky, whether in clouds or vastness of blue, and breathe in the contrast between above and below, reminding ourselves we are experiencing both. In this field of vision, we allow ourselves to receive much more than we may feel capable of comprehending, which is simply being with the expansion of who we are beyond the focus in the singular or this body. This is a very simple technique for times when we are feeling lost to the complexity of energies that arise in our circumstances. Not only will it relieve the pressure we may feel in overwhelming energies, but by allowing ourselves to be with this space of expansion, the soul will draw attention to specific parts in need as they are ready to be addressed with our awareness. And although this process takes place naturally, as we awaken, we will find it necessary to become more involved with our awareness for nurturing care as the ego slowly dies. The difference in perspective here is that although our personal journey continues to accomplish all that we have come here for, we will either fulfill an experience of absolute terror, or exhilaration, depending on how we embrace our evolvement.

Back around 2016, I wrote a very large post-it note for myself to see every day, saying, "A year from now, don't wish you had started today." There was deep pain, uncertainty, and walls crumbling about me that for a very long time held a different reality, which the universe began deconstructing on my behalf. Everything had conspired in events to bring me to feeling extreme loss, aloneness, and an incredible tipping point of powerlessness. As I sat in my cabin, deep in the forest amidst snow-covered hills with cold winds howling outside, two very powerful realizations surfaced: first, that *to fight any further was futile, because the universe had arranged everything*— it was too perfect, and second, that even though in deep pain, and feeling unbearably alone at times, *I was not alone.*

There is an unmistakable friendship with the universe, one that brings us to a place of facing the shadows, and those parts that for many years were just outside recognition's view which may have been denied or avoided for a more comfortable reality. And when we feel those parts approaching within, all that is left is to see those places that were once refused acknowledgment or that we managed to believe were somehow separate. Some nights may be filled so full of tears that it will feel as if the ribs will burst from our sides, and others we may find ourselves on the floor curled up in a ball wailing, the heart feeling the weight of an unimaginable force as though we would be pulled into some great abyss. Yet, I Am convinced in my experience of faith that the same love that sat with me in the darkest hours of intense suffering and bore witness to something miraculous in transformational healing is within every one of us, waiting for our evolvement.

Beholden within each soul is the care, comfort, and inescapable destiny that love has in store for us precisely as we are ready to receive it. We all have our life paths, some are very brief, others full of toil, but each has requested entrance in coming here to heal, express, and explore on levels we may or may not be unaware of. In the most unexpected of places, love permeates the walls of former constructions for their eventual cracking, leaving shattered pieces which cannot be recovered and fulfilling sacred contracts. This utter devastation conspires to bring forth life from the dead, as a new creation sprouts among the broken places of these intense energies. The dumbfounding beauty of it all is that often, universal forces do for us what we believe we cannot, or would not, choose for ourselves consciously and will move in the recesses of the shadows, working with each desire.

But this path is always one in which we are called, and therefore must rely on universal arrangement for timing. Although we may perceive the shadows as something to cast light upon, some shrouds are meant to bring a feeling of comfort and ease, granting a space by their covering until we are ready to proceed in the depths of their surround. Exploring the dark is necessary in healing, but not all darkness is afflictive in nature: some parts are simply dark as it is well for us to be in the absence of light, which gives a space of ease in the quieting of brilliance. Just as there is a void of space between stars in the universe, there is also purpose in our deep shades of night, where the chambers of the heart find solitude in an ancient peace; shadow work is not about vanquishing the dark but befriending it as part of who we are in greater journey. As we give ourselves the gift of the eternal through the moments we spend with our infinite selves, we discover this same presence in all facets of our being: the love we share incarnate with both the earth and spirit transcends any perceivable boundary, unfolding a balance of harmony through every contrast, and utilizes everything for creative expression of being. Once we are awakened to this, we begin to see the value in both darkness and light for everything which has happened exactly as it was supposed to, and that all is for our highest interest, with every circumstance alive in meaning. So we flow, as the great river teaches, that all things above and below, although impermanent, and ever-changing, are still river before us flowing, and that even in loss, we never are lost by love.

Chapter 10

Healing

When traveling on the road, frequently we stay overnight in rest areas, and although well-lit with many RV's, cars, and trucks, there is a cautious sense of investigating our surroundings. We observe our neighbors, feel into the environment, and assess our sleep for the night, listening for insight as best we can.

One night as we pulled into one of these areas, close to the facilities under a pavilion there was a biker snoring, so soundly, fast asleep that it more than drew our attention. He had laid out his sleeping bag, hand radio, and lamp with seemingly not a care in the world to interrupt his rest. Viewing him restfully at peace under these circumstances, I found myself feeling a little disturbed and strangely comforted by his presence; I was disturbed because his restful sleep challenged a deeper personal trust within me in relation to the universe, and I was comforted by the light of his surrender in the night. There he was, living life freely, content under the pavilion, a beacon for all to see, his brilliance staggering.

Often in universal reflection, when we are challenged by feelings that arise, they do so in connection with our innermost desires— not because we have done something wrong or we are inadequate, but rather because it is our higher Self attempting to emerge. If emotions are afflictive or disturbing in nature, they are directly linked to the vibrational threads within us that long for resolve. As we are challenged in circumstances, emotional messengers come forward in relation to those parts of us which are asking for faith, ground, and love. When viewed in conjunction with healing, this can be a very difficult teaching because it supposes that all of creation is a reflection of ourselves, and if rooted in egoic construction, often we may find ourselves in resistance to light; but if this is so, how can we possibly embrace the dark? Often in humanity we will find ourselves dangerously impotent to the nature of our relationship with the universe, which is why we ease ourselves into this belief system, learning the communications of universal arrangement and forming a relationship with greater self as we are ready for revealing. When learning what we are both transmitting and receiving vibrationally, love is and remains the most important factor in any shift of perception or otherwise.

Angels frequently approach us with unconventional circumstances, their light provoking the depths, and appear often as demons in the faith that they will be heard for a more intimate relationship with the soul. Any healing begins with the vulnerability we allow in listening to these parts, especially when we feel insecure, unworthy, and unwell. Although it's easy to assign blame to outer circumstances when we feel our sense of peace has been compromised, in the nature of these intense energies are the forces necessary for resolve. Blame is a common tool the ego utilizes repeatedly to stabilize reality when we become overwhelmed, focusing on outer circumstances in an attempt to solve how we feel. Conversations such as, "If only that were like this, then I would be happy," or, "It's their fault I feel this way," become second nature in this reality, where we may even blame the weather, gas prices, who is president, or God for what is felt. Recurrent endeavors at altering outer conditions only compile what we feel, and as time is spent trying to rearrange environments, relationships, jobs, homes, and pets to just how we want them in hopes to somehow satisfy, this leads to further irritation, anxiety, and depression; anytime we blame, the heart feels the energy of what is being said and the finger pointing outward. Saying, "if only *that* were like this," is really heard within as, "if only *I* were like this or that."

Essentially, blame perpetuates a dynamic of unworthiness in the frequencies of our vibrational field, and the heart becomes a prisoner of walled constructions by the ego in order to do its best for protection. Many of us have carried this vibrational thread from lifetime to lifetime until we were ready to address the pain that arises from these specific frequencies, and ironically the karma we experience in the habitual patterns from them are viewed as unassociated plagues that we have somehow earned from not being good enough or deserving in our current life path. But this egoic logic only serves to stabilize reality until we are 'worthy' of a shift in perception or awareness, and the deeper levels of blame begin to be revealed in a shift from our perspective of outer circumstances to directly inward in what we are feeling; in a sense, the love that we are at our core is always greater than any perception or paradigm based in unworthiness or ego and eventually must manifest in its true form. This may lead to more intense anxiety or depression that will not be healed by any conventional means but only through ascension along our evolutionary path.

Although we may find ourselves in the mire of our feelings, asking what we may do to receive help or support to shift our position for the better, the key to easing our pain in the evolutionary process is by the allowing of love to come to the forefront of our practice. When thoughts or feelings plague us and we find ourselves going further into blame, we don't fight what we think or feel, but instead we grant ourselves permission to think or feel while we embrace the heart in a loving manner. A simple yet very effective practice with this is to return the hand, placing it upon the heart for nurturing, and affirm its wellbeing, saying, "Even though I feel blame, I want you to know that I will not abandon, or reject you. I am here for you, and I love you." What arises as we do this is the emotional debris stored in our cells, necessary for both clearing our energetic field and resolving vibrational threads simply by the feeling of what we need to feel through a safe channel of travel. We no longer withhold or resist what we think or feel, but by holding the heart in compassion we have given our karma the opportunity to be acknowledged, and in essence we begin to clear repeating patterns by the love we offer.

Becoming aware of the necessity for allowing emotional debris to surface as needed for resolution can be one of the most difficult life paths we will ever live. Events, people, and places are all a part of a purposefully perfect manifested reality for the triggering or activation of both clearing cellular memories attached to our vibrational threads and exploring or expressing our most intimate desires that surface. The body works in conjunction with the universe by providing a vessel in relation to this, where habitual patterns of karma surface as part of the ascension process. As we practice being with ourselves, feeling what is felt while holding the heart in loving compassion, we provide a space for allowing emotions to flow and root inward upon the ground to who we are as divinity. The ego only begins to fall away from its stance of attempting to solve any uncomfortable energy as we are ready to embrace the love of who we are. This is where healing really is observed in reflection, but only as a byproduct of love— never as direct resolve, which is perhaps why healing can seem so elusive; the pain we encounter for resolution tends to challenge a belief system based in what wholeness looks like three-dimensionally or along egoic lines, which is only one facet to a much larger universe in understanding. In other words, when we desire healing, there is always something underneath asking for resolve, and we may view healing as the solution to how we feel, but if the underlying vibrational need is not met, 'dis-ease' or affliction will always return in some form.

In all of mankind's journeying, there has been the common theme of seeking dominion over our environment, whether it be in the body of healing, a space for growth, food for survival, or the need of connection with greater meaning. The deeper mystery of our humanity is that these desires are closely related in the nature of each inward path: places for expansion that we may thrive, nourishment for the soul, wholeness, and relevance in purpose. Frequently though, 'dominant relevance' is misunderstood and carries with it a fairly large stigma, especially when we are overwhelmed or in emotional duress. But like everything in the universe, it serves a purpose in leading us to more prolific desires. This isn't to say that any healing we seek is unwarranted, but rather that beneath the surface is a wealth of discourse attempting to reveal itself in what is coming forth in feeling. When we feel turmoil, discomfort, and pain arising, a part of who we are is asking to be fulfilled, but if we are incapable of hearing these communications, often we will seek authority over them simply in an attempt to feel better. From an early age we may tell ourselves anything to quell our fears, pain, or uncomfortable feelings, but in our quest for relief, egoic construction upon egoic construction is built in a pattern of inadvertently ignoring what we feel, commonly stuffing or acting out in emotion. As we do so, a reality is formed based on shifting sands— one which can be potentially dangerous when solely from a three-dimensional point of view but is necessary as a part of our metamorphosis.

Eventually, we will begin to question reality, experiencing an increase in irritation, resentment, and projection of blame for what is felt. We may attempt to arrange our day-to-day life to feel better, but no amount of control we exert will convert the energies we feel in us, for they do not desire to be dominated, rather *the dominion of being heard.* Each attempt to do so only works for taking us deeper into that which we desire. It is only through the acknowledgment of our truths that we will begin to experience some relief. There are a variety of emotions that may manifest, but anger in its various forms is one of the most common as it is close to the surface.

Often once we do begin to acknowledge our needs, there may be strong waves of unworthiness that coincide with the love we offer. This may ostensibly be the opposite direction of where we wish to go for resolve, but as we allow ourselves to experience the ache of what we are feeling on a deeper level, the attachments that once stabilized our reality will challenge it. Cellular memories will frequently arise in a torrent of panic and emotion, attempting to turn any exploration into a defensive posturing; it is the death of a belief system which served us well for the gestation of energies to become ready in creative power. If we are in this place, it is very much like Jesus had said in Matthew 19:24: "…It is easier for a camel to go through the eye of a needle, than for a rich man to enter into the kingdom of God." We must lose the certainty we may have grounded in upon shifting sands in order to evolve in the faith of who we are as divine love; what we think we know, how the universe is believed to work, and any grasped conception of what or who we are as a species is subject to revision in this place. The key here is in loving the heart with a childlike humility, abiding through each experience with nurturing kindness, and feeling the emotions necessary as part of embracing a shift in reality rather than what we have believed to get by.

As we allow ourselves to feel, to see those parts that are hurting, and we are with them in love, a fulfillment of contracts begins to occur; the love that we give resonates in abiding with strong emotional energies that we feel, and the universe responds to this with the "authority" we have been seeking by the arrangement of energy fields for well-being. All creation works in relation to a natural system of order and balance, and chaos serves in every circumstance for harmonious development. In other words, we can't change the laws of attraction, or have dominance over them, but we can allow them to work for us as we embrace those parts that are wanting. As we do this, in giving the passage necessary for uncomfortable feelings to flow, the same visitors which once plagued us reveal themselves as guides to a new reality or creation where we experience the relief of expansion in it.

The bottom line is that healing doesn't always look like healing and may be perceived as grotesque, harmful, and even painful. There will be times when everything that arises seems to do so in opposition to our wellbeing, but once we see through the disguise of circumstances, we become aware that these afflictions have only come to align or shift our vibration in resolution; honesty does not have to be brutal, but it does need to be embraced for the allowing of energy to pass as needed for resolve. And one of the more painful realizations is that honesty is not about others or pressing them to know our truths, but about ourselves, what we desire, and who we are in coming to know our life path intimately.

In the beginning stages of resolve, some touches of compassion may feel so unfamiliar to us, and especially if we have been ignored, abused, and deeply hurt, we will recoil painfully, even as love approaches us. While we may not come from abusive homes, *or if we do*, neglect can severely darken our world, producing deep wounds that are in need of nurturing care if we are to recover. When working with past trauma, loss, grief, or abandonment, love can feel foreign, even enraging us as it draws near, but as we receive the touch of tenderness, although it may feel uncomfortable at first, over time our vibrational field shifts.

Recently there was a video that came up online of a dog that had been terribly abused, taken in by a caregiver, and shown compassion for the first time. The animal was a little older than puppy age, maybe about a year or two, and as the young woman approached the dog in a holding area, the animal cried out in pain, cringing tightly in a corner of the pen. She slowly reached out with a soft hand stroked the dog as it cried out, but with any touch it felt the former pain of abuse. The caregiver moved with slow movements, but the dog cowered further into a corner, tail between its legs, peeing itself, as if it were being beaten, continuing to wail while touched. After some time, the agonizing cries became whimpers as the worker continued her light strokes of compassion while whispering soothing tones, and looking into the dog's eyes, anchoring love in the room. The dog began to settle slightly, where you could see an apparent shift, realizing it was not being abused, but still felt the strokes upon its body with revulsion, very difficult to receive. Time-lapse video showed the dog in a few weeks, a little skittish, its tail still tucked, but now playing with other puppies, no longer hunched fearfully in the corner. Another lapse showed the same dog now playing with the caregiver, running, licking, tail wagging, living a completely different life from much of the abusive terror it had previously suffered.

Healing can be one of the ugliest experiences we may ever go through, tormenting even, and at first we may do everything we can to cower away in some corner, full of fear by the uncertainty that we face. But as gentleness, kind words, and the tender hand enter into our life, they begin to soothe our wounds; once we recognize love as a force of possibility, although we may feel the pain of our past circumstances, our perception of the world begins to shift in relief. We may doubt, resist, or fight the tenderness we feel, but pain only arises in longing to be released. In identifying the agents at work in our outer circumstances, love is revealed among them attempting to provide a path for resolve. At first we may resist this greater arrangement of love because of egoic mind, but as we move into the shadows, our heart gains a newfound footing in faith by trusting the universe when facing uncertainty. With each unraveling of egoic logic, we are brought closer in relationship to our divinity, where we gain clarity as a byproduct of the ascension process— not by overcoming habitual patterns or karma, but by developing trust in the relationship of who we are as divine self in the layers of our experience.

As we allow it, this faith grows to become unshakable, and we learn new ways of processing energetic information that arises, which is no longer held in habitual paradigms where we saw ourselves as victims of circumstance. In this shift, we begin to cooperate, coordinate, and express on a level universal in reflection that opens us to an ever-deepening intimacy with life; an increased longing is merely part of our journey in self-discovery, as those places deep within the soul manifest in the body energetically to be recognized as communications coming forward for attention and love. The human life is nothing short of divine potential manifesting in experience, even though we may be unaware of who or what we are.

As we awaken, it is common for energetic guides to present themselves to us with feelings such as frustration, irritation, restlessness, and discontent, which represent aspects of our vibrational character which come forward as previously unacknowledged passions. As we begin to interact with ourselves in a state of deepened awareness with love, what we receive is based on our most inherent need of finding our way back to greater self. Innocence serves as an excellent intermediary with these guides, as once darkened parts reveal themselves as necessary for our wellbeing. Its purity softens the intensity of what we feel energetically, which allows for a more fluid integration. Although we may not always view strong emotions that arise as 'gifts', they are here to help us resolve those places in need within us. As we learn to feel into each circumstance, embracing our experiences as teachers, we are heightened in awareness, intuition, and clarity, both through the clearing of emotional debris that were once lodged in our cellular memories and by the furthering of connection with universal self.

We slowly become accustomed to working with the flow and creative process in which the universe moves for resolve, and our perspective shifts with the love we offer and receive in reflection. Just as everything in nature works together for the greater benefit of the whole, so too, on a macro scale, each life path labors in a finite existence for the greater infinite of who we are. This doesn't mean we will not reap the benefits of an expanded life on a linear timeline, but rather that what we reap we become aware of as we are ready to receive it. How this manifests dimensionally will always be in relation to what our best interests are, not necessarily for immediate wants of comfortability.

About twenty-five years ago, I wore glasses for my eyesight, which felt awkward, unnatural, and physically painful. My nose would develop an indentation from where the ridge of the frame rested, my eyes were frequently sore, and just outside in peripheral view was a world of blurry, irritating taunting. Being a sensitive from early on, this was all magnified in experience and became a consistent reminder of where my beliefs stood in relation to what I desired universally.

One day while riding in the car with Mother through our small town, I decided enough was enough, and that if I truly believed in the power of prayer, healing, or any divinity, the glasses had to go. So in an act of faith, I quietly lowered the passenger window and abruptly threw off my 'oppression' to the curbside. Mom yelled at me, "What did you just do!?!" And in a quick, confident, stand-fast sort of reply, I said, "I threw my glasses out the window!" Of course it didn't help matters any that this particular pair was brand new and that Mom had just bought them, or that at the time my life was in a place of deep recovery and I was very much dependent, living at home.

Sheepishly I did my best to try to explain this move while being the recipient of a stern talking to. And the next hour, Mother vowed we would find the glasses, even if she had to drive me up and down the street all day looking for them. But my reply again in an act of faith was, "They're gone Mom, most likely broken somewhere in the grass of someone's lawn," confident that the actions I took would lead to a healing of my sight. But true to her word we drove back and I was instructed to start looking, and she even made me go up to the first house we stopped at to ask. The universe has a funny way of working with us, and often what we expect or think along lines of resolve isn't always the case for resolve. This doesn't mean we are not heard or that manifestation is not in motion, only that our best interest is always at heart.

As I walked up to the first house and was about to knock on the door, it opened and a lady said, "Did you lose a pair of glasses?" I was dumbfounded. How could the universe turn on me like this? And why would I be met with flat refusal when acting on such faith?

The next day I sat with the emotions of seeming failure in a local community meeting. As everyone shared, I looked from face to face, watched their gestures as they talked, and felt nothing but defeat. After some time though of sitting with these feelings, it occurred to me that I was not a prisoner, and even though my mother had instructed me not to throw away my glasses, I could simply take them off, especially if I was physically hurting. Upon doing so, everyone became blurry, and it became difficult to recognize once familiar faces. The first emotion that came forward was fear, which arrived in many forms that were surprising: fear of rejection, fear of unworthiness, even fear of others in that I couldn't tell who was sitting across from me and didn't want to insult them by not recognizing them. So I would put the glasses back on, return to 'normal' living, and proceed with my day. But sitting with these feelings intrigued me, and I wondered if there was something more to the healing process than the physical redemption of sight. So over and over I would return to removing the glasses, sitting with these feelings, loving the heart while with them, and exploring the uncomfortable sensations the body that I felt as they arose.

Frequently I would meditate for long periods, simply being with the breath, blurry vision of a hillside, and fear at not being able to see clearly. At times the sun's rays felt so intense, it was as if they were penetrating the retina in a brilliance of healing. Intuition would arise in connection with these experiences, urging me to allow energy to pass in the form of emotional debris while slowing down in the breath of loving the heart and receiving the sunlight as an adjustment vibrationally to the eyes. Moreover, each year I had an appointment with an optometrist who, although reassured me no healing could occur through these actions, was baffled at my sight slowly becoming clearer and would simply state, "Whatever you're doing, keep doing it because your sight is improving!"

This process took a period of about seven years and gave me an incredible wealth of patience, self-love, and faith in the slow, steady path of resolve; although we may not always understand how the universe works for resolution, healing is only one byproduct of a much deeper scope where our wellbeing is concerned. Today, though I can see the forest hillside crystal clear, the issues vibrationally that were in need of resolve gave me a much more profound gift in the faith which was received over time, especially in the teachings of uncertainty, abiding, and integration of doubt, which would not have occurred through a quick healing on command. Let me be explicit here, if we desire healing from any physical duress, it is never in question or 'wrong' in wanting and will always lead us deeper in resolve, but if we seek healing only as a means to resolve, although we may be healed physically the vibrational issues may not. These energies are the underlying fabric to any reality we live in and can only be adjusted eternally as we are ready to acknowledge, abide, and integrate with love. When fear, doubt, or anxiety surface, even though we may view the feelings in connection with an event, person, place, or thing, they work in conjunction with manifestation for revealing the parts within us vibrationally that are in need of love. As we learn to love ourselves through all that we feel while holding the heart, the heart responds to being held by the safety it feels which is needed for expansion and allows a more infinite view in finite circumstances we perceive on Earth. This extended field of awareness opens our potential for a larger life than we have been living, creating a dynamic relationship with the soul and the universe for manifestation to proceed in ways we never previously imagined possible. We not only learn to trust this process and the universe but begin to see our doubts, anxieties, and fears in a new light: afflictive emotions no longer are something to be overcome but rather revered as messengers of our impending transformation. Not only are they harbingers of deep metamorphosis, but the desires that have been dormant for many years begin to shine expressively as we realize love's power in working through them for our benefit.

As listening into feelings becomes more and more abundant in daily practice, the stored energies of habitual patterns begin to reveal themselves, which are often triggered by outer circumstances. Each event, environment, and relationship is a part of the universal vibrational response in reflection that we may both love those places within us in need and explore or express what we feel. If we were to view these energy threads that arise as our karma being revealed to us, we not only become more aware of our vibrational path, but the inner work involved in relation to the outer universe; from a fifth-dimensional perspective, there is no separation within the universal body— everything works in coordination and is all-inclusive beneficially. What we often experience as synchronicity or outer arrangements of circumstances for resolve are really vibrational responses to what we desire. Because we are often limited in what we see three-dimensionally, these appear as forces beyond our manifestational capability, but as we open ourselves to the simplicity in practicing love, a natural evolvement occurs as intuition is honed by interacting with the universe energetically in each known reality.

A fine-tuning of sorts unfolds in sensitivity as we abide with strong emotions while holding the heart in loving compassion, which in turn creates a safe passage for the clearing of emotional debris as both work together in transformation to shift reality as we evolve. Not only are previous energies that were too overwhelming for the nervous system integrated, but they become potent instruments for a heightened awareness.

Holding the heart becomes our mantra in all that we feel as emotional debris stored in cellular recordings are played and released for passage, which in turn shift vibrational threads as desired. Slowly we will begin to feel this shift in vibration, much the way a sliver exits the body as part of the process for wellness. As this happens, even though painful at times, we become open to experiencing life on a much more expansive level, creating room for the soul, deepening our connection with the vessel, and gaining clarity to

160

sense multi-dimensional existence. However, ascension is not held to the confines of progression, nor is it goal oriented in any way, which is where lofty ideas of egoic mind may interpret 'high vibration' as evolvement (even though we are in ascension to fifth-dimensional awareness, divine potential exists as infinite in energy, and as such we are never walking the road to it, but we are already of it).

Where once we may have had the perception of the body or the third dimension working against us, they now support us informatively. And as such, we may open in awareness to new sensations of energy, allowing ourselves to feel not only what we need for our wellbeing, but exploring the landscape of manifestation for the love we are in benefiting all beings. As we become accustomed to a world we are immersed in without barriers, the beings that we are serve in relationship with our environment to help guide evolvement and deepen our energetic understanding of divine expression. Really what we perceive as an imbalance to any reality we are living are the forces in motion to rebalance or align us with what we desire as vibrational beings. Our bodies are encoded with this imbalance through a variety of circumstances when we incarnate: gender, race, ethnicity, even our DNA, and the overall environment we are born into contribute to our process. Whether this is natural in our humanity or a phenomenon as we ascend dimensionally along the evolutionary path, as we acknowledge divinity coming forth, the clarity we receive is our adjustment to higher vibrational frequencies of love in the body. Gender, race, culture, etc., all play a role in this process, but often for them to be most effective we are unaware of their impact in evolvement. And really understanding this or its purpose is not as important as the relief that arrives when we begin to offer love to the one in process.

In our current society, the heart becomes incapacitated by these imbalanced energies (which only do so in order to rebalance) through the many layers of emotional debris stored in cellular memory, causing a cascade of what we perceive as mental illness where the ego attempts to forge a new reality in what is felt as the absence or hidden aspects of our divinity. Most of humanity is prone to this except possibly in a few rare exceptions of remotely isolated indigenous societies, where from an early age there is a balancing/rebalancing of energies. There has also been much talk or focus in the New Age community that if one is not in 'high vibration' that somehow they are in a lower caste or in darkness as to what love is and how well they truly are. Let me say from my own experience as one who has healed, is a healer, and continues to work with the universe in reflection intimately: this is a half-truth presented by ego to boost morale among the prestigious elite based in the world constructions of 'other'. Indeed, there are times when ALL of us will experience the shadows of lower frequencies which are part of the divine nature in us coming forth. The Buddha, Mohammad, and even Christ moved among the dark world and saw these experiences as part of the divine process, where evolvement came disguised in affliction or strong emotional upheaval. The resulting effect is that once we begin to embrace these energies within, we also become vulnerable without as our awareness catches up to the multi-dimensional living we are capable of and the ego slowly dies. And although this state may be viewed as nothing short of what we call schizophrenia or the likes of it, as we are ready, when approached with loving compassion, it begins to become clear as multiple dimensions are experienced simultaneously. To the uninitiated or the perceptions of only the third dimension in understanding, this will most certainly feel insane, but to those that have undergone the transformational integration of energies a higher consciousness or awareness, abounds unfettered by previous boundaries of how the universe works. Throughout this metamorphosis, there is no goal upon which we can focus on but rather a state we are in realization of as we come to know our infinite divine self.

In my own experience early in youth, life produced a steady flow of struggle (which, being a sensitive, frequently led to feeling overwhelmed), and at times there was such incapacitation that in order to survive the overstimulated nervous system, defensive mechanisms were developed as an egoic cocoon of sorts to protect self-identity or a functioning reality. In doing so though, these layers of protection encased the heart with an egoic wall of considerable fortitude which was virtually impenetrable. But as with all things, the creation utilizes everything for wellbeing, even egoic construction; every event, relationship, and environment ever experienced contribute to the metamorphosis within, and eventually the shell begins to crack under the weight of itself using the energy of its collapse for the divine to emerge in transformational power.

Although not all of us may be sensitive, everyone is sensitive to some degree and there will come a time when through no uncertain circumstances each cocoon is ripened as part of our evolvement. When this happens life will begin to feel very surreal, like it is being witnessed from a distance, and even though we may do our best to stay alert, awake, and sane, this will only fuel the realization that we have been asleep. Nearing this place, not only will we experience the pain of an egoic reality weighted by illumination but also the relief as life moves in transition. This process may lead each of us through various circumstances, and at times we may feel utterly abandoned, but as we abide with the energies that are coming forth to be felt, we will sense something else manifesting in form. The challenge becomes one of feeling into the layers and allowing ourselves to explore into those areas under the surface where we may become despondent, especially as the mind attempts to reason why events unfold in what we may perceive as not in our favor. Any insistence that something is wrong or that there must be a mistake is a perception based in duality, which serves to bind us in comfortability or familiarity to our former reality. The fear that is felt here is nothing more than the ego sensing its death, and it will struggle to survive and fulfill its contract as guardian in making sure we are ready for expansion. In this transition we are reminded of the impermanence in all things, yet of the permanency in love; although loss may visit our life path, it is also the creation of space for that which is to come.

Once we become accustomed to the practice of abiding with love, many of us will find that in most situations we are more uncomfortable than mistreated, and even if the latter is the case, once we are safe we may move into the past to feel what was felt when we are ready. Even in the most extreme circumstances where an injustice has been done, if we are grounded in compassion we may ease into the pain with gentleness and will begin to feel an alteration in our vibration as we hold those parts that are in doubt, fear, and desire of resolution. Although none of us would choose trauma as a means for resolve, the loss experienced from it can be a powerful component to spiritual evolution which leads to our humanity being fully embraced. If we ask ourselves, "What are we are ready for?" and, "How much are we willing to see?" what arises in feeling rather than thought will render exactly where we are at in readiness for resolve.

By allowing ourselves to be with the feelings commonly experienced as pain, we take a step forward into a larger capacity for love and are able to hold space for the one who has suffered where an integration of energies takes place on a level necessary for eternal shift in vibration. True healing in a teaching such as this can be a messy business, one which often comes in disguise and can take us off any well-known trail into seclusion, darkness, and a deconstruction of life as we know it. But what we perceive as failure, ugliness, and a derailing of our path is often necessary in the steps of resolve, where the derailleur actually works to shift gears to a more fluid experience of who we are as divinity. This path is difficult because it requires perseverance in something that seems to be in opposition to what we desire and frequently makes no sense to the world we live in. And we will not push through, force change, or awaken on our timetable; great faith is not grown by greater deeds— it has always been sown fully contained within any seed. Although we may feel as if we need to do something, the something we need is contained within us and arises to be felt and offered safe passage while we love the heart for wellbeing, which is the most valuable ground for growth in any life path.

Even when we perceive hints of encouragement nudging us on, until we provide the space necessary for abiding, nothing will be of lasting resolution and the heart will continue to be plagued by doubt, anxiety, and depression as an urging to what we are capable of in embracing who we are. These feelings are a culmination of our efforts on an outer focus, and as life becomes overwhelming, they turn us inward for reconnection, resolve, and deep healing. In essence, we often lose who we are through our determined attempts to shift outer circumstances, and when we do, how we feel is an indication of our soul, body, and the universe working in coordination with each other to bring us back to divinity. We may view the ache, depression, or sadness we feel with disdain, but as we come to know our darkness and the afflictive emotions that we experience in it, we not only come to find value in these shadows but our own value in loving ourselves enough to abide with them for resolve.

It's normal to want to feel healthy, vibrant, and alive, abundantly experiencing all life has to offer in complete contentment. Sometimes though, the deeper path is one of sickness, brokenness, and darkness, where we go into those places, journeying beneath the layers to embrace the demons of our derision. Although self-care of the flesh is a part of self-love, when it becomes our sole focus, we side-step what we are desirous of in resolve; by believing only restoration or wholeness of the body is what we view as healthy, we inadvertently trap ourselves in a three-dimensional paradigm, and those places within us that are in need of resolution, which we have incarnated here to allow our humanity to reveal for us, go unacknowledged.

When large wounds have been festering for years, possibly even lifetimes, vibrationally they are in need of extensive attention, the kind that only comes when we are facing extreme or terminal conditions. Often we become more flexible in the nature of the heart, allowing unresolved energies passage through our bodies when facing potential finality in a life path. This does not mean that we ignore the flesh, but rather that we go into the darkness of our affliction, allowing ourselves to embrace through a deeper sense of listening to what is being asked for, offering space to what arises in emotion with loving care. We do this by the foundational practice of holding the heart, abiding with the strong emotions, and telling our heart as we would a dear friend, "I love you, and will not abandon you, nor reject you, but I am allowing myself to feel all that is necessary for loving resolve of those places that are in need of my attention and care." When we view resolve as a priority, even more so than the circumstances life presents as itself, we move beyond any former perception of what life has to offer into something unimaginable in living.

By Our Design

By Our Design

Chapter 11

Multi-Dimensional Beings

As a species we are evolving beyond a three-dimensional paradigm of living in which, as the constructs of an egoic reality die and are integrated in transformation, we are becoming capable of living in a world without boundaries, free to interact with the universe from multiple points of view as we explore the infinite in our ascension process as divinity.

When we look at the known history of mankind, even more so in just the last century, with all of the war, poverty, devastation, and outpouring in suffering, it becomes clear that we are a species in deep dissension, confused by our moral right as children of the stars, each of us exploring in pilgrimage along lines of human existence. When we begin to review our life path as a whole, taking stock-in-trade of our ancestors, we find an energetically diverse past full of trauma that has triggered everything from abandonment to betrayal, rejection, and unworthiness. Instances such as the Irish Potato Famine, the Holocaust, and the disease plagues to the Native Americans followed by centuries of genocide and displacement by European settlers have had rippling waves of effect as emotional debris lodge themselves in our DNA. And whether in race, gender, sexual orientation, social status, or culture, there is a mass exodus of people searching for identity, resolve, and expression. Globally, parts of humanity are awakening on a scale never witnessed before as unresolved issues conflict with the lives being lived and are coming to surface at an unprecedented rate in human awareness. Potent questions arise for this age: "How do we navigate the deep vibrational trauma, resolve what seems unresolvable in our current reality, and embrace where we are destined from here?"

In this present time, we are learning the responsibility we have not only to ourselves but our ancestors and future generations as we proceed to cross a dimensional rift in our evolution. Although facing the uncertainty of our species, the soul in each of us is well aware of our needs both collectively and individually. Inherently our first impression will simply be to survive, but survival itself has layers both in feeling the trauma that arises in our cellular memory and living through whatever is necessary as any activation occurs. Those that are 'chosen' are absolutely ready, but as dimensional beings, often balk in willingness until awareness catches up with what is necessary to undergo the pain of transformation for spiritual evolution. Whether in journey as 'light workers', 'shadow walkers', or 'anchors of love', when ready we will grieve our humanity but celebrate it and undergo great sacrifice and extreme loss to a former world, finding a new one awaiting in the wings. And as we learn to love every part that calls out for resolution, this path is one of such magnitude that it will ripple out upon the sea of all beings, shifting vibrational frequency in compassion multi-dimensionally.

What we perceive as time and reality are merely constructs of our ascended selves, created in order for awareness to awaken through experience. In a sense we are growing into who we already are, which is a being who has expanded beyond a third-dimensional view. And as we do so, what we often undergo in this expansion may feel insane, impossible, surreal, or unrealistic by the expectations placed on reality viewed solely from a three-dimensional point of view. This is where the opening of the universe in understanding appears to be very small and incomprehensible, because when seen through a tiny view, well, it is. But we can start from a point of view we are familiar with, such as the traits we inherit from our parents.

Many of us may have observed ourselves standing in a certain way, saying certain phrases, and reacting similarly to how our family members would. In youth frequently we may have denied association, or even vowed that we "would never be like them" only to discover the apple doesn't fall far from the tree. While in some cases this might be a heartwarming nostalgia, in others these traits may be incredibly difficult to process and connected through cellular memory to deep wounds of trauma or fear. And even in some circumstances there may be recordings of abuse being heard emotionally over and over again that we may be completely unaware of. So it really needs to be stressed here that going beyond this life path where we have incarnated can wait if there are other immediate issues arising in need of loving care. As we begin to resolve those, we can move in exploration to a deeper level that we find through our DNA which has stored previous ancestors' trauma as well. Regardless of how we came to be in this timeline existing vibrational pattern, the human experience we are receiving is exactly as needed for what we desire to resolve. As we come to know ourselves and the energies that arise in our field, we experience the manifestations stored vibrationally in us as recordings of our ancestors, while also seeing them in relation to outer reflections as spiritual evolution taking place.

When we become aware of those places within us that we have inherited, as we are ready, we claim responsibility for healing by offering resolve in the form of love for the needs that have arisen. Not only is this an adjustment for our own vibrational needs, but as we evolve there is a shift across dimensions through time and space both in past and further generations to come. We contribute by hearing the needs that have been called forth within us for attention and by feeling what we feel while holding space for the heart in love. Although thus far this has been our personal practice, we see the implications of our shifting energy field across timelines and dimensions for every lineage. Just as a pebble may be dropped in a pond for ripples that may affect the entirety of the pond, so too we begin to understand as we evolve how our energetic field may shift or affect the entire universe, even beyond three-dimensional awareness.

One of these aspects in an evolving multi-dimensional life is the application of time travel. Whether we realize it or not, on a consistent basis we are going back, moving forward, visiting both past references and future points of potential along our life path, which are stored in the cellular memory of our incarnation. Although three-dimensionally one of the constructs which develops in the ego is the appearance of time on a linear scale, on a quantum mechanical level the soul works in coordination with the universe to navigate a field of choices that arise knowing which will suit all points in time and serve our innermost desires fulfilling destiny. This has not been thoroughly discussed thus far in that the mind tends to reason out possibilities, becoming both a distraction and overwhelming the nervous system at the implications upon known reality. But what is discussed here will either move one further inward, feeling (even if overwhelmed) the nature of what we are capable of, or if uninitiated may be immediately compromised by the ego as it attempts to stabilize thought along more familiar lines of known reality. There are several practices though that may be embraced, which will surface naturally as part of the evolutionary process in ascension, so mainly my position in opening the discussion of time travel here is to affirm the desire to go deeper into them or introduce ones that may already be in place but are vague in practical application.

The first opposition which may be found when exploring time travel is the 3-D representation of physically moving through time and space; although moving around physically may seem implausible, ironically it may feel much easier than what is presented here for practical application. So how we approach each landscape of reality for resolve is always determined by the soul, and while fanciful flights of bi-location or visiting pivotal pints in history may be desired, underneath these are vibrational requests which always take precedent. And how the universe works in relation to the mind, intuition, and resolve are as much a mystery as what we are ready or capable of receiving. For our purposes here we will move into commonalities that many or most of us may be familiar with in experience.

There are times we will receive a strong indication in feeling of what is about to happen, and it may or may not unfold exactly as was predicted. Often the mind will struggle with this information and move back into past recordings, frequently becoming lost in a sea of contemplative pathways while attempting to solve what was felt. Some of the most prevalent questions that will arise again and again in this process will be, "Was there a better choice? If so, how can circumstances be corrected?" or, "Was what happened predetermined, where we have little or no say in determining the future?" In some faiths, practitioners will be in preparation for many years before approaching these and other questions that may arise as awakenings in potential. Although we are only ready when we are ready to receive what we receive, preparation serves two parts in that it forms a discipline to support the nervous system when overwhelmed, and it creates a space where love may freely move about in us as thought arises. Paradoxically, the undertone in any practice of preparation is also the revealing agent in it, meaning that many times when we stop looking so hard, we find what was seemingly lost.

An example of this in Zen Buddhism is when masters would give their students unsolvable problems, or riddles in the form of 'koans' such as, "When both hands are clapped a sound is produced; listen to the sound of one hand clapping!" When the student focused on solving the riddle by the use of logic, it led the mind to a place of exhaustion, which was exactly the point. In other words, when we think in three-dimensional terms to solve a higher dimensional equation, we will never come to a solution, which paradoxically is already there because we live in a universe that is completely connected and aware; the issue of life isn't that we don't know the answer, it's that we become too overwhelmed and distracted in our seeking to find or solve it. The mind is an incredible powerhouse of computing power, so much so that we become overwhelmed by the software at our disposal. But utilized more along the lines of an antenna or receiver to the void of creative expansion in coordination with the body and soul, the human experience becomes a conduit for sensing beyond the realm of the third dimension. Just as the space of preparation is utilized on multiple levels for receiving what we are about to hear, when we allow abiding space for what we feel while holding the heart in compassion, creative potential is granted room for us to become aware of relief as we engage our deepest desires. Often three-dimensionally humans view the void of emptiness for what they see it as in 3-D: empty. But multi-dimensionally or from an ascended point of view, it is abundant with potential, where we may even connect with our future as we come to know the one coming forth in us. In other words, the mind doesn't need to learn to navigate life on a quantum level, but rather is utilized as a tool for trust, observation, transmission, and reception to what we are already are as incarnations of divinity.

Although the past in particular can hold a wealth of information, as energies circulate themselves within us, often manifesting habitual patterns stored in the physical body, the future in relation to who we are in the next moment, year, or thousand years vibrationally can counsel us if we are open in connection. The loops that occur in our mind and patterns of behavior are merely an indication of what has occurred as well as what in potential is coming. And as we learn to embrace ourselves, granting space for the energies that present themselves, although we may be experiencing the past energetically, we can also draw on the inward reserve of the one who has already felt what we are feeling presently. Although we may feel alone or left to fend for ourselves in moments when we experience energies for clearing and transformation, these feelings are guides to the depth of trust where universal arrangement provides faith as an exchange in the love we offer. The sacred practice of holding the heart and leaning into what we feel transcends time, allowing us to shift eternal threads vibrationally that will not only serve our past self but the one we have already become in the future.

As we experience a rollercoaster of feelings, thoughts, and relationships throughout life, we will observe that sometimes we receive comfort in difficult situations, while in others we may feel utterly destroyed and might wonder what terms we are on with the force which is at work in our lives, how in some of our most vulnerable moments we feel watched over, while in others left to fend for ourselves. This becomes a matter of exploration as we evolve, and as we come to know ourselves as multi-dimensional beings how we meet life can be very complex or confusing as reality shifts in perspective. In short, the most difficult answer to hear is that everything will work out and there are necessary hardships we must survive in order for evolution to take place as infinite beings. We make agreements, contracts, and vows eternally that many times affect our life paths whether we are aware of them or not.

Sometimes they are passed on genetically, environmentally, or circumstantially, but all of them are being vibrationally fulfilled even when in question. Manifestational insight assumes we are the ones creating our path we are about to meet, and it is valid, but again when we expand beyond this point of view to a multi-dimensional interaction, we begin to see a myriad of relationships working in synchronicity for each and every part as needed. At first although this may seem complex or confusing (because of a natural filtering by the egoic protections in place) it can be simplified in amplification if we focus solely on the relationship we have with our self. Our relationship with the self which simultaneously touches and is touched by all others may be considered a nexus for any shift we experience manifestationally. In learning how to give love to all aspects of self through each and every darkness and the most vulnerable, insecure moments we may face (many of which we may feel as the ache of loneliness), we provide an expanding compassion for what we are capable of— not only in three-dimensional terms, but by time itself becoming a tool we utilize fifth-dimensionally. In other words, if calamity occurs, there are reasons beyond third-dimensional reasoning, and it will always serve love to greater purpose. This doesn't mean we are not loving based on choices we make as these events unfold, but rather we are given considerable opportunity for deepening self-realization as dimensional beings of support through the one they are occurring for. Although this type of relationship may be daunting in discovery at first and may even feel more like an imaginary friend of sorts from the future or past in application, and as we evolve we slowly begin to realize moments of deep intimacy with our past or future self in resolve.

One of the most basic practices is to move energetically into the past to moments where we have deeply desired that someone could have be there with us and place the hand upon the heart, share that moment with our past self in support. Once we start to feel the energies of what may be past trauma or a difficult time, we ask ourselves what some gentle words of encouragement are that we would have wanted to hear— not to change circumstances, but simply to be with the one in suffering. Maybe we even place our hand on their shoulder, telling them we won't abandon them, or simply say, "Even though this is a difficult time, everything will work out, and it's going to be ok. I will love and abide with you through this in all that is felt, and you are not alone."

Whether we realize our capability or not, practices such as this build an energetic bridge with our former self and allow resolve on a level which can shift both our vibrational thread at the core and establish a relationship with who we are that we have intimately desired in depth. Even in what we perceive as unresolved trauma, once we begin to offer the loving support necessary to feel often intense and overwhelming energies we have experienced in life, the heart opens in the safety of our care allowing us to integrate what was calling out for attention.

Not only can we move back in moments of time to abide with ourselves in loving support, but as a natural consequence, a relationship with our future Self unfolds to reveal an unlimited source of faith, wisdom, and compassion as well. Amongst any present chaos, where we may feel tossed this way and that, there will be times when we observe the same presence of support we have offered to our past self in practice. And as we feel, we become more self-realized, gaining insight by the depth of our surrender and innocence, which allows expansion into a much larger verse of reality where we are never alone and are *always* being held, even in the most difficult of circumstances. This path requires vulnerability and sacrifice to what we think we know in how the universe works, the kind that can only be given by loving compassion, or our divinity. But once this door is opened, the very ground beneath our feet forms a new relationship with us in connection with all things, and as we further an intimate bond with ourselves going into the places that scare us, we begin to feel the warmth of relief as our future self stands by us whispering counsel as the one we already are.

Although this concept of who we are as divinity may seem a bit solitary in practice, the more we expand in self-realization, the more we find of ourselves, not so much as a singular entity in self-form, but rather a wholeness where everyone and everything is both a part of this identity and living their own lives in journey. 'God', or 'Love', which was previously seen in three-dimensional terms or by egoic constructs as 'other', which may have been worshiped, praised, and deified as a principle or power beyond being human, becomes a force of who we are in relation to all life. Just because we may be unaware of who we are doesn't mean we are inconsequential or separate, but proportionately that we are in the process of resolve.

In ancient times almost across any major spiritual culture there was a belief that if a knock came upon the door, it could be a master of a great house, or an otherworldly being such as an angel in travel. If they desired fellowship, to warm themselves by the hearth's fire, or to wash the dust from their feet, you addressed them with the utmost humility and respect because you might be entertaining beings far beyond what they have made known. This custom is not far from how we may perceive ourselves in unawareness. Not that fear should govern us, but in our fears we find the desires of the soul, those places of wanting that are expressed as they reveal themselves in our experiences. Even though we may be unaware of it, within our humanity is a built-in exploration of this 'otherworld', where each desire works cohesively with universal reflections to fulfill our dreams which would not come to surface if it was not meant to be a part of our soul. Although we may find ourselves shrouded in the darkness of incarnation here on Earth, carrying certain traits that seem bound to specific circumstances, our environment, the body, or family we have chosen to be born into, they serve for the purpose of unraveling those parts of our vibrational thread ripe for expansion. Even when we take issue with another religion, race, or cultural view, it isn't so much because of the doctrine, color, or beliefs in that society we struggle with, but rather those places within ourselves stepping forward by the opportunity presented for the clearing of what we feel arising in our energetic field proportionately. In other words, the stronger we believe in something, the more we are attempting to love that part of the self which is emerging. It is only through the connection within our self and others as we perceive them that we begin to find the necessary fuel for enlightenment or to evolve beyond three-dimensional experiences. Once we open our hearts to this process, we will find that any perceived loss we experience in our judgement, or belief system is only creating the space needed for any expansion as multidimensional beings. As Jesus once said, eternal life, or heaven, is not a closed system for the wealthy, but stands as an open gate for those that are 'poor in spirit'. The key as always is not needed to unlock the door, but rather to hear the passage being offered with love as our agent to walk through it.

One of mankind's most curious qualities in relation to expansion is in the nature of our manifestations and the darkness we must wade through in order to see them; the same desires that frequently seem to taunt us in life are the very ones asking for fulfillment. When we observe justification, projection, and expectations as frequent guests in our house, the energies in them are purposefully linked to paradigms which are shifting and have surfaced as both carriers in clearing space for expansion while also doing their best to claim reality ensuring any love we offer is grounded as we approach a much larger world in perspective. Often what we feel as the pain of unfamiliar ground or uncertainty that shrouds us is the real work in piercing the veil, as thoughts, patterns, and energies surface for us to feel while we gently hold the heart in compassion. When we embrace truth unconditionally in love, this allows desire to be expressed, and in turn expansion fulfilled. It is the most basic purpose of existence as we come to know ourselves on a more intimate basis and where we often witness vibrational threads shifting on a three-dimensional plane of circumstances as the universe reveals them for well-being. Those parts we may struggle with, dislike, or desire to be different are the very parts awakening us in awareness for the love we have to offer. And as we integrate, those parts that have served for expansion and spiritual evolution will occur in what the three-dimensional or rational mind would deem impossible circumstances to do so.

When doors open into the fourth and fifth dimensions, to the uninitiated they can feel terrifying, to say the least, which is why they must be approached with love for any type of multi-dimensional living. Throughout the transformational process, it is only once we start to settle in that a much larger verse than we previously thought possible reveals itself, where we may begin to feel into the details energetically of each experience. Our foundation in compassion serves to bridge the energies that arise, so that even when we may feel afraid, upset, or overwhelmed, by utilizing the body as conduit while placing the hand upon the heart, we allow strong currents of intensity to move as necessary. Simple affirmations such as, "I will not abandon you, nor reject you, even though I feel _____, but I will hold you as you have desired to be held, through all that is felt. I love you."

Remember, most of us that are in this transformational place will not recognize it as such in order for it to be most effective. What will often be experienced is the sensation of loss in one form or another, and it will frequently be associated with three-dimensional circumstances. Initially we may feel shock, disorientation, or sickness as we attempt to process intense emotions which may be viewed as pain. The mind will try to interpret what is happening, most likely from a three-dimensional point of view, and if what we feel is too overwhelming for our nervous system, either the ego will begin to create an alternate reality, or we will shut down until we are able to feel what has unfolded at a later time. The more difficult teaching in this is that the universe is in complete management of these circumstances, and however awful (or wonderful) we may feel, there is always potential for our divinity to utilize everything for our highest emerging of self. Multi-dimensional living is not something that we see as a result of our incarnation, even though the experience of the flesh works tirelessly to prepare and reveal energies for exactly that expansion; what we perceive as a lifetime of interaction is a blink of an eye from an ascended perspective, and the universe works both paradoxically and inclusively to our benefit in this. So many of us may live a multitude of life paths before ascension occurs, with the universe patiently waiting for energies to gestate and ripen in coordination with the perfect circumstances for awakening. Although we may interpret this process to be a horrific rollercoaster of emotion at times, as we open in expansion, we will see that it is one of many steep climbs, sudden drops, gentle glides, and loops of amazement. And it's not so much that we regard our investment with little care as it is that we give care where our attention is drawn to in the asking for love.

We may regularly observe our spiritual growth along two paths: the first where we tend to feel oppressed, experiencing an ache of emptiness or loss (which is frequently necessary as a gestational primer for our fears and doubts to manifest for eventual clearing of emotional debris, and fuel for the transformational process), and the second that as we become conscious of universal arrangement taking place on our behalf, manifestations reveal themselves as our most intimate desires bringing us into alignment with a higher quality of existence. Both paths are necessary parts in experience of divine unfolding and contribute to the nature of who we are as human beings.

Whether we embrace our fears, or they overwhelm us, we move into the depths of who we are in the process created both for our incubation and our evolvement. What we may view as pain, or barriers of some sort, the universe sees as the husk or shell which can only be traversed by its breaking; each reality is purposeful in its construction for the furtherance of life, love, and resolution of desire. Even what we may resist or refuse to choose in the darkness or mystery of our incarnated life path, the soul willingly suffers for a more fulfilling reality which is emerging. Pain is merely an indication of this transformation in process, and although we may tend to grasp at familiar or former realities of construction, once emotional debris begin to clear and awareness catches up with the vibrational shift taking place, relief wells up within, revealing those places that have been asking for expansion. This is where the potential of who we are as divinity allows room for greater possibility, as we are no longer held to the third or even fourth dimension of reasoning. When we have reached the pinnacle of any devastation, there is a tipping point, a clarity that only comes as we are ready and open to receive 'the end', abyss, or emptiness of what we perceive as loss. Although pain may be excruciating at times, it is the narrowness of the path we feel, and this will eventually expand, but while in these intense energies they provide a transformational quality like no other in unexpected places. The practice of staying in and with the body while holding a space of compassion as each sensation washes over us grants desire an opportunity for the resolve in both inner and outer circumstances.

As a discipline, relaxing into the body also works as an offering in listening, which allows a sacred space to be formed for those parts of the soul that are asking for nurturing care in order to fulfill our desires. The energies that arise in us throughout the day, whether they are triggered by circumstances or revealed through the reflections that manifest, only do so for resolve. And although resolve is frequently viewed as being 'whole', or in more alignment with who we are, it is also the expression and exploration of the creative nature of the universe; a flower sometimes is simply a flower, and it unfolds its faith as love resolving an expression of beauty. Where we may experience pain while in process is through the shifting reality as the one who is emerging within asking to live the life desired. When we begin to see that we are more than the darkened circumstances of past traumas, wounds, and uncomfortable life events we may have experienced —not rising above them, but by the love we offer as integration of them— then we ascend to embrace the fullness of our potential in receiving divine nature.

It may sound ridiculous when we ponder our circumstances and life events that have led us to where we are now, but the underlying tone of humanity has never been one of unworthiness, rather that we are afraid to fully engage the value of who we are. Comfortability tends to find cause in coming to know ourselves by some form of resistance, but if we embrace those aspects that arise in ourselves through the ease of allowing space to be with the body while we experience strong energies, the divine will both nurture and pierce the veil of any discomfort by the love offered (which is, on a side note, the feminine and masculine energies in harmony). This is the resolve sought by humanity since the beginning of creation, both in the struggle of realizing who and what we are, as well as our inability to live in the uncertainty of an existence based in faith. And where doubt became overwhelming as a part of evolvement, an alternate reality developed until we were ready to receive the fullness of who we are.

181

Love allows us to evolve beyond judgements and opinions by the acknowledgement, abiding, and integration of them, where we may move into the energies of each circumstance itself exploring the dimensional rifts of our innermost being (although this might seem like division, it is actually expansion into the many facets of who we are as infinite beings). But this only happens as we establish a connection energetically with the universe, and as we are ready to receive insight into reflections, there are no short-cuts; what sounds easy can be incredibly difficult in feeling as emotional energies arise for resolve. Even so, as we move into this process with compassion, what we formerly perceived as barriers will begin to be resolved through integration, which in turn shifts inward and outer reflections vibrationally. Where we once saw only a small portion, or a single piece in the puzzle, we begin to see a bigger picture unfolding.

Although many practices shared here sound simple —and they are— as we love ourselves, we discover the nature of depth coming to surface in us, which can be both revealing to the process of evolvement, but also frightful in the sense that we become aware of just how transparent we are. We begin to see the importance ego has served in 'covering' us, and that any former reality lived was a necessary part to evolutionary lines of ascension. This may become slightly challenging in that underneath the experience of our circumstances, and what we believe in thought about them, we begin to observe that vibrationally we are always transmitting our desires which we may not fully know: in essence, we cannot lie, even to ourselves. This is where unexplored depths require us to anchor deeper into the love we offer, which knows the truth of what we are transmitting; honesty and openness may be targets in any discipline of self-awareness, but as we come to realize more and more of who we are, love is always the arrow we aim with.

Nature operates within the same sphere of energy which benefits all inhabitants, bringing both desire and creation together in what may seem like terrible chaos at times, but the resulting flow of life force always manifests for evolutionary harmony; a universal law of parallel opposites exists as a part of creation, which consistently moves on a multi-dimensional level in coordination for a balanced process. This can be seen in the balance of feminine/masculine energies, or something as profound as a tree. If we are fortunate enough to live in a place where we have access to nature, we are surrounded by wonderful teachers of wisdom that will guide us deeper into our divinity. We may be drawn to a river, rock formation, mossy grass, or open field, but for the purpose of this teaching, we will allow our focus to be a tree.

The following meditation will support an exploration in awareness of energies which may feel at times as if they are in contradiction, but they are actually moving in resolve as a natural process of life. We never look at a tree and say, "it must be out of balance today," or "it needs to be aligned," yet as humans we consistently view ourselves in this context which we believe prevents our embrace of divine unfolding. One of the simplest practices for connecting in an understanding with these energies that are frequently viewed as in conflict, is 'rooting' with trees.

This particular meditation may be done just about anywhere, but it will have greater effect if done in the presence of trees among the quietness of nature. Often, we can be overwhelmed and even desensitized by egoic constructions of the civilized world, but when moving among nature an ease will immediately allow for an integration of illusion, similar to a fish returning to water. As we move in this environment, we allow ourselves to be drawn to one of our tree kin and ask permission to approach, feeling any sensitivities in the heart field (more often than not most trees are open to this, and we will find this space of asking for permission is really within ourselves). Upon initiating contact, we focus on the breath in combination with reaching out with our emotions, perhaps closing our eyes and placing a hand softly on the tree. While we listen in presence, it is helpful to allow our senses to engage the tree, noticing what we are drawn to: maybe the height, color, or vibrancy of the leaves, the texture of its bark, possibly its smell. What is it we appreciate about this tree? As we do this, we may compliment those parts we are drawn to: maybe how magnificent the crown is, or the beauty of its foliage, and we gently give our fellow traveler an embrace if we feel an openness between us.

Once we have settled and allowed our energies to come together, we step back and begin to root beside our friend. Bare feet upon the earth works well, that we may feel the ground underneath them. As our energetic roots slowly move downward, gravity works for us, sinking us inward to find a well-balanced center. Dropping our hands to the side, slightly bending the knees, we breathe in, out, in, out, feeling our own limbs slowly lift towards the sky, our hands slightly turning palm up to receive the nourishing light and warmth of the sun. With a gentle focus on the tree, we feel the many subtle ways of a tree: the branches swaying with a wind, yet their connection to the roots for a good ground, strength but not straining as limbs with many thousands of leaves which allow absorption of the light, the faces of each one gently receiving what is needed, then transmuting and giving back oxygen in release. Perhaps we feel the base of the trunk holding up all its arms, always centering in a natural rhythm with all parts for balance, or the roots of the tree set in the earth, each holding ground in the dark, not only nourishing, but communicating in subtle ways to the whole, both within and without where it has grown.

We settle in our roots, breathing with the tree, balancing, receiving, giving back as a part of a greater eco-system. We listen to the tree's wisdom, hearing the journey of faith and the simplicity in which it's walked. We feel into the various parts of this presence, and when we are ready, we open our eyes, slowly bow with prayer hands to the heart, acknowledging divinity in our connection for this sacred time with tree.

Paradoxically, although we awaken in awareness to recognize growth (similar to a tree) as necessary when maturing spiritually, the concept of a finite experience can be difficult to process for infinite self which has incarnated (what we perceive as our struggle with coming to terms as us being infinite is really the other way around as the illusion of incarnation). When we are born as infants the experience is so overwhelming in comparison to our previous existence in the abstract or multi-dimensional realm that we quickly lose ourselves to the over-stimulation of being present in a body. And as the body grows from an early age, the ego develops as a measure of protection for the over-stimulated nervous system. This allows us to function in the world of three-dimensional living, but also begins to inhibit what many of us may remember as very young children: 'pretend friends' (which often we refer to as angels, ascended beings, or spirits), seeing higher-dimensional realms (often appearing as sparkling lights, fissures in comprehending a three-dimensional reality, and energy waves of transmission), and an unshakable faith in universal arrangement (the belief that anything is possible). And although some awakenings as to who we are can be frightful once we have formed a relationship with a three-dimensional timeline, others can be blissful, but all are there to serve our greater sense of self in realization of discovery to those parts of the universe we are in anticipation of receiving; just as an infinite being has incarnated in a seemingly impossible finite existence for experience, so too what we view as our finite road of exploration will always reveal well-worn paths of eternal love.

We may feel uncomfortable about viewing the mysterious intersection of multiple timelines, realities, and dimensions, especially when we sense we have been 'here' before, but the relationship we have with ourselves will only evolve with compassion no matter what choices we choose or have chosen before. And as multi-dimensional beings incarnate, some parts are only capable of shining through the uncertain depths of repetition, where the three-dimensional landscapes we have come to know linearly by the stability of ego are perfect for emerging into a larger existence of experiencing time or our awareness differently. Déjà vu or similar experiences are only one facet to a much larger world of multi-dimensional living, but because of an often-limited perception from a reference point of what these experiences might mean to us as humans, we have a tendency to box up those places we feel uneasy in, creating judgements and opinions about circumstances that are only trying to reveal misunderstood feelings, all of which is the soul's way of bringing attention for expansion in love.

Although this can be one of the most difficult passages in the human journey and may even seem complex by what we understand three-dimensionally, what often takes the form of conflict is simply reconciliation. What we may view as behaviors or previous actions that were developed by the ego in order for us to function in a three-dimensional reality (i.e. the person we view we once were or may now be struggling to love), are only indications that come to light as we become aware of our identity in divinity. The balance, resolution or relief that we desire is in the offering of love we provide by abiding with our past, present, and future friend, who was, is, and will always be serving to unfold and fulfill our highest destiny.

By Our Design

By Our Design

Chapter 12

By Our Design

Although what comes in our life path may or may not be to our liking, and at times feels awkward, strange, different, and challenging to many parts of human psychology, what appears is consistent in relation with our innermost pleas for self-love; we may feel like a victim of circumstances in certain experiences when viewed through the lens of ego, but dimensionally every paradox maps the road upon which we travel as beings of divinity. Time, space, and energy are all relative to the soul contracts we have come to fulfill, which is why manifestation can be so difficult to understand. What we see as A+B+C=D in three-dimensional terms is only one small account of a much larger picture or language in transmission, and when applied out of context can severely hinder insight. This is by far one of the most difficult teachings to receive and will undoubtedly cause division in belief systems as egoic constructions are unraveled, which is why the shamans, mystics, and ancients worked with the world on a scale of continuous connectivity in partnership instead of seeking to connect only for specified outcomes. In other words, if we desire to manifest, or understand the circumstances of life as manifestation in its unfolding, we focus on improving the nature of our relationship with all things in reflection to our journey. This can feel very difficult in a world of egoic construction, because the protector ego is only concerned with stability, and as guardian to that reality it will defend the gates of transformation until death. But, when the energies themselves recognize the time of their season, they are like a seed sensing the warmth of the earth in the spring, which cannot be contained by the shell which was only meant for a protection in planting, and must come forth by design. This doesn't mean we will

189

not experience fear, bewildering emotions, and loss, but as these emotions arise and are felt with compassion they lead to a pause in possibility, where we may emerge among the fields of infinite intersection, recognizing the nature of a higher-dimensional relationship we have with perfection in all things, even when what we perceive is misunderstood or uncomfortable. As we learn to trust the process of turning inward and listening, even when confused by what arises, we may experience a sense of ease simply by the acknowledgement of what we feel in compassion. And as simple as this one teaching is, time and time again in human experience it may be so elusive that we will question our resolve and place in coming here.

Throughout human history we have gazed at the stars, entered deep into caves, or built structures in one form or another with the express purpose of hearing our 'meaning' on the canvas of what we know as reality. And while each act brings us to a new scene in evolving consciousness, similar questions are provoked within our sphere: "Who Am I? How did I come to be here? Is there a God or Higher intelligence that made the creation? Am I, or are We alone in the universe?"

As someone who grew up playing outdoors with no cell phones, computers, or video games to occupy the mind, the imagination was free to roam in the backwoods of Pennsylvania as far as it went. As a child my best friend and I would 'pretend', creating various adventures from Saturday morning TV shows, and frequently found ourselves on other planets exploring the surroundings or fighting for our lives as the narrative in each drama unfolded. Although present day may seem much different with our 'modern' advances in technology, each generation will find we are not that dissimilar in exploration from our ancestors' stirrings. In my childhood we had radio, record players, and television where it was common to find the family gathered around the nightly news, watching the TV intently as if staring into the embers of a campfire. Today, with the advent of video games, laptops, internet, podcasts, and cellphones, although many would argue we have somewhat disconnected from each other or our imagination, collectively humanity has gone deeper into the embers, personalizing each search for meaning, but still gathering around the digital fire in its seeking to fulfill affairs of the soul.

And while often we may or may not be aware of the writing on the walls about us or the level of communications taking place in our sphere, we are beings of energy, consistently transmitting and receiving in connection with the hero's journey of our ascent. We have come here in need of fulfillment, where each adventure or challenge that arises has been perfectly coordinated to explore the depths of what it means to be alive. And when we feel or experience a transmission that resonates with us in relation to life, curiosity streams the flow of greater potential that has desired to emerge in the life paths we are walking. It's in our DNA to strive, but not necessarily for the constructed reasoning of solely the third dimension; what we may perceive as accomplishment or 'better' is really the reflection of life asking for evolvement within us as we awaken. Watch any child pretending, playing by themselves or with others, and there is a glimpse of another world of being in the innocence of manifestational powers available to us as we are ready: a virtual playground of imagination raised up in the dust of our bodies, in all that we may feel, express, and experience more deeply. But how we allow ourselves to hear and see is the quality of life we come to know, even in the most uncomfortable or unpleasant circumstances.

Everything from where we live, the family we were born into, to the graffiti on the walls and the melodies that accompany moving lyrics, or the colors, textures and smells that permeate our senses are purposeful in design for our most fulfilling reality. Even on the surface of unwanted experiences that we may have, the emotions that come forward are meeting universal arrangement on our behalf, as a necessary part we have been longing to embrace. And even though we may feel alone at times, or that we are breaking, desperate, and that no one understands, life is listening, watching, and hears each groan that we utter.

Encoded in all things is the very essence of their nature: just as a tree never learns to become a tree, but simply does as it is, so too we gravitate towards that which we already are. And as we reach out in a myriad of ways to ground, everything cycles in culmination for us to open where we expand in recognition to the truth of who we are. Love works in coordination for, with, in, and alongside each of us unfolding every life for this greater expansion. And just as a tree is known by its trunk as a focal point for balance, the heart becomes our focal point, as every issue that arises only does so for our benefit; as we encourage, reassure, and nurture the heart, the vibrational field of each body adjusts for continued inspiration and evolvement. Once we begin to realize the magnitude of this process and our larger Self moving in conjunction with all that is mirrored in our sphere, fear slowly fades as we fall into the depths of our being; whatever circumstances may unfold for us as we are consciously introduced to our deepest desires, we awake to find they are exactly as we have asked for on an energetic level.

In ancient times, individuals of authority or power were depicted with wings and often glowed in their presence of being. But in the more modern world of witty inventions there is much to do in preparation for flight: we check our controls, fuel, and destination, then await to be cleared for take-off. Even so, in that moment of release when there is only the air under our wings, we revert to something primordial within us, a force of instinct profound in origin. Deep movements of overwhelming surety guide this connection, making it unbreakable in the force or energetic sense of who we are at the *core*. What many of us may experience as a newfound habitat in an extensive ground of uncertainty is where the fires of life are more fully engaged as they are called into being by faith.

Whether we believe we have chosen our life path or that it has been thrust upon us, the universe remembers each contract, plea, and reason in coming here. And although we may feel alone, many others walk in step beside us even if we may not currently see them. With every holding of the heart, compassion moves for our benefit, traversing universal currents with humility and innocence on our behalf. And eventually what we have known from the beginning reveals itself: as the path narrows, we instinctually surrender, judgements and opinions lose importance, and we are brought to the precipice of a new life arising from the ashes of the old; as the world we once knew collapses, an ever-unfolding universe expands, and by moving into it we find relief.

When we begin to become aware of our inward journey, the universe knows exactly how to proceed. Everything has been carefully orchestrated for our flight, our path unfolding with such intricate witness that we begin to sense a relationship with ourselves on many different levels: we see ourselves in others, synchronicity is commonplace, and we experience a feeling of safely being held by our larger self, even in the direst of circumstances. But what we undergo in transformation cannot be unearthed before we are ready, for in its secrets are the very soul of transformative power and the energies necessary for our shift. The movements of these energies connect consciousness on multiple levels in awareness, but they only do so when we face uncertain ground, where time is held in a sphere of potentiality awaiting each desire for its emergence in creative life force; the fears that are felt are the shadow side of each being and add the quality of intensity to each request that has come forth to be expressed in resolve.

What the birds of the air present as being so effortless and ubiquitous once may have seemed burdensome in the nature of their realm. Similarly, what at times may feel like useless appendages or aberrations in our life always have depth in meaning and will yield greater fulfillment when viewed along the evolutionary path. Although this does not come without cost, and the price may feel high, the sacrament of pain is often a rite of passage in each entrance to a new world; what we perceive as being impossible, irrational, and irregular in darkness is frequently the gateway to claiming responsibility for that which presents itself to us in potential. When we see the pain of humanity by feeling it first in ourselves, each unique path we experience holds tremendous power, and as we allow it to unfold, moving at a pace we have chosen, we find ourselves learning to navigate with the currents, utilizing them for lift rather than our former oppression.

We may be challenged in our beliefs as the very ground beneath us falls away from our feet, but this is only because that which has served us is complete, and we are entering a space of retrieval. The practice of abiding with our emotions in compassion allows entrance to a world beyond the governance of fear, into the 'self' of those we encounter that reflect our humanity. Even though we may feel despondent in a world of, "if only I had this or that then I would be content," as we acknowledge the despondency of what we feel, we offer the love necessary for resolve, which in turn opens the potential of becoming aware of how the universe works and coming to know each outer circumstance as the reflective nature of our inner qualities, those parts within that desire fulfillment, even those we are unaware of in depth. It may seem counterintuitive at times, but the feelings that are afflictive as human beings are only there to raise attention to those parts of ourselves that are in need. And like despondency, both anxiety and depression are not an indication that we have done something wrong, or that we are less than healthy, but rather signs of our highest nature at work in adjusting, shifting, and rebalancing reality on our behalf. The struggles we feel are merely those parts or vibrational strands pressing to be acknowledged in love, and as they do so, even though we may feel the uncertainty of our evolvement, there has already been a space created for expansion which is the paradoxical nature of how the universe works. So when we are challenged by thoughts of the environment we live in, or financial circumstances and the relationships we desire, the practice we focus on is not one based in outer circumstances, but in the feelings that surface as our truths are revealed while holding the heart in loving compassion. Our abundant nature will naturally step forward through this acknowledgment as emotional debris clear with the love that we offer as previously unloved parts begin to resolve, which allows for greater clarity to the manifestations of what we are both transmitting and receiving.

Previous questions such as, "what are we transmitting for these manifestations to appear?" "How are they relevant to what we desire?" and, "Can we approach life differently in revelation?" will begin to gain insightful traction. This is where spending quality time with ourselves becomes an apparent ongoing love practice in which we can offer ourselves the space necessary for rest, time to be with what we feel, and freedom to be ourselves *which is the very foundation for our spirit to thrive.*

It's very common though when we start to really get into the substance of our life path to feel overwhelmed by the reflective nature of these relationships. For many years, the ego has worked diligently at constructing an identity unique to each of us in order to help shield the nervous system so that we could immerse ourselves in the third dimension. But, when we move deeper into this design, we become aware of its existence as a form of protection, a necessary shell until we were ready to come to terms with reality on multiple levels dimensionally. This is where the practice of abiding with strong energies in love is needed, but with gentleness as we allow time for our nervous system to adapt from many years of shielding. The body, in all its wonderful wisdom, will work with us as a powerhouse of information through the emotional recordings of events past which are stored on a cellular level and reveal the desires we have come to resolve in their energies. Once we acknowledge the universe as a larger aspect of ourselves, we see how the love we offer is the most impactful action we can give in the development of trust for universal timing in this process. By granting ourselves permission to observe, abide, and act with compassion, we become a caretaker of our journey rather than a victim of circumstances, holding ourselves accountable in judgments and opinions about present and past relationships.

This in-depth intimacy sends an unmistakable message to the heart that we are ready to discover our roots and that any previous actions were not made with malicious intent, nor were they unforgivable sins of separation to our self or others, but rather pleadings of pain only attempting to fulfill unmet needs that have been crying out for love. Our soul has no other way to communicate these energies, other than to work with the universe in arranging circumstances vibrationally, subconsciously or consciously in life. So if we are craving attention and love, or want to be treated in a manner of respect, this might be the exact person, situation, or opposite we attract in reflection, either in how we have treated ourselves or how we desire to be loved in attentive care.

When we are challenged emotionally, these energies are one of the highest indications that we are ready for a shift in reality. What we view as our self or the reflections we see in others can be terribly difficult to process as we start to ask questions about who we are, the nature of our life path, and the meaning in our choices. Furthermore, the power in these energies is not to be underestimated: it is both purposeful in its nature as a vacuum allowing us to go deeper into the fulfillment of desires we have come to explore, express, and experience on Earth, as well as carrying us in the current of transformational resolve to the precipice of flight.

Often though, it is a very confusing time, and if we are unwilling or incapable of moving into the energies of these questions, we will find the ego provides a solution of grasping, which will interpret what arises however it can for stability, focusing on outer circumstances as a measured solution. But as beings of energy, light, and awakening divinity, temporal measures will not satisfy the inherent nature of questioning that arises; just as a seedling must break its shell and move through the darkness of the earth towards the warmth of the light, we too must come forth in our season. The universe works in such a way that whatever triggers us or shows up in our life is intentionally for this benefit, even in painful or afflictive circumstances. However, the provision of choice can be one of the most provocative feelings we face, especially if the ground we grasp is based in the security of illusion. Many of us wander through life asking the same or similar questions, hoping for answers and the guidance of something or someone who will gift us with the insight into the choices that will best meet our desires. And although we are vibrationally entwined with our incarnation of experiencing a life in human form, we are consistently reminded that it is fleeting in comparison to eternity.

In part, our lack of remembrance to who we are has purpose in that we might be fully immersed in experience for integration as humans, but often we become so involved with our choices that we overwrite the value we have in them, our focus being solely on outcomes rather than how we feel as we choose them. The mind will add to our confusion by attempting to reason out a solution and strive for a logical deduction of circumstances until exhausted. Meanwhile, we sink deeper into every energy of transformative power until we are ripe for vibrational shifting; what we frequently approach in unawareness is the awakening of awareness as we proceed. Likewise, we live in a universe full of evolvement where consciousness is in experience or some part of deep integration, and as each life path fulfills its contracts it comes to know itself as an integral part of destiny. But the relief sought by so many will only appear as the heart is held in compassion, where fears, ache, and pain are met as allies in awakening an intuitive, meaningful, deepened relationship with ourselves, each design, and what we desire; the one misconception we have as humans is that life is static, but really it is dynamic, vibrant, and abundantly creative. When perception expands for loss to also be seen as the creation of space, dimensionally one reality fades but another becomes apparent. And how we choose to receive any expansion is based on the love we offer to the one in experience.

If we were to imagine walking up steps into a great hall, similar to an enormous library, where every human event, word, thought, intent, feeling or otherwise occurring in the past, present, or future is recorded, and sitting down with an ascended master as counsel to open a 'book of choices', the conversation might go something like this:

"IN ORDER TO PROCESS YOUR REQUEST, THERE ARE SOME VITAL QUESTIONS TO CONSIDER BEFORE WE PROCEED. THEY ARE STRUCTURED IN SUCH A WAY THAT YOU MAY KNOW ENERGETICALLY WHAT YOU ARE READY FOR. PLEASE FILL OUT THIS FORM:"

1) ARE YOU DESIROUS TO MOVE INTO THE DEPTHS OF EACH CHOICE REGARDLESS OF THE OUTCOMES THAT MAY HAVE, ARE, OR WILL OCCUR?

2) ARE YOU READY TO RECEIVE INSIGHTS THAT WILL POTENTIALLY SHIFT EVERYTHING: HOW LIFE IS EXPERIENCED, WHAT YOU BELIEVE, AND THE VERY FABRIC OF REALITY?

3) ARE YOU CAPABLE OF EMBRACING TRUTH AS IT PRESENTS ITSELF, EVEN THOUGH IT MAY LEAD TO EXTREME DISCOMFORT, PAIN, AND A COMPLETE UNRAVELING OF IDENTITY?

IF YOU HAVE ANSWERED NO TO THE ABOVE QUESTIONS, PLEASE PROCEED NO FURTHER. THE UNIVERSE WILL CONTACT YOU WHEN IT IS TIME, AS YOU ARE READY. BUT IF YOU HAVE ANSWERED YES, AND FEEL THAT THE TIME HAS COME TO ACKNOWLEDGE THAT WHICH HAS BEEN ASKING TO BE HEARD, HERE IS WHAT YOU HAVE BEEN DESIRING:

The ascended master opens the book before you and reads its transmission:

"The universe is an energetic construct made by you, the Divine One. You may not remember, because you chose to allow yourself to forget for this journey. But you desired to contract this incarnation willingly, not only for your benefit, but for the benefit of all beings. The choices you are in deep thought about run below the surface of your circumstances, and each pulse of the nervous system, even your cellular memory into the vibrational frequency of who you are, which is precisely why they feel so difficult.

What you choose is merely the outcome of every potential timeline you have ever felt or contemplated in your deepest desires, and is only waiting for an exploration of it as you are ready. Each moment is a culmination of your vibration working in conjunction with the universe to bring about a fulfillment of reality, and as you feel into and integrate each experience, the intimate relationship you are forming with you is the choice you are looking for. This is the choice that you desire above all others, and it is the opening of all expansion in divine nature. Every other choice you are pondering or possibly agonizing over is leading you to this choice, the one of giving yourself all the love that you long for regardless of what path you walk. As you embrace this choice you are emerging in awareness that universal energy is shifting to meet you in every unfolding moment and will open to you as a reflection of your innermost desires, manifested in each truth, both of those places dark and light within which reveal as they are heard, seen, and expressed in the uniqueness of love that you are."

As humans in journey on Earth, while we may continue to struggle with our choices, seeking some prognostication of what they may yield, ultimately once a choice has been activated we learn to surrender in trust to the universe, or not. Even though a choice may seem not to be held up in support, we ourselves are always held up in love as each life path unfolds. And although certain outcomes may seem better than others, the more powerful transformations occur in abiding what we feel in the choices themselves. Often, uncomfortable choices move us deeper into the layers of difficult places where uncertainty has had a need of resolve for years. When we become more familiar with the energy of each choice, darker aspects begin to surface in them, and we see beneath the surface into the governing vibrational patterns of them. By abiding with these energies and each place that calls out in need, we begin to see that the choices we have made are miniscule in comparison to the need they are consistently implying energetically for resolve. When we are open to these teachings, we also become aware of the enormous theft to the present moment or time spent in a confined perspective along linear lines in an attempt to decipher our choices.

As an example, imagine yourself as tree, being told as a small seedling, "You will someday stand a hundred feet in the air, with branches providing places of rest for various birds and animals, shade for those under your canopy, your trunk large and round, virtually immovable by all but a few creatures or elements on Earth, where roots stretch deep into the recesses of the ground holding firm your mighty girth." It might be rather consuming if we were to learn of what we are from a point of view with such magnitude. And if we were to observe ourselves consistently looking towards this future, we might become obsessively focused and find ourselves driveling away the necessary energy for growth. Sometimes the simplest path, event, and state we struggle in acquiescing to is the one that pervades over us manifesting our future. It is the here and now which provides the wealth of needs for our continuing evolvement and expansion, and although often unsophisticated, it is the seemingly irrelevant places of discovery which open us to a new world full of possibilities. There are certain tones of life we tend to be born into that many times are purposefully beyond comprehension until they are ready to be fulfilled. However, as we maintain daily practices that serve in offering love to the heart, not only will we find relief, but our vision will expand naturally, whereas even if we are resistant to believe what we see, what we experience is given the opportunity to integrate vibrationally. Just as that which becomes the mighty tree carries with it all the source code and faith necessary for its eventual fulfillment, our eventual unfolding is pre-determined as divine beings.

In any relationship, it is common to look back in review, pondering how we felt, what we might have done differently, or even the desires we have for each future, but as we evolve, this reflection will expand to reveal the higher nature of our connection dimensionally as beings of design, our design, and those we have signed soul contracts with to manifest in mutual benefit. With no designation between the lines of 'good' or 'bad', but simply receiving energies as allies in forging a deeper relationship with the soul, we realize that without people, events, and circumstances unfolding as they have, we would be incomplete. This brings us to the gates of mass consciousness, where we may find comfort in the one who is always in acknowledgment and will pause in reflection, providing an opportunity of support where we may move deeper into the nature of each relationship with the soul. Universal forces always work in conjunction with circumstances in assessing vibrational needs, so regardless of where we are at in evolutionary process, the energy itself communicates with collective awareness.

The precious time we share with ourselves or those we have chosen for our investment are colleagues within the scope of love. And as we learn about ourselves, the body we are in with all its intricate workings, and the circumstances of each life path, we discover a web of infinite interdependence much more than three-dimensional origins in design. With each interaction we come to realize the purposeful space of all life and the importance of abiding in the simplicity of experience— where we hold the one asking to be held in love as desired. So as we abide with both the darkness and the shine of life, we come to our godhead in all its various forms, circumstances, and beliefs, receiving the fullness of design as intended by innocence. In layman's terms, we feel what we feel, experience what we experience, and abide with all of it in the simplicity of the heart, acknowledging where we have been, where we are, and where we are going as the one we already are in the light of loving compassion. We are they who are honoring the one coming forth in us, however that one chooses to appear, in benefit of all beings.

∞ In Conclusion ∞

A while back we were camping at Denby Point campground in Arkansas after a fresh rain, and the sun came out for a spectacular sunset. I was walking around in shorts, a pleasant 74 degrees, my sandals a bit wet, clothes slightly damp, but very much enjoying the time in nature. My adventure partner was making some soup, I had just finished rewiring our electrical hookup to the camper, and I decided to walk down to the lake to receive some fresh air. This might sound very peaceful, and it was, except for the disconcerting noise that continued while I was on my walk for the next couple of hours. It was very barely audible, almost like a wheezing, and I would stop every now and then in an attempt to pinpoint the source with no luck.

Some things just tend to wear on you, as if there is no resolution, and might just send the day into such a frenzy of irritation that life loses all sense of stability. With this sound it was certainly the case, and I just had to figure it out. My mind tried very hard to reason what it could be, "maybe an animal, or person in distress in the distance? Or maybe it's me having an unusual health issue? Could it possibly be some sort of weird mechanical device at the park not readily seen?" Then there's always the thought of the odd place or two of conspiracy like, "I'm picking up static transmissions from the government or aliens..."

Every time I would stop to give a bit closer ear, it would abruptly stop with me, and it was gone. After several periods of this process, I finally became exhausted mentally and surrendered, abiding in acceptance with the wheezing while walking, simply observing, and feeling its peculiarity in moving with me. Surrender has a mysterious way of working with what we feel, and it creates the opportunity for compassion: to be with the one experiencing irritation, uncomfortable sensation, and flavors of life we might normally move away from. It creates an opening to simplify what we may view as complex or not understandable, and allows the seeing of truths that may have been incredibly overwhelming otherwise— kind of like my peculiar sound that seemed to elude me throughout the day. I had envisioned it as everything from "I'm dying," to "aliens are in my brain," but when the truth was revealed it was so very funny I burst out laughing, and could barely tell my partner who lost it too.

It was my sandals.

Yes. The perplexing sound that sent me in so many different directions was the wheeze of wet sandals as I walked.

So maybe it's not so important that we discover every piece of the puzzle to our irritation, fears, or disconcerting circumstances, because most likely it isn't the large things or prized developments we think of, but merely the soles of our feet walking along the path. And with a little love, abiding, and tenderness, we may even find the greatest of challenges produce a smile from time to time, or an awkward burst of laughter to just how simple life really is.

By Our Design

Chapter 13

The Thirteen Love Practices

I: Survive

It may not sound like much in the form of a practice, but as we learn more about the energy systems of the human body and the interactions we have in reflection with the world, we come to know a deepening relationship with ourselves in the form of loving the one who made it here. Often the distress we experience in our life will crush, dishearten, and leave us frenzied in perplexity, where we will struggle to find any meaning or purpose in what we feel. Although we may be capable of leaning into universal arrangement as a truth, we only do so as we are able, our first priority being to survive. There will always be moments where we may listen, acknowledge, abide, and receive informational downloads, but sometimes the journey simply requires us to live through what we feel.

When the most painful, uncomfortable, and oppressing sensations engage us the heart can feel challenged, unloved, and ache as if it is breaking. Simply being with the heart in these times is one of the most profound actions of compassion we can offer. This may be an adjustment to our physical position, care in the form of rest, or stillness, but the nurturing hand of compassion provides love unparalleled in relief. Frequently distress is charged with currents of unresolved, overwhelming vibrational energy that must come to surface as a part of the human evolutionary process, and just by surviving them to some degree the body itself acknowledges and integrates these energies, which may not seem actionable on our part, but living through this process it is the most loving participation we can offer.

In the times we believe we are failing, frequently we are learning and gaining the experience necessary to move further into the acknowledgment, abiding, and integration necessary for our soul contracts to be fulfilled— even with distress or pain. When physical distress visits, once we have survived, we listen to what our body has to say, breathing into our circumstances and allowing it to share its most intricate workings through the holding of the heart, but *we never underestimate the value in simply surviving.* By honoring the one who made it here, who survived so many experiences, we offer compassion to life itself and revere the journey we have chosen as part of a greater cosmic force working in benefit of all beings.

II: Showing up

A few years back my partner and I camped for about a month with Burfir and Maggie, the parents of a large family that had chosen a nomadic lifestyle which consisted of homeschooling and a core set of values that reflected uniquely in each of their five children. One of the most prevalent practices they shared on a daily basis was whenever one of the family would "put themselves out there" (as the father Burfir would say), meaning, share some insight, wisdom, or express how they felt however the outcome, a comment was made, "you showed up." Watching the parents and children utilize this practice with each other in their distinctive personalities challenged each member of the family to embrace a higher dynamic vibrationally: competition was replaced by cooperation; disagreement or argument became an attempt at communitive resolve.

As we learn to be with ourselves, abiding with what may arise in energy, when an emphasis is placed on 'showing up', simply that we may with each breath and beating of the heart, we transmit a vibrational signature, distinctly offering the gift of who we are and what we have come to reveal— those parts that have eagerly incarnated to shine.

When we practice the acknowledgment of 'showing up' in ourselves or others, we create a space of safety for each of us to be vulnerable, effortlessly being who we are. And as we allow these energies to come forth in expression, we find fulfillment, even in times of deep resolve where emotions may feel afflictive, and these frequencies communicate purpose in manifesting.

When we celebrate 'showing up', we are being the best we can be in any moment, no matter the outcome, grateful to share this time as both a witness and a recording of gifts that have been purposed specifically for us to embrace in our unique human form.

May the humble phrase, "you showed up" be an inspiration, exploration, and expression of the love you already are, that burns brightly in you as nothing else can.

III: Rooting

"Rooting" is an ancient practice that can be found almost anywhere in the world to varying degrees, from sacred rituals to spiritual disciplines, as well as culturally, societally, and generationally passed down traditions in one form or another. Even in everyday activities, from work to play or family, rooting can be found: athletes commonly use rooting practices to prepare for a big game, or when centering to shoot a ball; fisherman root when their line is cast in the river, feeling for the perfect spot to drop the bait, and then giving just the amount of tension needed, sync with their surroundings awaiting the bite of a fish; mothers, when cooing a baby, sense the appropriate tones, movement, and amount of nurturing to offer their infant in love. Rooting is a purposeful connection to the realization of life and something greater than the details, but within them, where we receive support, centering, and affirmation of the balance flowing with all things.

Throughout the day many of us subconsciously return to the practice of rooting, often unaware of the connection taking place in various forms. It is an inherent, primordial instinct to ground, both in turbulent circumstances as well as in the calm of serenity. But in practices such as yoga, meditation, qi gong, and tai chi, the connection of rooting is consciously purposed by intent and is much more pronounced as a liberation from the accumulation of attachment, or the energetic debris of permanency the ego creates in order to stabilize an existence in the third dimension. Whether we utilize any of the before mentioned practices, or develop our own sense of connection in rooting, regardless of where we are at in our circumstances, rooting will provide a ground of discovery to the deepening nature in relationship with the self, who we are, and the integration of experiences we have come to embrace.

Some days we may awaken with a long to-do list of things in our head or on paper, where we may feel a disconnect to the body and spirit, which often may haunt the mind and emotions with a query as to the purpose or meaning of the life we are living. For stability, the ego will place the value of self-worth on what may be accomplished through productivity, rather than who we are in being. Nevertheless, our true divine nature is love, and as we are ready to move deeper into what we feel, rooting will support the life we've come to live, its purpose, and the liberation of self to a much larger reality of who we are in expansion. When we create space for intentional rooting, we open ourselves to the cosmic mystery of standing firm yet flexible in each circumstance, consciously trusting love as the source of our ground.

IV: Embracing the Sacred

The Native American people at Three Rivers in New Mexico left no massive monuments of their civilization, no written record, and little evidence of existence other than the petroglyphs upon the rocks near the remains of a few simple dwellings of their small community. There are archeological findings that many families buried the dead in the floors of the places where they lived, perhaps to keep them close and draw upon ancestral energies, or maybe as a simple reminder to the spark each life holds which in time transcends all boundaries of earthly perception. But as you stand where they stood, walking paths they once walked, and touch the pictures they left, you find yourself immersed in the sacred, where a profound sense of self arises in acknowledgement to the preciousness of life.

Sitting on one of the small hills in an area filled with petroglyphs, looking out on the once fertile valley, there is an ease that comes over the soul of a time when life may have been more difficult, but carried with it a deep sense of connection in knowing the land, each other, and the sacred in everything. The petroglyphs contain carvings of wildlife, masks, handprints, sunbursts, and geometric designs suggesting a revered expression in relationship with life, one in which the abstract and the tangible met in form upon the rocks. Although today we may find ourselves surrounded with technology or the busyness of life, moving at a speed where we often may lose any sense of self, when we grant the space necessary for receiving the sacred, we soon discover the sacred emerging; even in the most troubling of circumstances, if we allow the sacred to come forth, we will feel a part of ourselves deep inside reflecting this acknowledgement, empathizing, and revering ancestry for all beings universally where we see something more than the mere passing of time.

The practice of "embracing the sacred" in the reality we know may be challenging, which is often why visiting sacred places can help in support by the energies they naturally provide, where a deep connection can develop in opening a different relationship with the world. That said, we may intentionally move into the sacred on a daily basis, perhaps with a simple ritual, offering, or acknowledgement of what we hold dear to our heart. Like the thousands of testimonials etched in rock at Three Rivers from a people long ago, who left small, seemingly unsubstantial traces of animals, forms, and feelings, we too carve out moments in time with energy signatures or expressions that are felt in the absence of our human vessel. When we allow ourselves to connect on this level in communion with life and honor the relationships that are inherently a part of who we are, we observe the interdependence of all beings in the experience we have come to receive.

V: Developing support

In tribal society, the love, intimacy, and safety that is naturally shared from being a part of a community has proven to increase health, happiness, wellness, and a higher sense of purpose in living. One of the key elements in any support system is in the fellowship of familiar empathetic identification. Whether we realize this process or not, from an early age our family or those of our immediate environment become our first bonding agents in familiarity, until eventually we begin to expand based on friendships, social status, and groups of similar need or interest. But in each circumstance, empathizing with other human beings is essential for spiritual growth and reveals an inherent wellness emerging from connection. This not only allows furthering a relationship with the self, but as we are energetically ready opens a dialogue with the universe or greater self on fourth- and fifth-dimensional levels, increasing awareness of the potential in who we are. It is common for questioning to arise as a part of this process, where often we will turn to our tribe in reflection: *regardless of where we are at in our journey, if we utilize emotional identification rather than intellectual stimulation, we feel a sense of support from any community we find ourselves in.*

However, this doesn't mean we must stay in our current situation, but rather as we offer the love being asked for in resolve, our confidence, inspiration, and vision grow where we may try different tribes that better support our expansion. Initially the field we have incarnated into is always the one most suitable in reflective power for activation of unresolved energies, but as we evolve, so does our support system. And those we intentionally gather with support this evolution, opening their energy field interdependently, working with us much like cornstalks growing in a field full of corn; we begin to realize the necessity for naturally leaning on each other in high winds, but ultimately each of us is responsible for our own energy

212

instead of becoming solely reliant upon others, and we learn to ground in a system of growing in and amongst them for mutual benefit.

Although we may change our tribe multiple times throughout life, from family to friends, groups, or even career relationships, listening to our needs as we evolve is paramount in seeing the opportunities that present themselves to us. Exploring how we feel in our tribe can be difficult (as the ego does an excellent job in protection, or assuring we are energetically ready), but many of us have found when we are inspired to venture forth from familiarity or comfort a reality has already been constructed and is awaiting our arrival in support. And as we grow in the love we have been offering, divinity also grows our tribe in expansion, where we will want to connect on deeper levels energetically in experience. The tribe that will support our evolutionary path is the one listening to our needs as we feel them, where holding the heart becomes a communal action benefiting those being held, as well as those offering support.

VI: Slowing down

Sometimes we may find ourselves moving through life on autopilot, with set schedules of work, play, and sleep that leave little to no room for the heart to explore what the universe offers. Or we can become so involved with making progress that we lose any sense of self to the line and order of goal-oriented thinking. With either, when the pressure builds, increasing in pain, often we too will increase our stride, moving faster in an attempt to overcome distress. While this may provide a brief respite in fortitude for better production and keep us on schedule, the realization soon arises that this pace is unsustainable to healthy living. Eventually if unheeded, the nervous system will become overwhelmed as energies course through it, and with the body unable to process what is felt, physical, emotional, or mental collapse becomes imminent; but in our distress we come to know that part of us that is coming forward to be acknowledged.

Slowing down is a profound step into a much larger world of abundance, clarity, wellbeing, and fulfilled living. Although when we do so it may feel in opposition to our goals, resisted, or impractical, paradoxically our desires are met at a much faster pace. By giving ourselves the space and time to engage this moment, we immerse ourselves more fully in it, where the experiential energies wash over us in manifestational potential. This allows us to connect with the flow of life in an expanding space of awareness and to move with the resources available for fulfillment, rather than working against them. The simple act of focusing on the breath, placing our hand upon the heart, and acknowledging what arises in our energetic field will calm the nervous system, ground us, and help to align the body with what the soul is asking for in love.

The difference in experience when slowing down is one of intimacy, integration, and love of life, rather than meeting deadlines solely based on productivity for wellbeing. It is very much like a person traveling on a train from destination to destination, seeing the wonderful sights, but they pass by so quickly that although arriving at their destination, what transpired was contained to the train car. Whereas if someone were to drive, walk, and stop along the way, experience is deepened, places of interest may be explored, and an intimate relationship with life is created. This doesn't mean we will not arrive at our destination, only that a more fulfilling reality will occur in what we experience, rather than the one whizzing by in passing. Even though we may feel we should, could, or would be doing better with a more productive use of our time, what we might ask ourselves is how we want to live, what we desire to feel, and how we may open the door to resolution when we feel life is passing us by. What are the relationships like in our life, and in turn, what is our relationship like with our self? When we open ourselves to the practice of slowing down, we give permission for the space and time we have been asking for, offering love to the one that is simply being in this moment.

VII: Building bridges

Sometimes we give an accounting to ourselves for what we have been offering to humanity: those things we will leave in the ripple of our wake, as well as how we have treated others and our self in journey. We may view the relationships we have built with some comfort, and those we have destroyed with scorn, but in reviewing our life path with compassion what we will discover is that in every interaction not only did an opportunity arise for our uniqueness to step forward, but the vibrational essence of who we are that unfolded did so as necessary for what we desire to be made manifest. In other words, without our reactions and responses we would never come to know those places within us that are asking for manifestation, that desire the light to become apparent. We may not understand the reflections that appear, but as we begin to embrace each relationship with a certain sense of ambiguity, we allow expansion itself to reveal our integrity, innocence, and love that frees the heart to follow its bliss; building bridges is a practice in being filled with surprise and wonder, where other points of view may be seen as manifestational qualities of intricate interdependent energy, working with each other multi-dimensionally for resolve.

In a sense, everything we contribute to is for the betterment of humanity, even in paths of destructive force, but how we view each life path (including our own) is essential to the relief we receive from the choices we or others have made or are making. Life is a living stream of engagement, where each vibrational thread moves as it feels necessary to best serve the trinity of finite, infinite, and whole of creation. As egoic constructs fall away by the embracing of the heart, bridge building becomes a practice in energetic awareness or the self-realization of a partnership in relation to the universe, that both mirrors those places in need, and those parts that feel safe enough to express themselves. It is a shift in how we perceive the world that honors each choice as being the one most beneficial for everyone, even in disagreement, chaos, and painful circumstances. When we move into building bridges, we choose the way of surrender, empathy, and compassion for our feet, offering a substantial high ground to walk on that our soul has been asking for and desires to share with others in relief.

VIII: Tea Ceremony

When we are entering into a state of deep resolve, often we will be unaware of it, and feelings of anxiety, frustration, depression, or ache can be frequent guests in the home. We may try to act, look, and be "normal," but normal will feel elusive. Daily practices we have grounded in might seem automated, and comfort from friends can sound like an altogether different language, one so foreign in connection that we may wonder who they or we are. When every attempt to do something positive or pick up the pieces only yields further despair and we experience a sense of drowning, unable to consider our self, let alone others, the proposition of being abandoned by God is a fear beyond any reasonable fear. It is in these moments when nothing hears us or responds to our pleas that the nothing or emptiness felt is misunderstood as abandonment, and we will seek an alternative for a friend.

Attempting to fill the void in this weight of wanting produces an accumulation which can come in many forms: from the physical, mental, and emotional debris of the body to the outer circumstances of what we grasp for in our surroundings. Frequently this cycle will repeat throughout each life path until we are ripe for awakening, and the potent energies reveal themselves as our guide to inner transformation. Once we are ready, the resolve of accumulation becomes apparent in what we feel.

When in deep resolve, we may feel like we are dying, which is often why suicide becomes a consideration in the pain. Existence may be so grey in the condemnation of the mind that a purgatory of wandering becomes our reality, where thoughts jest at the cosmic joke of cruelty in what we feel. But in this space, there will arise an uncanny realization that even in suffering, it is all too perfect. This light of realization is so intense that there will be no doubt that

216

something has us in its grips, so much so that there is no escape, no place to hide nor appeasement to our circumstances— not even death.

In this darkness we will begin to receive a list of visitors along with the abandonment of what we feel to complete the malady: loneliness, unworthiness, betrayal, and rejection arrive as shadows, uninvited guests so they seem. They can appear as life events, sickness, or in relationships unique to each of us, and all of them trigger some part within. How we respond while feeling these energies can either distance us from the heart or provide an opportunity to deepen intimacy in relationship with our soul. When they come, we may relieve the oppression that often accompanies them by offering space, acknowledging their presence, and holding our heart in compassion. For me, one of the most effectual practices of love was to utilize the imagination, picturing each of them as old black and white horror monsters of the cinema: Frankenstein's monster, the Creature from the Black Lagoon, the Wolf Man, boogeymen, and vampires from the abyss knocking on my door, and I would invite them in for tea.

The practice of this "tea ceremony" grants the space for familiar feelings of affliction to be heard, held, and embraced that for much of life many of us live with in an unresolved state, or repeating cycles of pain. One by one as I pictured what was felt, they would come to sit at the kitchen table in my offering of tea, their subtle mood of nightmarish, stoned-faced glares staring at me from across the table. This would always give way after a time, maybe because they were black and white, or most of their character was based in movement rather than sound, but it allowed me to be with them in a way that wasn't too overwhelming to the nervous system. And even though these apparitions were scary to me as a child, in this context they just didn't seem to be that horrific. Usually, they visited me in the early hours of the morning —a bit inconvenient— but when they arrived, I would invite them in for tea, welcoming them, saying, "Hello friends, come for another visit?" Sometimes with tears in my eyes, or with a hesitant reluctance in my voice, but always with a surrender in love for my heart, and the necessity to feel what was being felt for resolve.

Each in turn was pictured entering through my front door, coming into the kitchen, and sitting down at the table for tea: Confusion seemed to fit the character of the Wolf Man nicely, Loss was a vampirism quality, and Pain went well in the longing which always seemed to accompany Boris Karloff's face as he portrayed Frankenstein's monster. Space was made for them in my home as they felt compelled to visit, but none of them ever drank the tea offered, and sometimes they would bring other uninvited guests which were assigned attributes. After a time of abiding with them though, eventually one by one they would stand up, walk towards the door, and leave. Maybe I had made them feel so welcomed that they decided they had better things to do, but frequently I would see an awkwardness in their faces or sense some uncomfortable feelings about staying to long where love was offered, and I would say my goodbyes politely. "If you guys really have to go, ok, but you're welcome to stay as long as you like." So with a slight grin, I thanked them for coming and for the visit while walking them to the door. The look on their face was priceless in this process, mostly blank as if they couldn't figure out how this had happened.

These are the places we must go if we are to ascend, the places where we are shattered, where we cannot pick up the pieces, which are purposely made for us in order that the love we are may be offered. Although ascension is an elevation to high vibration, we find *that* vibration in the depths, where we come to know ourselves, our substance, and learn to love as the essence of who we are, emerges. If "normal" eludes us, we are indeed ready to receive the love that we are. And when we allow the light of the universe to shine on those parts that are in need, the ones that feel out of place, abnormal, and unacknowledged in their role, we come to know them intimately, holding them as we hold the heart, telling them, "Even though it may not feel like it, relief is coming, all is well, and it will all work out. I'll make tea."

IX: Finding value in the voices of failure

Some of the most difficult emotions to process are the ones where we feel the ache that may arise as we view our circumstances with a sense of failure. At times we may feel so overwhelmed in the loss that is felt that we can become completely incapacitated. Although this may seem to work against us, these energies that overwhelm are a part of a greater restructuring vibrationally in fifth-dimensional potentials of awareness and allow us a pause for integration which leads to expansion. When we experience a sense of failure, it is nothing more than the people, events, hopes, dreams, and circumstances of our life path come to call on those parts within us that are asking to be recognized in value; any part of us that has endured the weight of measurement judged by success is only desirous of relief— that no matter what the outcome of any circumstance, we will be loved beyond them.

We find value in the voices of failure by acknowledging those parts that may have silently suffered in a perception based on an underlying tone of success, that without which we were somehow incomplete, unworthy, and rejected. When offering attention in the form of compassion to these energies, we establish a practice of nurturing care to the heart that has felt unworthy in each measurement. When ready, we move into this practice by learning to love ourselves where we are at: loving the one who is overwhelmed, who may feel loss in their sense of worth, or self-esteem, and by presenting support to a point of view which sees all things as purposeful, especially those which move us into a deeper intimacy with the soul.

As we are ready, we will hear the voices of failure as valued messengers of the soul whose only desire is to be loved. We do this by befriending them in conversation, listening to what they are sharing with us emotionally and energetically rather than logically on the surface. We ask ourselves, "How can this serve me? What is arising to be heard?" and, "How may I love the one in experience while feeling what is felt for resolve?" If we continue to feel failure

219

or perceive circumstances as failed life paths, it only means we have not found the value in what we have endured as failure and will do so once love is offered in abiding with whatever we need for our process. This is a principal teaching for the one which has come here to unravel the greater potential of what an eternal life path may unfold or has felt previously limited in vibrational expansion. By finding the value in our voices we hear ourselves as beings of expressional vibration, exploration, and resolve, benefiting multiple dimensions of reality, which await with eagerness the fulfilment we have come to offer in love.

X: Learning our language

Many of us carry the burden of doubt throughout the day— it reveals itself in the tones of our voice, how we interact with others, and in the reflections that materialize. But one of the most common threads we will begin to notice is through the habitual patterns that manifest in the conversation we consistently have on vibrational terms. Just as we may have learned a language in the environment we were raised, with certain customs, behaviors, and nuances, so too we receive a communication differential in how we treat ourselves based on the conversations we hear or have inherited. For example, if our ancestors frequently suffered from a point of view as being "less than" in reference to social class, "less than" vibrationally travels from one generation to the next until resolved. This may not be apparent in our awareness for some time on our life path, but our heart, soul, and body are always aware of it. And after some time of living with a certain amount of reference to our incarnation, we begin to feel the effects of how we have been living along our life path. For some people, this may be incredibly sound with a feeling of fulfilment and an internal recognition that leaves little room for doubt; most of the human race suffers, though, with a feeling of deep loneliness, either in undertone or on the surface, striving for contentment, purpose, acknowledgment, and love. The universe responds to this in turn by manifesting events, people, places, and circumstances to provide opportunities for us to address what we are feeling in whatever life path we are living.

One of the ways that may either provide support or relief in any life path we are on is by first observing the conversations we have been having, with the intention being both to hold space for how we feel in the words themselves or the worlds from which they transpire. This often draws our attention internally to places of self-doubt where we will begin to notice a direct correlation between what arises and the amount of faith we live by in the life path we are walking. Knowing the direct circumstances three-dimensionally in our past is not as important as addressing these energies in acknowledgement and abiding with loving compassion. As we do so, we open ourselves to resolve by learning the language of the heart, soul, and body, where we can begin to offer any places in need a simple statement of loving support for our journey. This statement may sound something like, "I Am here for you, through all that you feel, whatever doubts you may have, I Love You. I will not abandon or reject you but will encourage you in any choice you choose. I Am learning the language of the heart, soul, and body, and I have faith that everything that has happened, or will happen, is both for my benefit and the benefit of all beings. Even though at times I may doubt, I Am learning to hear doubt as a messenger of faith, a teacher of my vibrational needs. I Am here with you, for you, in all that unfolds. I Love You."

As the heart becomes accustomed to hearing this conversation, the body will also respond by providing a sense of relief, and the soul will begin to shift reality to a more faith-centered vibration. All three begin to know on a deep level what the mind may not comprehend, and with a childlike innocence they encourage us to believe that it will all work out, it's going to be ok, that our highest destiny is unfolding. Within all of us is an unabridged, unbroken, valid connection to faith, where a love beyond our understanding works tirelessly to release any burden of doubt. But we must first embrace the language we are learning with loving acknowledgement to breach what we perceive as any communication gap, and as we do so, we discover an unwritten language in connection with all things, where love, faith, and fulfilment reside in resolve.

XI: Mind, No Mind

The mind loves a great puzzle, so much so that even when there isn't something to be solved, often it still does its best to figure things out. Paradoxically we live in a universe where everything is perfect down to the smallest of details, with each moment working in synergy with creative force for continuity. So we may ask ourselves, "Why the mind? If everything is in order, perfect in its arrangement, what purpose would the mind have in such a universe?"

Interestingly enough though, like many things in the universe, the mind does not exist to itself, although sometimes we may like to think so. If we were to look at the brain as computer, the mind is like the software, receiving sensory input from the body, storing information, and managing data much like our PC software— only incredibly more powerful. The body similarly, like the mind does not exist to itself and is a part of its environment, functioning in accordance with its surroundings. And our surroundings (the earth, moon, sun and solar system) are a part of a much larger universe working in coordination with it also. Does this mean we are slaved to a much larger system of life with no free will of our own? Well, that might be one way of viewing things, but another is to perceive life as dynamic flow of creative informational energies, working in partnership with our soul as a manifestational beacon of awareness, both unraveling unawaken parts and restoring connection for our benefit with the mind as a partner to a much larger consciousness of being.

As we come to know our body, mind, and emotions, we are opened to a much more substantial experience, one where existence is not limited to the third dimension. This dimensional expansion comes at a cost though, in that eventually old egoic patterns of protection must be integrated in order for us to receive the vast amount of data being transmitted for downloading. If we continue with the PC/software analogy, older computers required much more room, and the software was capable of doing a tiny fraction of the calculations that a cell phone can do today. In other words, our previous finite experience, which required much more energy, a larger sphere of operation, and was limited in calculation, has the potential to be upgraded, utilizing less energy with a smaller room in functionality but an infinite potential dimensionally. Where the mind comes into this is in our belief systems, or software, and the PC components for processing.

Wherever we may find ourselves at in our journey, *daily meditation* will support this process. It is one of the most valued components in relieving the mind of "non-essential programs" for receiving an alignment with what we are ready for in our experience. And although the mind may continue to step forward saying, "Let me help you with that— all those feelings you're feeling, don't you see how uncomfortable that is? I can figure it out for you," as we abide with loving compassion through what we feel, slowing down and focusing on the breath, receiving the void of uncertainty for room, our heart will acknowledge the love that is being offered, which in turn will create an adjustment to our vibrational field. The universe responds to this by adjusting our reflections, which allows us to explore into the depths of our desires manifestationally. This opening to a larger observation in perception is the liberation or unraveling of those parts in our vibrational thread that the soul has desired to resolve, whether in the exploration, healing, or inspiration we have longed to express.

XII: Embracing Death

In Tibetan Buddhism there is a practice of being with death, or rather the uncomfortable feelings that arise when abiding among where the deceased lie. In certain places the ground in Tibet is so rocky that it's very hard to penetrate, so when someone would die, their body would be chopped up into pieces and laid out upon a cemetery of rocks for the birds to come feast in "sky burial" fashion. As you can imagine, this is a ghastly sight, and one very difficult to process, where former loved one's bodily remains are scattered across a barren rocky mound becoming food for the fouls of the air. Being with death in this manner leaves no room for doubt as to what awaits the body, and it is intended as a practice specifically for abiding with difficult feelings or acknowledging the impermanence of the body.

In the West, we tend to avoid the uncomfortable energies that are felt when we see sickness, old age, instability, and death. We desire to overcome, fight, and master the physical as an obstacle to be dominated instead of a friend in journey with us. When we experience the difficult feelings associated with impermanence, the point of this practice is to abide with the strong energies that arise as a part of our development in loving compassion, which will support us when we embrace egoic death. The nature of uncomfortable energies in our body helps with this process to prepare us for what might feel like an actual physical death as the ego begins to die. Often in our current culture, if we are unaware of what is happening and have suffered for some time with depression, anxiety, or chronic pain, we may struggle to see and be with this process of support that exists in transformation, and thoughts of suicide become common. In many tribal or indigenous cultures, there would be a mythos or ritual to support the individual as they approached this nexus. The old patterns of energy would be rallied as transformational power into the new, guided by the insights and wisdom of the elders. Although our current society may seem bleak comparatively in this type of support, as always, everything is purposeful in circumstance, even in what we might label as ignorance. The relationships we have are working in coordination with the universe to grant us the most effective use of our time embodied here. And the emotions that are a bridge between our awareness and the circumstances that unfold in our reality work with the soul to reveal what we have come to adjust, resolve, or express as a part of our pilgrimage here.

But if we are among those receiving initiation in abiding with strong energies, we begin to recognize the application of this practice when egoic patterns begin to die. We need not fear death or our coming forth as divine beings, and what the world will look like as we ascend, because the love offered through this process is the one component that has permanence as we transform.

Sometimes this may feel like we are living two lives, one that has interactions in relationships of all sorts with family, friends, driving to work, employers, eating, paying bills, and such, the other immersed in dreams, meditation, and observing the space between "you" and "me" where consciousness expands and contracts in awareness. For years we may observe these two different realms of existence with a sort of wonderment, being carried away in imagination as to what life really means. There will be moments of preponderance where we feel our circumstances are only necessary steps in a much wider vision, yet the ego will quickly move to reorganize any thoughts which may cause confusion. And as we carry unrecognized or unacknowledged feelings in undertone for longer and longer periods, they may feel like a small pebble might when it affects our walk in a shoe, only not troublesome enough to stop and investigate. But once a door has been opened within us for the potentials that exist beyond the third dimension, often through trauma, pain, or discomfort of some sort, we are met with an ongoing obligation to the soul in receiving what arises for our inward journey. When this happens, the nervous system may become overstimulated and overwhelmed, and we will grasp to anything familiar as old patterns, behaviors, or insecurities become inflamed. Life will feel like something has released a whirlwind and placed us on a rollercoaster without consent, where in our over-stimulation we will want to escape, considering almost anything to stop the ride. When we are in these moments, spending time with ourselves is essential, being alone with the heart if needed, relaxing into the body, and breathing compassion into the feelings of what arises. We welcome support, but only in the context of loving compassion, without restraint to what we are feeling as it allows emotional debris to clear, working in transformative power as necessary. Once our ego begins to die, life in physical form may feel like we are dying also. The walls of the world we live in will begin to fall like scales from our eyes, and the illusions we once fought to maintain will slip away even if we grasp onto them. Awakening, transformation, and becoming aware that we are aware of our process can be both exhilarating and frightfully painful as we embrace what is happening— but love will never fail to see us through, even in what may seem like the direst of circumstances.

By developing a practice of embracing death, we nurture both the vessel and the spirit through all that we might feel in potent energies of transformation. This can be difficult in practice, so we remember to be gentle with ourselves and that our vibrational field is literally shifting to align us with what we most deeply desire in the fullness of who we are. As the ego unravels, we open our arms to embrace the one coming forth in us, allowing space for reflection, however that one may appear.

For purposes of this practice, we will utilize our imagination (rather than viewing the spectacle of a graveyard as described above) to proceed in shamanic journey. As we have chosen to incarnate in a life path where mortality looms in some future for us, one of the elegant ways we may embrace our current life circumstances is to befriend our physical end. This paradoxical practice in guided meditative journey is a wonderful introspection into these moments where, as we abide with the body in death, we gain insight to the love we are capable of offering in life; as we learn to sit with the setting of life, just as the sun warms the body giving contentment to the heart in the lit hours of the day, when night comes, with all its hues upon the sky, we may embrace the contrast with our presence. Although this may seem difficult in comprehension to our physical reality, who we are as eternal love does not fade even though day and night come. By learning to abide with the strong energies of transition we allow ourselves to fully embrace awareness in relation to our mortality (as a reminder for this practice, thoughts are only utilized as a guiding tool to our feelings, once we are present with what we feel, we simply allow ourselves to be with what arises while holding the heart).

For this practice, when we are ready, we find a quiet place where we may be, nature being optimum in setting if we have access, sitting under a tree, or in a field where we may be with the body. If we can lie down comfortably we do so, as this will help us to relax more fully in our engagement of what we feel for this particular journey.

We begin by settling into our breathing, filling our lungs from the belly first then allowing the chest to rise, and exhaling in reverse. This may feel like a slow wave of water bringing in the tide, and back out to sea. If we are in nature during this meditation, this only adds to our experience as the earth naturally rebalances energies by its magnetic field. We continue by simply focusing on the breath and allowing ourselves to be in the body, relaxing any tense parts that we feel. We notice the colors, smells, and sounds of the earth, gently reminding ourselves that it's ok, trusting in the love that we are as we gently hold the heart. We feel ourselves breathing, being immersed in the field, or under the tree, and observe the sky briefly before closing our eyes.

We imagine passing through death, and how we would like our corpse treated: would we like it washed, held, our hair combed, to be viewed by others?

How would we like the physical remains cared for as they decompose?

Would we like to be buried in the earth? In a mausoleum? Set afire? Or maybe placed on a pier under the sky?

We imagine what we would like, and we allow ourselves to be with that experience, remembering that this is our vessel and it has served us well on our journey.

After abiding for a short while in this space, we then move on in the timeline fifty years or so into the future and feel the remains of the corpse: what do our hands feel like? do we still have eyes to see with? has all our skin rotted away, and what does our chest feel like, absent breathing?

Once we have sat with our vessel, feeling its end and how the energy is returned to the earth and air, we gently bring ourselves back to now, feeling what we feel from this experience, but doing so with compassion while holding the heart. We breathe in the rising motion of belly first, then up into the chest, filling our lungs, and exhaling in reverse, envisioning the tides of an ocean. We acknowledge the preciousness of this moment, the gift of our body, and the experience of being incarnated here to explore. Although we may have felt some very uncomfortable feelings, whatever we felt, we focus on the gift of this moment we now have. We grant ourselves reprieve from any affliction we may feel, simply being with the breath, opening our eyes, and receiving the beauty of our divine nature in all things.

XIII: Above all else

There is one practice above all else that will open doorways in life that may otherwise elude us— however we may feel, or whatever circumstances we find ourselves in, this practice will never fail to resonate and align within the depths of the soul. It will rejuvenate the body, provide inspiration to our journey, and remind us why we have chosen to come here; our eyes will open to potential pathways we may have previously been unaware of, and we will see brighter with each experience than we have ever seen before. Even old adversaries will greet us as friends, and previously unwelcomed guests shall be invited to sit at our table. Paradoxes will reveal their curious gifts and grant insight into the mysteries of the universe. What once troubled our heart in perplexity will lay itself bare in simplicity, and we will find ourselves encountering the wonderment of joy as we begin to notice a much larger world working in love with us.

The times where this practice may be most beneficial are the troubled days where we least feel like applying it: days when we awake to a myriad of thoughts, issues, and unresolved emotions, where we feel like staying in bed, or rushing off out for the day with distraction as a sensual life partner. The ego will attempt to fill any void which may arise, and although it will provide moments where we are numb from what we feel, avoidance will eventually yield to the places that are in need of attention. It is not necessary to fight, overcome, or even let go of these spaces, because their energies work for us as an incubation to the love which desires to come forth.

The practice we have come here for above all else is to deepen in relationship to ourselves. Some of us have come to resolve, others to express, many of us to explore parts previously untouched in the soul. How we do this is by spending time with ourselves: our feelings, this body we are in, and the dynamic relationship we engage in with life. Although our tendency as human beings is to focus on the outer circumstances, attempting to arrange, modify, or manipulate in hopes of a happy or comfortable life experience, we do so many times unaware that we are ignoring the one asking for love. While the outer world may be (and is) part of the solution, if it is solely focused on for meaning, it can have grave results leading to mental, emotional, and physical instability.

How we resolve the unresolved places is by offering ourselves the one gift that no one else can: love on an interior level of intimacy or involvement as we evolve.

Although this may be very uncomfortable at times, it is only so in the context of unfamiliarity. As we spend more time with ourselves, we begin to explore our likes and dislikes, how we feel, and what the desires of the heart are. We find ourselves becoming open to expression, voicing the love that we are, and expanding in divine nature. Above all else, the one who is asking for love is the one we wisely give our time, attention, and nurturing care to. May we develop a practice of self-love that suits our needs daily, where we acknowledge both the one coming forth in us and the one we already are as we deepen in relationship with the soul through each holding of the heart, one "I Love You" at a time.

By Our Design

By Our Design

∞ ACKNOWLEGEMENTS ∞

First I would like to acknowledge the many souls who, whether they were aware of it or not, contributed to this work of well-being in sharing so much with me— specifically, Miss Ciara Whipp, my traveling companion, editor, and all around mirror of depth, who encouraged a deeper listening for this life path to shine more brilliantly than I thought possible. Thank you, Ciara, for being who you are and for your tireless desire to stand in the love that is coming forth in your light.

Next, two of my most avid supporters, Pamela McGarry MS LMHC and Gwen Woodin MA, Counsler, who have helped to carry the current of this message with their belief in it, and have supported me personally through their involvement again and again. Both of you have been unwavering in resolve to build a better world through each Zoom meeting, workshop, and transformational discussion, often with difficult teachings that challenged the fabric of your reality. Thank you for such wonderful passion, holdings of the heart, and shared unwavering confidence in the simplicity of love.

Finally, as always, thank you to my unseen friend, who has been with me this entire journey, whose touch, whispers, and wisdom have calmed the nervous system when reality unravels to reveal a much larger verse. Thank you, my friend, for supporting this path through often intense experiences and abiding with it, but not rescuing me, as we continue to walk in the light and shadow of exploration, expression, and resolve. I Am eternally grateful for all of it.

By Our Design

ABOUT THE AUTHOR

James Anthony Curtis was born a sensitive and has had intuitive interactions all his life. From an early age, he felt the energetic fabric of his surroundings on a deep vibrational level which often overwhelmed the nervous system affecting physical, emotional, and mental wellbeing. Growing up he consistently questioned the nature of human existence, and sanity in relation to three-dimensional living. Frequently he experienced rifts in reality, where energetic conversations would take place beyond his comprehension at the time; these communications led to a sense of both comfort, and confusion, where he began to seek relief believing he had an overactive imaginative mind.

At the age of thirteen he began to drink in an effort to calm the nervous system, but by the end of high school and early into college, this turned to a full-blown drug addiction. Repeated attempts to cover, avoid, and quell his overly sensitive nature ironically helped to surface the deep places within his soul asking for attention. This eventually led to a passionate quest for the truth, which began a journey of inward exploration and transformation.

James became homeless for several years, living on the road where he continually received visits from otherworldly beings, which he describes as 'agents', or angels, spirits, and energy guides in nature. It was in these years that the doors were opened to vibrational teachings as he allowed himself to move into dimensional rifts. Communion revealed the nature of habitual patterns, and he became an experienced shadow worker

235

through his own resolve at healing, which led to a deeper path of awakening, granting insight into the substance of faith as an evolvement process.

Coming back to his home state of Pennsylvania in 1993, he joined a 12-step recovery program, which is based in fourth-dimensional teachings and has been the cornerstone that would launch him into fifth-dimensional resolve. Ever since, he has gradually embraced being taught by ascended masters, future self, and universal consciousness as it manifests for his ongoing expansion in self-realization. His drive to share the nature of the universe, and more specifically how it works manifestationally in coordination with the human soul, is his passion. Currently he works as an insightful guide, spiritual advisor and support in helping others to embrace emotional debris, see their manifestational process, offering practices such as holding the heart, shamanic journeying, and abiding through difficult or painful feelings in the ascension process.

James continues to write daily, inspired by the teachings in his sensitive nature, guided by loving compassion for all beings. For more information, or to engage him as a speaker, guide, or personal assistant in ascension, and to continue following his writings, please visit at: deeplyrootedinlove.com